HARVARD HISTORICAL MONOGRAPHS

XXXII

Published under the direction of the Department of History
from the income of The Robert Louis Stroock Fund

Oscar Handlin, Editor

Disarmament and Peace in British Politics 1914–1919

By
GERDA RICHARDS CROSBY

CAMBRIDGE, MASSACHUSETTS
HARVARD UNIVERSITY PRESS
1957

All rights reserved

LIBRARY OF CONGRESS CATALOG CARD NUMBER A57-8623

Printed in Great Britain

Preface

During the early years of World War II, Gerda Richards Crosby began a study of international relations and British politics for the period between the two World Wars. This developed into a study of the influence of politics, particularly British politics, upon the movement for limitation of armaments. The period covered began with the First World War and extended to the coming to power of Hitler. It was planned to have the work in two volumes: the first to cover the period from the beginning of World War I to Locarno, and the second from 1926 until the mid-thirties.

When Mrs. Crosby's untimely death occurred, only the first part of the first volume was in such form that its preparation for publication was feasible. Part of the remainder of the volume was in first draft, and much of the material had been collected for the second volume.

In the autumn of 1952, Miss Ellen Guild was helping Mrs. Crosby in her research work. During the winter, when it was learned that Mrs. Crosby did not have long to live, Miss Guild concentrated all her efforts upon completing, under the supervision of the author, the manuscript for this volume. At the time of Mrs. Crosby's death, April 6, 1953, there was still some writing to be done in connecting and concluding certain sections of the manuscript, and, in addition, the bulk of the references had to be looked up and all of them had to be checked.

The writer cannot adequately express his appreciation and indebtedness to Ellen Guild for her care and devotion in preparing his wife's manuscript for publication. Special thanks are due to Professor Sidney B. Fay for his very helpful advice and for reading the manuscript.

IRVING B. CROSBY

July 23, 1956

Contents

I. The Disarmament Ideal   1

II. British War Aims and Disarmament, 1914–1916   10

    British Ideas and the World War
    Early Plans for Peace
    "A Fight to the Finish"
    The Development toward Total War
    Feelers toward a Moderate Peace
    The Knockout of Moderation

III. British War Aims and Disarmament, 1917–1918: New Theories of International Relations   38

    Currents of Thought, 1917: Disarmament in the Background
    "No Annexations, No Indemnities"
    The Reichstag Resolution and the Pope's Proposals
    Lord Lansdowne's Letter
    Labour's Aims, Lloyd George's Concessions, and Wilson's Fourteen Points
    Party Alignments and Britain's War Aims
    The Growth of the League Idea and Its Relation to Limitation of Armaments

IV. The Disarmament Idea from the Armistice to the Peace Conference   76

    Negotiations for an Armistice
    The Armistice Terms
    The Khaki Election
    Interlude

V. Disarmament in the Peace Treaty 103
The Paris Peace Conference and Disarmament
The Drafting of the Military Terms
The Press Campaign
Final Decisions on the Military Terms
The Naval Terms
The Air Terms

VI. General Disarmament and the Peace Treaty 131
Article VIII of the League Covenant
Pressure on Lloyd George
The German Counterproposals
The Treaty and its Critics
Postwar Europe and Disarmament

Appendixes 165

Bibliography 169

Index 179

Disarmament and Peace in British Politics 1914–1919

Chapter I

The Disarmament Ideal

Some part of all the designs for abolishing war among nations or for mitigating its ravages, toward which many men have labored, necessarily has been concerned with the future of armaments. In the main, those plans which preceded the French Revolution envisaged complete disarmament as the result of international pacification which would be achieved through some federal organization or system of arbitration or a combination of these schemes. Armaments would wither away when the necessity for them disappeared. The tendency in these utopian schemes was to use the word "disarmament" in its literal sense as meaning the turning of swords into ploughshares. The rational plans for international federation to keep the peace, both of the Duc de Sully and of William Penn in the seventeenth century, looked toward the achievement of disarmament as something which would necessarily follow after their cherished systems were in working order.

Almost as soon as those twin forces, the Industrial Revolution and the French Revolution, began their transformation of the world, plans appeared to use international agreements on arms limitation as a means toward achieving relief from war, rather than to accomplish complete, or almost complete, disarmament as a result of peace attained by other means. This conception of disarmament was later apparent in the 1920's, when General von Seeckt wrote: "Taking the road, which begins at the signpost, 'To Permanent Peace, Distance Unknown,' the traveller must be content to reach by nightfall the little village whose inn bears the sign 'Disarmament.'"[1] In its

[1] General Hans von Seeckt, *Thoughts of a Soldier* (London, 1930), p. 48.

use here, the word "disarmament" has acquired a more restricted meaning which it now generally bears, and in which it will be used in this study; that is: the limitation of armaments by international agreement.

The progress of the industrial and commercial revolutions created the means to utilize the technical inventions which have made the growth of armaments so formidable. And, at the same time, the social forces of egalitarian democracy brought into being the mass armies which employ these weapons. The French Revolution created the "nation in arms." The dual forces of mass democracy and of nationalism, then set in motion, carried potentialities for the use of the products of the Industrial Revolution not perceived in the early years of the great transformation.

The fashioners of the utopias, who looked toward the achievement of complete disarmament as a final product of their schemes, were on sound ground in their assumption that, in order to bring about any mitigation of armaments, a general atmosphere of tranquillity was essential. The basic settlement for Europe attained at the Congress of Vienna, at the end of the wars set in motion by the French Revolution, was a relatively successful one. In spite of all the domestic disturbances and foreign tensions, no general European war broke out for a century. There is good reason to believe that this was due to the moderate character of the settlement itself, with France admitted to the council table as soon as she relinquished the conquered territories. In the comparatively tranquil atmosphere following the Congress of Vienna, plans for disarmament, as well as other designs for peace, appeared more generally than they had before. A proposal was even made by the Czar to Castlereagh for a specific international agreement on arms reduction, but it was not seriously considered.[2] Moreover, the great powers embarked on a succession of international conferences which formed the "Concert of Europe," with a tacit understanding that consultation among the powers would at once follow any threat to peace.

In Britain, the Liberal philosophy, which during the nineteenth

[2] C. K. Webster, *The League of Nations in Theory and Practice* (Boston, 1933), p. 180.

century conquered the public mind and the English statute-book as far as domestic policy was concerned, accepted peace and retrenchment as basic to its aims. Particularly the Manchester school, headed by Richard Cobden and John Bright, demanded disarmament as a part of this goal and suggested definite schemes for achieving disarmament. Gradually, the idea came to be accepted by a large section of the Liberal Party and especially by the nonconformist element, which formed an important section of the party's support, and which continued to be interested in the Cobden-Bright proposals.

In the middle years of the century, a succession of peace society movements kept these ideas alive. After a decline of interest in the 1860's and after the setback to peace movements by the War of 1870, the dangers of resurgent imperialism and of increased nationalistic forces in Europe stimulated a renewal of activity for peace which reached a new height of intensity in England in the nineties, particularly in the middle years of that decade. The nonconformist churches became particularly active. In these years, international agreements on arms limitation—that is, "disarmament" in the sense in which the word is used in this study—first received wide attention from the public. The activities of numerous unofficial groups toward this goal were even reflected in a few abortive official moves.

The first of these attempts was the Hague Conference of 1899, called by Czar Nicholas II, who suggested that the nations of the world meet in conference to direct their efforts toward "the maintenance of universal peace and a possible reduction of the excessive armaments which weigh upon all nations."[3] When the delegates of twenty-six nations assembled in May 1899, it soon became evident that Russia's concrete proposals for the limitation of military and naval budgets would not be accepted. Accordingly, the question was laid to rest by a resolution asking the various governments to study the proposals made at the Conference as the bases of a possible agreement.

Nor were the conditions for a settlement more favorable when the Second Hague Conference convened in 1907. The Czar, fresh from

[3] Merze Tate, *The Disarmament Illusion* (New York, 1942), p. 169.

defeat in the Russo-Japanese War and anxious to build up his nation's military power, purposefully omitted any mention of arms limitation in his invitation to the Conference and instead emphasized the importance of extending international arbitration and the Red Cross rules of war. Circumstances, meanwhile, had caused Great Britain to cast a more favorable eye on arms limitation agreements. If a settlement could have been reached at that time preventing further increases in naval construction, her naval supremacy could have been maintained. Britain was nevertheless conscious of the general opposition to limitation proposals and therefore closed the short discussion on disarmament with a resolution confirming the resolution of 1899 and suggesting that the various governments resume examination of the question.[4]

The Hague Conferences thus had no direct results significant for the movement for limitation of armaments. Nevertheless, the fact that the possibility of agreements on limitation had actually been brought before a great international conference marked an important advance in the place such a conception held in the public mind. It had ceased to be merely a theme for pulpit and pacifist oratory and was now a subject upon which kings and ministers had, momentarily at least, been willing to deliberate.

As the international tensions increased in the years before the outbreak of the war, opportunities for the application of the disarmament principle became more limited. Both public and official alarm in Great Britain at the rapidly increasing German naval expenditures initiated conversations on several occasions in the prewar years in an effort to bring to a halt the race in naval armaments.[5] However, owing to uncompromising policies and pressures for a stronger navy

---

[4] In the light of public opinion, Germany bore the blame for the failure of the two conferences because of her outspoken opposition to the consideration of the armaments question. However, only German methods and not policy set her off from the other powers who, being subject to the criticisms of pacifist opinion at home, were more cautious in expressing their attitudes. Tate, *Disarmament Illusion*, p. 342.

[5] The Kaiser and Lord Hardinge, 1908; Bethmann-Hollweg and Sir W. E. Goschen, 1909; and Lord Haldane's Mission to Berlin, 1912.

in both countries, there was little possibility for agreement. To the naval leaders in England, the *Dreadnought* meant safety, either by peace or by victory,[6] while, on the other hand, Admiral Tirpitz believed that German determination to increase her fleet would, in the long run, make England more tractable on international issues.[7] The views of professional navy men in both nations had a powerful effect, both direct and indirect, upon the tempo of naval expansion.

In 1909, the competition in capital ship building was intensified. First Lord of the Admiralty McKenna's inaccurate predictions of future German naval strength created a public panic in England which precipitated a campaign for increased production of *Dreadnoughts*.[8] Such increases in British building played nicely into the hands of German large fleet advocates. Thus, Admiral Tirpitz succeeded in overcoming the opposition of the moderates and liberals who saw the dangers of the great Navy Laws. When all Anglo-German conversations failed, the Liberal government in England, although originally pledged to a program to decrease arms expenditure, had no course left open but the maintenance of the "two-power" standard of naval supremacy. Naval competition had created an atmosphere of tension and suspicion, on both the official and national levels, which fostered pessimism regarding the possibility of an agreement and defeated all serious attempts toward that end. After the failure of Lord Haldane's mission to Berlin in 1912, the proposals by Winston Churchill, then First Lord of the Admiralty, both in 1912 and 1913 for a year's "holiday" in naval construction were but gestures, however sincere, in the direction of a hopeless goal.

In spite of the foundering of the disarmament principle in these years, it nevertheless remained in the background as a part of the Liberal creed and was actively espoused by European Socialists who were especially suspicious of private armaments firms. There was, indeed, evidence that this suspicion was well grounded: that certain

[6] Philip Noel-Baker, *The Private Manufacture of Armaments* (New York, 1937), p. 412.

[7] Winston S. Churchill, *The World Crisis* (London, 1927), I, 112.

[8] Noel-Baker, *Private Manufacture*, pp. 466–477.

private manufacturers on the Continent and in England were instrumental in accelerating the armaments race in order to create more business for themselves. In the spring of 1914, Philip Snowden, an Independent Labour Party leader, in Parliament denounced the undue influence of private firms over the government's armament policy and attempted to expose the questionable methods they employed. A notable instance of such activity by munitions manufacturers had been the Mulliner campaign of 1909, in which the director of a large ordnance firm, H. H. Mulliner, brought pressure to bear on the Admiralty and the Cabinet for an increase in naval production. Working through the ranks of the Conservative Party, Mulliner supplied the Cabinet with "information" on German building which painted an alarmist picture of Britain's position in the naval race. Together with McKenna's predictions of German production, Mulliner's agitation helped create the national panic which was so beneficial to the armament firms.[9] Snowden, moreover, pointed to the interrelated character of British firms as well as their connections with armaments firms in European countries, including potential enemy nations.[10]

The influence of private manufacturers upon national policy was not confined to Great Britain. Similar instances of pressure and intrigue were discovered in both Germany and France.[11] But also universal was the realization and condemnation of the firms' activities by Socialist members of European parliaments.[12] Certainly, the

[9] Noel-Baker, *Private Manufacture*, p. 448–510.

[10] *The Parliamentary Debates*, 5th series, *House of Commons*, LIX, cols. 2135–2146, March 18, 1914. Hereafter *The Parliamentary Debates* will be abbreviated as "*H.C. Debates*," for the House of Commons, and as "*H.L. Debates*," for the House of Lords.

[11] Herr von Gontard and his "French Machine Guns," which caused a machine gun appropriation in the Reichstag. The Poutiloff Affair in France, another scare on false grounds. See Noel-Baker, *Private Manufacture*, pp. 372–377.

[12] Jaurès and Thomas in the Chambers of Deputies, January 1914. Liebknecht and Erzberger in the Reichstag, April 23, 1913. See Noel-Baker, *Private Manufacture*, pp. 372–377.

Socialists were suspicious of high finance in general: the activities of the private manufacturing interests were, for Socialist purposes, an excellent verification of their mistrust.

The rise of Socialism also involved other phases of the question of arms limitation. With the growing number of Socialist representatives in the Reichstag and in the Chamber of Deputies, the hope had become widespread that, if war should break out, its continuance might be prevented by refusal in the parliaments to vote war credits. In Britain, the Labour Party, though it was affiliated with Socialist organizations, had not yet declared itself a Socialist party. However, the pacifist spirit pervaded the Labour Party and, to a certain extent, the Liberal Party as well. Along with the rise of Socialism, demands for increased expenditures on the social services were ever increasing, and conflicts between these demands and the inroads of increasing arms expenditures on National Budgets were already appearing. Nor were the Socialist parties the only groups stressing the need for increased social services. The British Liberal Party, which may be taken as indicating the general tendencies of Liberalism everywhere, had taken on collectivist ideas, as was clearly demonstrated in Lloyd George's budget of 1909. A large section of the Liberal Party had become Imperialist as well, and by 1909 this section dominated the Cabinet. The affinity of these ideas with the general Socialist trend is illustrated by the similarity of aims, as well as of personalities, between the Liberal Imperialists and the Fabian Society, the Socialist organization of the British intellectuals. Both these groups hoped for governments with more far-reaching mandates and authority to plan the economic development of Britain and the Empire. The tendency of these movements was to create an atmosphere in which changes in the nature of warfare in the direction of "total war" were to be more possible.[13]

---

[13] Since the advent of nuclear weapons, the phrase "total war" has acquired a different meaning from the meaning it carried during World War I or during the interwar period. Although now "total war" suggests war by nuclear rather than conventional weapons, in the earlier period the phrase was used only in order to distinguish "limited war" for "limited objectives"— the concept which prevailed in seventeenth-century and eighteenth-century

As British Liberalism created an atmosphere favorable to ideas of general arms reduction, so the situation of Great Britain in the world gave her a key position in the movement for disarmament. In 1894, the Arbitration Alliance of Great Britain addressed to Queen Victoria a memorial praying that her government should take some practical step toward the international reduction of armaments. They wrote:

> The neutral policy of this country, the smallness of her offensive armaments, her insular position, the commanding personal influence of Her Majesty, and the friendly relations in which she finds herself with all European Powers, appear to give her a unique opportunity, and to impose upon her in this matter a unique responsibility.[14]

While not all these factors continued to operate, if indeed they were operating in 1894, in the years following the First World War as in the nineties Great Britain did occupy a key position in international affairs and sometimes, it appeared, the decisive position.

An examination of Britain's domestic politics and opinion upon the problem of disarmament and the formulation of her policy thereupon makes a focus of study for the whole question of limitation of armaments. Not only did her world position in the crucial years affect the importance of the movement, but also certain factors of Britain's economic and political development made disarmament significant as a domestic issue. In every respect her connection with the developments of the problem was close. For Britain was the home of the Industrial Revolution which created the technology which now rendered arms limitation essential. And in Britain had been nurtured, and there flourished, the particular brand of Liberalism of which the disarmament idea was most clearly a part.

As the ideas of universal peace, to be obtained through federation

---

Europe—from "total war" in which the means and objectives of war become limitless, in which total military victory is required to ensure the accomplishment of war aims, and in which many facets of domestic life are drawn into the war effort. When we refer to the tendency toward "total war" in the World War I period, our reference is, of course, to the World War I–interwar period meaning of the phrase.

[14] Quoted in Tate, *Disarmament Illusion*, pp. 103–104.

and arbitration, bringing disarmament in their train, had developed in the atmosphere of eighteenth-century rationalism, so had the ideas back of the Liberal philosophy. The idea of limitation of armaments was indeed a rational idea which grew in men's minds at the same time that the rationally based Liberal philosophy was developing. In the period following the end of World War I, when an attempt was made to apply the principles of nineteenth-century Liberalism—then on the wane in the domestic field—to international relations and organization, the principle of disarmament was to become, for a brief space, a matter of practical politics. It failed of successful implementation in a world where irrationalism, as a conscious philosophy, was, in fact, becoming triumphant. When it again becomes a matter of practical politics, and that it should do so appears the only alternative to the destruction of Christian civilization, it will mean that rational principles have once more entered the field of politics.

Chapter II

British War Aims and Disarmament, 1914–1916

British Ideas and the World War

In England, in the years just prior to the outbreak of the war in 1914, the recurrent attempts to force public attention on disarmament, which earlier had stemmed from the efforts of the old Gladstone Liberals in alliance with the "nonconformist conscience," received fresh impetus from the Socialist movement. While the old Liberalism was being pushed aside by the new Liberal Imperialism, the force of the Socialist societies was attacking the armament problem through two approaches: first, by encouraging distrust and suspicion of the activities of the private armaments firms, and second, by urging the necessity of arms limitation to achieve the Socialist purposes of internationalism and abolition of war. The outbreak of the war appeared to confound all the hopes of both Liberals and Socialists. The very fact of its outbreak, by ending the hope for an England set apart from continental struggles and devoted to "peace, retrenchment, and reform," appeared to defeat all for which the old Liberalism had stood. As for international Socialism, the belief proved groundless that its considerable parliamentary strength both in Germany and France would mean the refusal of war credits and therefore would make impossible a great war. No aim of these groups seemed more hopelessly lost than that of the principle of limitation of armaments. The triumphant ascendency of war and of nationalism had taken from it even such small claim to reality as it might once have possessed.

Nevertheless, the Treaty which five years later ended the conflict committed its signers, or so it appeared, to a policy of arms limitation. By Article VIII of the Covenant of the League of Nations, members recognized "that the maintenance of peace requires the reduction of national armament to the lowest point consistent with national safety" and charged the League Council with the formulation of plans for implementing this declared purpose. Nor did this article stand alone, since the purpose of the clauses by which Germany was disarmed was stated to be "in order to render possible the initiation of a general limitation of the armaments of all nations." By these clauses of the Versailles Treaty, those nations which for more than a decade were to dominate the affairs of Europe gave notice of their intention to take a rationally indicated step of basic importance toward the solution of their most pressing difficulties. A declared purpose, if not indeed a commitment, to implement agreements for arms reduction became part of the public law of Europe.

These clauses found their way into the Treaty as a result of the developing fortunes of Allied war aims. Since the intensity and destructiveness of the conflict had bred in all countries the demand for some system to prevent wars in the future, British statesmen were compelled to reconcile their people to the war's continuance by giving constant assurance that this would be accomplished, and this purpose runs as a constant thread through public discussion. The idea of limitation of armaments necessarily appeared as a part of such schemes, and at the war's end hopes had become widespread that its achievement would be forthcoming. To many, disarmament appeared as the hoped-for result of a long-continued peace obtained by other measures, but, as the war wore on, it was discussed more and more as a specific proposal in itself, for the purpose of making war less likely.

But assuring the people that this war was truly a "war to end war" was not in itself sufficient to maintain public opinion at the high emotional pitch necessary to bear the strains of a prolonged and total war. Toward the accomplishment of this end, myths were developed and slogans proclaimed whose endurance made impossible the creation of a real peace. By proclaiming the aggressiveness of the enemy to be the sole cause of the war and his "undemocratic" propensities the chief obstacle to future peace, not only did it become unlikely that the issues would be realistically faced, but the way was prepared for the continuation of the war by both economic and psychological means when the military hostilities were ended. While the war aims controversy resulted in fairly widespread agreement on disarmament as a goal, at the same time there was almost universal acquiescence in ways of thought in whose atmosphere the achievement of arms limitation proved impossible. And, at the same time that the war aims controversy was fashioning ideas and fabricating myths, the cleavages revealed in its course were foreshadowing the political alignments in Great Britain in the postwar years.

During the early months of the war, war aims were ignored. Instead, in Britain as well as in Germany and France, justification was first sought for the part played by the respective governments in the war's outbreak. In France, the wickedness of Germany explained everything. In Germany, the duty to the Fatherland was stressed. Great Britain was in the fortunate position that her stand on the violation of Belgium's neutrality presented an issue which gave the moral purpose on which twentieth-century nations have felt compelled to justify their military operations. A happy coincidence of Britain's own interests and of moral appeal was the result which almost at once, after her ultimatum of August 4, united an England which, during July, had been far from agreement on entry into the war.[1]

Before the die was cast, the great Liberal newspaper, the *Manchester Guardian*, and other Liberal papers had cried out against intervention. As late as July 27, the *Guardian* rejoiced in England's position of neutrality which should be used to save Europe. After August 4, however, all the Liberal newspapers cried with the *Daily News*, "being in, we must win."[2] Up to the outbreak of war it had generally been believed that there would be four resignations from

[1] Compare Kent Forster, *Failures of Peace* (Philadelphia, 1941), p. 15.
[2] Irene Cooper Willis, *England's Holy War* (New York, 1928), pp. 84–87.

the Cabinet if Britain intervened. When the moment came, only two Cabinet members—the ageing Gladstonian, Lord Morley, representing the old Liberalism, and the trade unionist, John Burns, representing the new pacifism—resigned. Within the Liberal Party most members accepted the government's decision to enter the war. Even so, the old Liberal vision of a peaceful world, with England apart from continental struggle and with peace the best interest of Britain, still maintained a strong hold on many men. To these, the war's outbreak, even though its necessity was not questioned, seemed a defeat of all that Liberalism had hoped for and all that it had stood for. Nevertheless, the rank and file of the Liberal Party was eventually reconciled to the war, first, by attributing to Germany all responsibility for its outbreak, and, second, by the apparent transformation of the war into a crusade for those same principles which its outbreak seemed to have betrayed. Within a week after the outbreak of the war, the Liberal dailies had seized upon such a justification and proclaimed the conflict to be a "war to end war."[3] This slogan, repeated so often during the course of the struggle that belief became almost automatic, carried with it assurance that the defeat of Germany would open the way to peace and disarmament throughout the earth. Without some such justification, it would indeed have been difficult for the old Liberals to accept the war so rudely thrust upon them.

It was, however, not only upon the minds of those Liberals whose visions were now lost that the new crusading idea took firm hold. From all sides, political leaders exploited to the utmost whatever contributions these new slogans might make toward victory. Apart from some of the old Liberals and new Socialists, most Englishmen had accepted the premise that physical force was the controlling factor in international affairs. They had become accustomed to the belief that, manipulated by a beneficent Britain, the principle of the balance of power would maintain the peace of Europe as well as the position of Britain in the world. To those accepting this view, and they included most English Conservatives, the means of securing

[3] Willis, *England's Holy War*, p. 88.

a peace after the war appeared clear and simple. Military and territorial settlements would prevent Germany from ever again becoming a world power. Toward the "fight to the finish" idea, the Northcliffe press put the whole weight of its influence, and *The Times* instituted a column with that heading. It was not long before the projected settlements after the war were openly proclaimed to have economic aims as well. "Trade we can take from Germany" appeared in the headlines of Conservative newspapers as early as August 1914.[4] The crusading aim of the war advanced the purposes of these believers in the sufficiency of armed and economic force, for they could now represent the achievement of their ends as the necessary objectives of a holy crusade for future peace.

In contrast to the relative unity of Liberal Imperialists and Conservatives in their views on the war, the Labour Party with its federal organization, as an alliance between two Socialist societies—the Independent Labour Party and the Fabian Society—and the trade unions, found itself in a difficult position. While in domestic politics the Party had not yet declared itself Socialist, it was linked with the Socialist parties abroad by its membership in the Second International: as a member, it had participated in the resolution of the Stuttgart Conference of 1907, which had proclaimed it the duty of the members to use all efforts to prevent the outbreak of war, and, if notwithstanding war should begin, "to intervene to bring it to an end."[5]

Just before the war's outbreak, the British Labour Party acted in the spirit of the Second International. On July 30, the Labour Party members of Parliament passed a resolution in favor of Great Britain's staying out of the war even if its outbreak could not be prevented,[6] and only two days before Britain's ultimatum, the Party held a huge meeting in Trafalgar Square protesting entrance into

[4] *The Times* (London), August 20, 1914, p. 7; August 24, 1914, pp. 8–9; August 28, 1914, p. 4; September 25, 1914, p. 107 (Engineering Supplement). See also Willis, *England's Holy War*, p. 184.

[5] G. D. H. Cole, *A History of the Labour Party since 1914* (London, 1948), pp. 6–7.

[6] Cole, *History of the Labour Party*, p. 17.

the war.[7] It was the task of the Party leadership to reconcile the sections of the Party which took the Stuttgart resolution seriously with those which did not and particularly with the more conservative trade union organizations, most of whose sympathies, as well as political connections and even support, were Liberal rather than Socialist.

The two Socialist societies, from which the Socialist inspiration of the Party came, differed in origin and in outlook. The Independent Labour Party, with 30,000 members and many branches, was largely working-class in its membership. It had served as the dynamo for the alliance which formed the Labour Party and put up candidates for Parliament. Of the two Socialist societies, it held more closely to the orthodox Socialist point of view on war. On August 6 its periodical, the *Labour Leader*, carried a heading "Down with the War,"[8] and a week later the I.L.P. issued a manifesto deploring the war and sending sympathy and greetings to the German Socialists.[9] Of its National Council only two members supported the war, but the rank and file of the Party were less united.

Quite different both in background and ideas was the Fabian Society, a band of intellectuals under the leadership of Sidney and Beatrice Webb, still "half a drawing-room society."[10] Although only one-tenth as large as the I.L.P., the Fabians had undertaken the task of changing the mind of England by their methods of "permeation" and "gradualism." With their confidence in planning and in the development of administrative techniques, they had found themselves in the early years of the century in sympathy with the hopes of the Liberal Imperialists to develop within the Empire highly organized interdependent units.[11] As early as the autumn of 1914, the Fabian periodical, the *New Statesman*, began to give

[7] Carl F. Brand, *British Labour's Rise to Power* (Stanford, Calif., 1941), p. 57.

[8] A. Fenner Brockway, *Inside the Left* (London, 1942), p. 45. See also *Beatrice Webb's Diaries, 1912–1924* (New York, 1952), pp. 29–30.

[9] Cole, *History of the Labour Party*, pp. 19–20.

[10] Edward R. Pease, *The History of the Fabian Society* (New York, 1916), p. 165.

[11] See *Beatrice Webb's Diaries*, pp. 228–229.

evidence that their views on the war also coincided in many ways with those of the Liberal Imperialists.[12]

With these divisions in the Labour Party clear, the executive of the Labour Party moved cautiously. During August 1914, groups within the Party declared themselves. The Parliamentary Labour Party, whose views were reflected in the decisions of the I.L.P., replaced J. Ramsay MacDonald with Arthur Henderson as its leader and decided to support the war and the recruiting campaign. At the same time, the Parliamentary Committee of the Trade Union Congress also voted support. The Party Executive then endorsed on August 29 the decision of the Parliamentary Labour Party to support the recruiting campaign. This foreshadowed the manifesto of October 15, issued by the majority of the Labour M.P.s, the Parliamentary Committee of the Trade Union Congress, and other labor leaders. This document, by putting all blame for the war on Germany and representing the conflict as a struggle of democracy against military despotism, accepted the view of the war's origin which had now become orthodox in England. It did, however, conclude:

When the time comes to discuss the terms of peace, all the Labour Party will stand as it has always stood for an international agreement among all civilized nations that disputes and misunderstandings in the future shall be settled not by machine guns but by arbitration.[13]

This reservation was the only hint in the manifesto that the position of the Labour Party in its acceptance of the war was far removed from the position of Conservatives and of Liberal Imperialists.

Early Plans for Peace

Although during the tense autumn days of the campaign in France the orthodox jingo view of the war appeared to triumph everywhere, groups soon appeared which attempted to appeal to public opinion on the basis of quite differently grounded ideas on

[12] "India and the War," *New Statesman*, III, no. 77, 726–728 (September 26, 1914); "Trust India," *ibid*, IV, no. 80, 29–30 (October 17, 1914).

[13] Cole, *History of the Labour Party*, p. 21.

international politics. In November, a society formed from an alliance of Liberals and I.L.P. members, calling itself the Union of Democratic Control, issued its first manifesto on proposed points for the peace settlement.[14] It aimed to become a propaganda and pressure group for democratic control of foreign policy. It insisted on four cardinal points for a peace settlement: first, the principle of self-determination; second, the ratification of treaties by Parliament; third, the abandonment of the principle of the balance of power for a concert of power which would set up an international council and machinery for guaranteeing peace; and fourth, a drastic reduction of armaments as part of the peace settlement, as well as nationalization of arms manufacture. These bases for a settlement were premised on the idea of a concert of nations, bound together by the force of international law and contractual agreements, whose democratically controlled foreign policy would be implemented by the force of world public opinion. While this program, insofar as it was noticed at all, met with almost universal abuse, it nevertheless outlined the same bases of policy later developed by President Wilson in his speeches during 1918, which won for him at that moment great adulation and with which the idea of arms limitation eventually became linked. During the early part of the war, the U.D.C. program was unique in its advocacy of disarmament as a specific aim in itself.

Most of the leaders in the organization, both from the Liberals and from the I.L.P., had been concerned before the war with the dangers of secret commitments on foreign policy and had favored greater participation of the House of Commons in foreign affairs.[15] The first impulse toward the formation of the society came from a representative of the Whig tradition in British politics—Charles Trevelyan, who had resigned as a junior minister on the outbreak of the war in August.[16] His family background—Lord Macaulay was his great-uncle and Sir George Otto Trevelyan his father—was

[14] *The Morrow of War* (U.D.C. Publication No. 1, 1914).
[15] Compare Arthur Ponsonby, *Parliament and Foreign Policy* (U.D.C. Publication No. 5, 1914).
[16] H. M. Swanwick, *Builders of Peace* (London, 1924), pp. 29–38.

close to the intellectual springs of British Liberalism. Arthur Ponsonby, who soon joined Trevelyan, represented Whiggish aristocratic family tradition. Ponsonby had formerly been private secretary to the anti-imperialist Liberal Prime Minister, Sir Henry Campbell-Bannerman. These Liberals set the tone of the U.D.C. meetings, described by an I.L.P. member as "bourgeois to their fingertips... They might have been lifted out of any gathering of gentlemen of England." [17]

The leadership of the Union of Democratic Control which drew whatever support the organization found in the country during the war came from its Independent Labour Party members like J. Ramsay MacDonald, who joined Trevelyan and Ponsonby as one of the five original organizers of the Union of Democratic Control. Among the I.L.P. groups of working-class men in the Midlands, South Wales, Lancashire, and Yorkshire and in Scotland, the U.D.C. was able to organize meetings and branches. Though the declared basic aims of the society—the democratization of foreign policy, a moderate peace settlement, and the four points of the manifesto—were those later adopted by President Wilson, such was the inflamed state of public opinion that its activities during these early years were considered treasonable by many Englishmen. In spite of this, the organization was of the very greatest significance in the political development of England. To a large extent, it was the decisive factor in the decline of the Liberal Party and the rise of the Labour Party after the war. The Liberals who became active in the U.D.C. during the war years led the way for many more who passed over into the Labour ranks in the early twenties.

During the early years of the war, limitation of armaments as a postwar aim was advocated only by the U.D.C., by some of the Socialist groups, and by the I.L.P., who, at its Party conference in April 1915, passed a resolution which followed closely the four points of the U.D.C. manifesto.[18] On the left, various groups during the early months of 1915 advanced proposals which had a good deal

[17] Brockway, *Inside the Left*, p. 54.
[18] *Report of the Annual Conference of the Independent Labour Party* (London, 1915), p. 88.

in common with the U.D.C. manifesto. On February 14, liberal and Socialist groups of the Allied countries met in London. Their resolution emphasized that the war was against the governments, not the peoples, of the Central powers and that the defensive war of the Allies must not become one of conquest. After stating certain specific war aims, such as the liberation of Belgium and self-determination for Alsace-Lorraine, they proposed peaceful federation of Europe and finally of the world.[19]

The need for an international organization to keep the peace was the theme of the studies of several groups in England, however, who had no connection with the Socialist movement. Most of these began private conferences almost immediately on the outbreak of the war, but did not come forward with any public announcement or organization until well into the following year. Some of the old Liberals met with the editor of *The Economist*, Francis Hirst. Another group of friends who centered around Lowes Dickinson and who were later known as the Bryce Group began, as early as August 1914, to discuss plans for future international organization.[20] Drawing its origins from this group was the League of Nations Society, which was first publicly organized in the spring of 1915 with Lord Shaw as President. While it began at this time to agitate for the principle of a League, it did not come forward with specific plans until much later.

The first organization to put forth a definite plan for international organization after the war was the Fabian Society. In January 1915, a research group was set up under the leadership of Leonard Woolf, and its plan was published in the *New Statesman* six months later.[21] In its main outlines, typical of several which appeared later, it advocated an international court to deal with justiciable disputes and a council for nonjusticiable ones. The council was to legislate, but under a weighted scheme which would ensure control by the

[19] *Report of the Fifteenth Annual Conference of the Labour Party* (London, 1916), pp. 31-32.
[20] *Beatrice Webb's Diaries*, p. 37.
[21] Leonard Woolf, "Suggestions for the Prevention of War," *New Statesman*, V, nos. 118, 119 (Special Supplements, July 10 and July 17, 1915).

great powers. There were also provisions for sanctions and for a secretariat. As was the case in the plans of all these groups, disarmament was not proposed as a specific aim, the hope being that as an international organization became established, arms limitation would come about of itself.

"A Fight to the Finish"

While these groups were concerning themselves during 1915 with the principles behind a peace of moderation and with the principles of future international organization, the plans which were developing in official circles and which were setting the tone for almost all press comment were in favor of a war à outrance and a Carthaginian peace. In April of that year, the London Treaty with Italy, the first of the so-called secret treaties, which was to create such problems for the Peace Conference, was signed. During the spring, Lord Bertie, then British Ambassador in Paris and high in the confidence of government circles, recorded in his diary informal conversations with different persons in Paris which reveal the direction in which the plans were developing. A talk with Delcassé, the French Foreign Minister, in the same month as the Italian treaty revealed that the opinion of both statesmen was that

. . . we ought to deprive them [the Germans], as far as humanly we can, of any power to injure us for as long a period as possible: there must be destruction of all their war-plant and weapon-producing factories, disbandment of their military forces, and every possible difficulty placed in the way of a resuscitation of those forces; an enormous indemnity must be squeezed out of Germany by a prolonged occupancy at Germany's cost; dismemberment, not by force, but by encouragement.[22]

These representatives of official or "inside" opinion, who saw the destruction of both German military and German economic power at the end of the war as the solution of all difficulties, found their ideas propagated for "outside" opinion by the most powerful section of the press. Not only did Lord Northcliffe's *Daily Mail* and Lord Beaverbrook's *Daily Express* dramatize such views for the public,

[22] *The Diary of Lord Bertie of Thame, 1914–1918* (New York, 1924), I, 149. April 15, 1915.

but in the columns of *The Times*, since 1909 under the control of Lord Northcliffe, the same ideas were more subtly presented to its more sophisticated readers. The political writers also assisted. During the summer a writer in the *National Review* advocated cutting Germany off entirely from the sea: Britain to take the coast from Holland to the Kiel Canal, Russia the section along the Baltic.[23] The course of military developments inspired new suggestions for the peace settlement. With the conquest of the German African and Pacific colonies in 1914 and the early summer of 1915, even the moderate, though Conservative, *Daily Mail* implied that German colonies taken since the beginning of the war should remain in British hands. By the autumn, the *Daily Mail* was assuming that it was a certainty that Britain would keep the German colonies.

Other groups which would have scorned such frankly jingo views as those of the *Daily Mail* or the *National Review* were nevertheless coming to conclusions which had something in common with them. Early in 1915 the group of Liberal Imperialists which centered around Lord Milner and included Philip Kerr, Lionel Curtis, and Winston Churchill, began to express their views on the war and the peace in their quarterly, *The Round Table*. They believed the war to be "the result of the rejection of democracy by Germany and Austria in the years 1848 to 1870" and ascribed its bitterness to the fact that the "two irreconcilable principles, autocracy and democracy," were struggling for supremacy in Europe.[24] From this premise, it was an easy step to the assertion that the "first and most essential object in the war is to compel Germany to admit utter and decisive defeat." [25]

Likewise the Fabian Socialists, who were the most readily reconciled of any of the Socialist groups to the war, justified it as a crusade for democracy, as the *Round Table* group had done. Their

---

[23] J. B. Castle, "German Territory for the British Empire," *National Review*, LXV, no. 389, 708-718 (July 1915).

[24] "The Schism of Europe," *The Round Table*, V, no. 18, 345-411 (March 1915).

[25] "Foundations of Peace," *The Round Table*, V, no. 19, 589-625 (June 1915).

attitude had become apparent in the pages of their journal, the *New Statesman*, by the autumn of 1914. By the spring of 1915 that journal, in an article curiously entitled "The Duties of the Allies," was proposing two remedies for the evils of the German state: first, to disarm it, and second, to force it to become democratic. To accomplish this, they suggested "one way is to forbid ... the manufacture of a single gun or warship or the training of a single battalion of infantry." [26]

Among men of all political faiths, from the intellectual Fabian Socialists to the "terrible simplifiers" of the *Daily Mail*, the idea became accepted that the necessary condition of a peaceful and happy international order was a complete destruction of German power. This idea had appeared in the first stage of the war in the Liberal press, since, to the Liberal mind with long-cherished dreams of international order, the war could be justified in no other way. From this it was an easy transition to the idea that the destruction of German power was *all* that was necessary for these ends. The old idea of wars as fought by the military alone, and only to the point where the ultimate military decision could be foreseen, was giving way to the new idea of war not between armed forces but between peoples, a "total war" with its object total victory.

In both Germany and France the politics of the war aims controversy had many parallels to the English situation. In Germany sharp divisions on war aims were clear and influenced postwar politics, as they did in England. The war was viewed as a struggle for the defense of the Fatherland, and this was the belief of even the majority of the Social Democrats. The modern views of that party on the war found adherents in high places. Hans Delbrück, the military historian and editor of the *Preussische Jahrbücher*, declared in October 1914, "that on land the balance of power must be maintained as it is, and that on sea a similar balance must be attained." [27] He claimed that this was also the view of the Chancellor, Bethmann-Hollweg; the Social Democratic organ, *Vorwärts*, observed that it

---

[26] "The Duty of the Allies," *New Statesman*, V, no. 110, 124-125 (May 15, 1915).

[27] Hans W. Gatzke, *Germany's Drive to the West* (Baltimore, 1950), p. 58.

was the Kaiser's view as well. With Germany's military successes in the west, however, ideas of postwar western expansion grew. The right bloc in the Reichstag was aided by pressure and propaganda groups outside, largely from among those independents who wished to extend German territory to include an iron supply. The position of the moderates was made more difficult, as that of the expansionists was made easier, by the increase of jingoist propaganda in Great Britain.

The military position of the French with their territory actually under invasion favored the acceptance of the idea that German power must be completely destroyed. At that time, too, the French desire to expand to the left bank of the Rhine was gaining headway, and, in May 1915, *Le Temps* ran a series of articles which advocated punishment of German individuals for war crimes. The peril of the French military position tended to give unity to French public opinion, and it was only from the doctrinaire Socialist groups that ideas for a league and for disarmament were heard.

The Development toward Total War [28]

When in the autumn of 1915 a military stalemate had again settled down on the Western Front, signs began to appear that there existed in England a desire for peace, despite the uncompromising official spirit and the widely accepted propaganda for a fight to the finish. In November, there were debates on the war in both houses of Parliament in which the idea of a negotiated peace was mentioned. The debate in the House of Commons was on a motion by Arthur Ponsonby, and almost all of those who spoke for it were connected with the Union of Democratic Control.[29] A similar debate in the House of Lords was made dramatic by a speech of Lord Courtney, now eighty years old and blind, who earlier had succeeded to John Stuart Mill's title of "the conscience of the House of Commons" and who held a position of great influence in the Liberal Party. Courtney now asserted that the progress of the war was destroying

---

[28] See the note on the meaning of the phrase "total war" as used in this study, Chapter I, n. 13.

[29] *H.C. Debates*, 5th series, LXXV, cols. 1450–1459. November 11, 1915.

all for which Liberalism had fought. Since, he argued, the war had resulted "in something like a deadlock of force" and had diminished the standard of civilization, the guarantees of liberty, and the "trustworthiness of law," and, since "what we believe is said in Germany with the same sincerity and same conviction as here," he was convinced that there existed an alternative to further strife.[30]

A few weeks later *The Economist* recorded that discussion of peace "has burst forth everywhere." Newspaper correspondents reported possible German terms; the Pope declared that it was time "to think of peace." Count Andrássy in the Hungarian Diet had called for peace at the first possible moment without waiting for a war of exhaustion.[31] In December, in the German Reichstag the Social Democrat Philipp Scheidemann asked whether the Chancellor was prepared to state "the conditions on which he would be disposed to enter into peace negotiations." While Bethmann-Hollweg made no proposals and stressed the "wild war aims" of the British press as a reason for not doing so, the speech was considered a "peace speech." By the end of 1915, everywhere many people were beginning to think of peace terms.[32]

In spite of these indications of war weariness and of hopes for a moderate peace settlement, new signs appeared around the turn of the year of the development toward what later came to be known as "total war." In addition to the professed purposes of total destruction of German power and changes in her constitution, new measures appeared to mobilize reserves for the total victory necessary for these purposes. In January 1916, England finally resorted to conscription. Asquith and some of the older Liberals had wished a further try at the voluntary system. By the end of the year, however, Lord Kitchener, who had earlier sided with Asquith, had changed his views; as a consequence, Asquith himself was won over. Only Sir John Simon, the Home Secretary, whose resignation had been expected at the war's outbreak, resigned on the issue.

[30] *H.L. Debates*, 5th series, XX, cols. 196–201. November 8, 1915.

[31] "War and the Peace Discussion," *The Economist*, LXXXI, no. 3772, 970–971 (December 11, 1915).

[32] Philip Viscount Snowden, *An Autobiography* (London, 1934), I, 430.

Far more significant for the advance of total war than this, however, was the discussion in the House of Commons on January 10 of plans for economic warfare after the end of the shooting war. Walter Runciman, President of the Board of Trade, declared: "At any rate, we must see to it that having ended this war victoriously we do not give Germany the chance of reconstructing her commercial production," and he later added, "it is in connection with this new economic campaign that it will be necessary for us in making peace to see that she [Germany] does not raise her head." [33] Later, in a press interview, Runciman explained that rather than "raise her head," he had meant to say "raise her helmet," but the phrase he had in fact used continued to be quoted.[34]

In February 1916, Prime Minister William Hughes of Australia arrived in England and during the early spring went about making speeches on the same theme as Runciman. At about the time of his arrival, announcement had been made of a forthcoming Allied Economic Conference in Paris to discuss possible economic measures, both during and following the war.

After this conference took place in June, the Board of Trade announced that, in addition to its plans for economic warfare during the war, it had passed resolutions in regard to a policy for the reconstruction period and the peace period to follow. For the reconstruction period the Board recommended denial to the enemy of the "most favored nations" clause and proposed protection against dumping and prevention of enemy subjects in Allied countries from engaging in industries "concerning national defense or economic independence." Further recommendations for the period of peace had the purpose of rendering Allied countries independent of former enemy countries in raw materials and essential manufactured articles.[35]

Enough of the older Liberalism survived in England to call forth protests both from the old Liberal journal, *The Economist*, and from a newer one, *The Nation,* on the reports on the Paris

[33] H.C. Debates, 5th series, LXXVII, col. 1368. January 10, 1916.
[34] Swanwick, *Builders of Peace*, p. 46.
[35] *The Annual Register, 1916* (London, 1917), p. 136.

Conference.[36] *The Nation*, under the editorship of H. W. Massingham, in contrast to the Fabian *New Statesman*, throughout the war counseled moderation and hoped for peace by negotiation. In accordance with this policy, it had begun to speak of disarmament as a concrete end in itself. In deploring the announced results of the Paris Conference, it wrote, "Apart from this Paris programme, if the settlement violates no reasonable claim of nationality, we should reckon some limitation of armaments among the more easily realizable hopes of mankind." Albert Ballin, the Hamburg shipping magnate, who had so often served as the Kaiser's mouthpiece, had recently declared, the editorial pointed out, that the chief talk of the settlement must be "to extirpate the fear of armaments." The editorial touched the crux of the whole question of arms limitation when it showed its relation to other war aims and said, "Disarmament is unthinkable if the world is about to inaugurate a new and more systematic use of force to achieve economic ends." The theme of this *Nation* editorial foreshadowed the postwar problem of disarmament negotiations, when its tie-up with the question of reparations was to make impossible the achievement of agreements on arms limitation.

Other moves to increase the demands upon the enemy were going on behind the scenes. The secret treaty with Italy of the year before was supplemented in the spring of 1916 by a secret agreement between Britain, Russia, and France to give Russia Constantinople and disrupt the Turkish Empire. The spirit of these official agreements was reflected for general opinion in an article by H. Wickham Steed in the *Edinburgh Review* in April. After saying that the settlement "should be the kind of peace which a strong chief of frontier police dictates to marauding tribesmen," he outlined terms following the lines of Hughes's economic proposals and, as the basis of territorial settlements, arrangements reflecting the terms of the secret treaties.[37]

---

[36] "The Paris Resolutions and Free Trade," *The Economist*, LXXXIII, no. 3802, 55–57 (July 8, 1916), and "What is our Policy to be?" *The Nation* (London), XIX, no. 16, 456–458 (July 15, 1916).

[37] "A Programme for Peace," *Edinburgh Review*, CCIII, no. 456, 373–392 (April 1916).

The Conservative weekly, *The Spectator*, continually urged harsh territorial terms in Europe, retention of the German colonies, complete destruction of Germany's economic and military power, with the ever recurring themes of punishment and no negotiated peace.[38]

Feelers toward a Moderate Peace

In spite of these official agreements looking toward increased demands, and the parallel tone of the Conservative press, the growing sentiment in most countries for an immediate and a moderate peace, and the peace feelers accompanying it, made necessary the development of new official techniques to counter these trends. In England, a movement, parallel to the efforts of the German Social Democrats in December to force a statement of terms, came early in February 1916, when the I.L.P. leader, Philip Snowden, put up a debate on peace terms in the House of Commons.[39] This was planned in the hope that Asquith might be obliged to comment upon the German Chancellor's speech of December 1915, on the Socialist interpellation for an early conclusion of the war. Asquith was only scornful, however, of Snowden's attempts to show that Germany might enter into conversations, according to Snowden's later account.[40] The purport of those who spoke for Snowden's motion was that, since there was a military stalemate, a desire for peace in Germany, and an increasing imperialism in British war aims, British aims should be stated and peace should be sought by diplomatic means.[41]

In Germany, not only was there evidence during the winter of 1915–1916 that a sincere desire for peace had grown among the German masses,[42] but in the spring the Center Party, which had hitherto "marched with the right," turned toward moderation.[43] Chancellor

[38] "Terms of Peace," *The Spectator*, CXVII, no. 4594, 64–65 (July 15, 1916).
[39] *H.C. Debates*, 5th series, LXXX, cols. 713–726. February 23, 1916.
[40] Snowden, *Autobiography*, I, 431–436.
[41] *H.C. Debates*, 5th series, LXXX, cols. 726–734, 737–742. February 23, 1916.
[42] Gatzke, *Germany's Drive to the West*, p. 111.
[43] Ebba Dahlin, *French and German Public Opinion on Declared War Aims* (Stanford, Calif., 1933), pp. 72–74.

Bethmann-Hollweg had always been for moderation; his struggle with the military had not yet reached its climax. In the spring, feelers went out to Russia,[44] and in April the German Ambassador in Washington, Count von Bernstorff, informed Colonel House that the German government was in accord with President Wilson's desire for peace.[45] Whether or not the British Cabinet was fully aware of these ventures, it was well aware through discussions with Wilson's emissary, Colonel House, on his second mission to Europe in the late winter of 1916, of the President's desire for a peace of accord. Meanwhile, the neutral press, particularly in Switzerland, was suggesting that while Germany was willing to treat for a moderate peace, Britain was forcing her allies to stay in the war. With all this as a background, Sir Edward Grey created a new precedent by giving an interview to the London representative of the Chicago *Daily News*. No British Foreign Secretary had hitherto spoken through a press correspondent. After defending in vague and general terms British diplomacy before the outbreak of the war and the aims of the Allies, he gave indications of the uneasiness of the British Cabinet at German diplomatic and propaganda moves by saying that Germany was trying to make the neutrals believe that Great Britain was forcing her Allies to continue the war against their inclinations. He, of course, denied the existence of any such differences of view. He believed that the German people after the war must take control of their government, "for a German democracy will not plot and plan war, as Prussian militarism plotted wars."[46]

A month later a speech by President Wilson set forth the basic principles of his ideas on foreign policy.[47] Delivered in the limited audience of the members of the League to Enforce Peace, it never-

[44] Forster, *Failures of Peace*, pp. 43-45.

[45] Document 2, April 11, 1916. *Official German Documents Relating to the World War* (New York, 1923), II, 971.

[46] "Sir E. Grey on Peace," *The Economist*, LXXXII, no. 3795, 886-887 (May 20, 1916).

[47] R. S. Baker, *Woodrow Wilson: Life and Letters* (New York, 1939), VI, 220-223.

theless started what really meant a new departure for the United States. While Wilson, since the early days of August 1914, had been active behind the scenes in efforts to make peace negotiations possible, the speech of May 27 contained a public declaration that the United States was ready to act as a mediator. Wilson still believed that the best interests of the United States would be served by a negotiated peace without either side being clearly victorious. Recent correspondence between Grey and House had shown that the British were not considering action to bring about a conference between the belligerents which had been discussed by House with them during the winter.[48] Also, Wilson, unlike his emissary, House, and his ambassador in London, Walter Hines Page, was not at this time free from suspicions concerning the purity of all the motives of the Allies.

Wilson's speech of May 27 further revealed the principles which he thought should be the basis of future international relations: first, self-determination; second, guarantees of territorial integrity; and third, freedom from disturbances of the peace through aggression. Given such bases, the interest of the United States would be in a League to guarantee them.

This speech by Wilson was the first of the series of his addresses which were to revolutionize the position of the United States in world affairs and create a new theory of international relations. Both House and Wilson believed the speech to be in conformity with the ideas of British Liberals, and Wilson had been provided with background material from speeches of Asquith, Grey, even a speech by Lloyd George in 1908, and some *Times* leaders of the early days of the war. These were supplied to House by Norman Angell, author of *The Great Illusion*, and an active member of the Union of Democratic Control. In his first speech, Wilson did not mention the question of limitation of armaments. Nevertheless, the new position of the United States in world affairs and the principles of foreign policy revealed in his speech provided the impulse without which the disarmament clauses would not have appeared in the League Covenant. Its significance was not, however, grasped in the Allied countries. In speaking of the war, Wilson had said, "with its causes and objects

[48] Baker, *Woodrow Wilson*, VI, 209-210.

we are not concerned," and it was this phrase which, particularly in France, caused great indignation at the speech.[49]

In spite of the critical reception of Wilson's speech, the increased interest in possible peace terms and proposals was evident in articles during the next months in several British journals. Throughout 1916, news items showed real interest in the idea of peace. In accordance with its hope for a peace of negotiation, *The Nation* on July 29 published two views of a possible settlement, one entitled "What England May Ask" and the other "What Germany May Expect."[50] Besides articles in *The Spectator* in July,[51] in September both the *New Statesman* and *The Statist* published a series of articles on a possible settlement.[52] Of propaganda value for a negotiated peace was the pamphlet by E. D. Morel, one of the founders of the U.D.C., entitled *Truth and the War*, which was first published in July.[53] Morel here developed a thesis of general responsibility for the outbreak of the war, as opposed to the generally accepted view of sole German responsibility, and, although the pamphlet was ignored by the newspaper and periodical press, 30,000 copies were sold.

During 1916 the military situation gave reality to moves for peace from either side. The German offensive of the winter had begun in the Verdun region, and in the summer the virtual stalemate there was paralleled by the results of the hideously bloody battle of the Somme, where the British had begun an offensive on July 1. The results gained during the summer seemed little in relation to the terrific casualties. Further, the naval battle of Jutland on May 31 had resulted in a kind of naval stalemate. The exception was, of course, submarine warfare. While Germany, faced by a virtual American

[49] Baker, *Woodrow Wilson*, VI, 223-224.

[50] "Two Views of Settlement," *The Nation* (London), XIX, no. 18, 520-523 (July 29, 1916).

[51] "Preparations for Peace," "Terms of Peace," "The Long Road to Peace," *The Spectator*, CXVII, nos. 4592-4595 (July 1, July 8, July 15, July 22, 1916).

[52] "An Allied Peace," *New Statesman*, VII, nos. 179, 180, 181, 183, 184 (September 9, September 16, September 23, October 7, October 14, 1916). "Peace Terms," *The Statist*, LXXXVIII, nos. 2010-2013 (September 2-September 23, 1916).

[53] E. D. Morel, *Truth and the War* (National Labour Press, Ltd., 1916).

ultimatum, had abandoned unrestricted submarine warfare in April 1916, nevertheless during the summer the losses from submarines were heavy. In many quarters in Germany signs were appearing of a wish for a negotiated peace. Then, in August, von Bernstorff renewed his approaches to Wilson to take some steps to bring about a conference.[54] Though not aware from American officials of the increasing German pressure for diplomatic approaches to a settlement, the British Cabinet doubtless knew of it through other channels. The prevalent war weariness had affected some members of the British Cabinet who were particularly jittery because of the submarine losses, about which they, unlike the public, were informed. The Minister of Munitions, Lloyd George, determined to meet head-on any pressure for a negotiated peace from his colleagues, from possible diplomatic moves, and from popular war weariness and desire for moderation. This he did by adopting the technique Grey had used in April; accordingly, on September 28, he granted an interview to Roy Howard of the United Press. It was, he said, "vitally important to throw out a sharp challenge to the defeatist spirit which was working from foreign quarters to bring about an inconclusive peace and which appeared to find an echo even in some responsible quarters in England." Further, the world must know, he continued, "that there can be no outside interference at this stage." He concluded with the phrase which was to be associated ever after with his name: "The fight," he said, "must be to a finish—to a knockout."[55]

The Knockout of Moderation

Signs appeared at once that Lloyd George had achieved some success in his purposes. Lord Bertie recorded a few days later what he considered the salutary effect of Lloyd George's "knockout blow" pronouncement on French opinion.[56] In England, the Cabinet ministers hastened to back up his pronouncements in somewhat

[54] Documents 13 and 14, July 13 and August 18, 1916. *German Documents*, II, 979–982.
[55] *The Times*, September 29, 1916, p. 7.
[56] *Lord Bertie's Diary*, II, 34–35.

more moderate terms. In a public speech on October 11, Asquith said that the war "cannot be allowed to end in some . . . dishonorable compromise, masquerading under the name of Peace."[57] Bonar Law and Grey made similar statements a few days later.[58] As a follow-up of Grey's speech, *The Times* on October 30 ran a letter to the editor which demanded complete destruction of German military power. About this time Asquith admitted privately to Lord Bertie that moderation was dead.[59]

Nevertheless, behind the scenes a Cabinet struggle was already in progress over the question of the possibilities of a negotiated peace. In November 1916, the consideration of over-all war policy resulted in the presentation to the Cabinet of two reports, one by Lord Lansdowne and the other by Lord Robert Cecil.[60] The first, by Lord Lansdowne, showed the difficulties which beset Britain and asked consideration of what continuation of the war might mean. Pointing to a memorandum by Sir William Robertson,[61] Chief of the Imperial General Staff, which had been circulated to the Cabinet in August, he emphasized that, since negotiations for peace might arise any day, the Cabinet should decide what their policy would be and explain it to the Allies. Suggesting that the achievement of a "knock-out blow" would be at the best remote, Lansdowne said "we ought at any rate not to discourage any movement, no matter where originating, in favor of an interchange of views as to the possibility of a settlement of the question." He added that there were many indications that the germs of such a movement were already in existence. Lloyd George regarded Lansdowne's memorandum as a sign that the "elder statesmen" were ready to put a real obstruction in his road and that there might be a serious movement to anticipate

[57] *H.C. Debates*, 5th series, LXXXVI, col. 103. October 11, 1916.
[58] *The Times*, October 13, 1916, p. 5, and October 24, 1916, p. 9.
[59] *Lord Bertie's Diary*, II, 47.
[60] The text of Lord Lansdowne's memorandum is in: The Earl of Oxford and Asquith, *Memories and Reflections, 1852–1927* (Boston, 1928), II, 165–175; and the text of Lord Robert Cecil's memorandum is in *ibid*, II, 175–178.
[61] Robertson's memorandum of August 31, 1916, is in *War Memoirs of David Lloyd George, 1915–1916* (Boston, 1933), pp. 264–272.

and force conclusion of the war. Further, he doubtless had intimations that German peace feelers were on the way.[62]

The memorandum by Lord Robert Cecil, then Minister of Blockade, was presented to the Cabinet on November 27. Basing his views on reports from military advisers that one more year of war might see a great military success, he advised continuing the war in any event. He believed that any agreement reached soon would mean a settlement close to the *status quo*, with the resulting increase of German power in eastern Europe. Outside of the Cabinet, powerful interests of the Northcliffe and Beaverbrook press were exerted at high pressure to force the formation of a government which would reject any compromises.

The resulting formation of the Second Coalition under Lloyd George on December 6, 1916, was one of the great turning-points of modern history. There could be no doubt that those British statesmen least able to sympathize with any movement for compromise were now in control and the "knockout blow" policy truly in the saddle. Along with Asquith and Grey, most of the other Liberals retired from the Cabinet, and those who remained or were newly recruited could be counted upon to follow Lloyd George. Of the new Prime Minister, his colleague, Winston Churchill, wrote: "Every day for him was filled with the hope and impulse of a fresh beginning. He surveyed the problems of each morning with an eye unobstructed by preconceived opinion, past utterances, or previous disappointments and defeats."[63] The objectives already clear in Lloyd George's public utterances were henceforth sought after in the spirit as described by Churchill.

More historically symbolic than the departure from the Cabinet of such Liberal leaders as Asquith and Grey was the departure of Lord Lansdowne. It signalized the defeat of the forces of moderation, as did the dismissal of Bethmann-Hollweg in Germany six months later. While Lord Lansdowne's own political career had been within the Conservative Party, he was the head of one of the great Whig families, but had left the Liberal Party when Gladstone came out

[62] Asquith, *Memories and Reflections*, II, 152.
[63] Churchill, *World Crisis*, I, 256.

for Home Rule. As representatives of the old Whigs his family had carried on both an aristocratic and a liberal tradition. Beginning with the Earl of Shelburne, his great-great-grandfather, who was Prime Minister during the negotiation of the peace with America in 1782, all but one of his ancestors in the direct male line had been members of a British Cabinet.[64] Curiously enough, Lord Lansdowne was also a descendant of Talleyrand, who had struggled for a moderate settlement in Europe after 1815. The dismissal of Lord Lansdowne from the Cabinet in 1916 marked the overthrow of the moderation of Whiggism and old Liberalism, and it came just at the moment when peace negotiations were actually under way and when there might have been some hope for success and for a peace of moderation during the succeeding months.

And, indeed, two peace moves were publicly announced within a few days after the formation of the Lloyd George Cabinet. The first, on December 12, was from Germany, followed six days later by an appeal to the belligerents from President Wilson. The German move had been developing since August, when the Chancellor had privately warned a group of political and military leaders that efforts should be made to gain peace. In October he persuaded both the Kaiser and the recently appointed Chief of Staff, General Paul von Hindenburg, to agree that a declaration should be made in favor of peace, and a month later very general terms were agreed on. At the same time, it was agreed that the declaration should take place only if the military situation were favorable, particularly in Rumania, and if the compulsory labor service bill were passed.[65] The bill was passed on December 2, and Bucharest fell on December 6. It was these dates that controlled the timing of the German peace note.

Many factors entered into President Wilson's move. The peace feelers made by Germany to Wilson, which had formed the background of Lloyd George's "knockout blow" pronouncement in September, had been pressed again later in the autumn by an appeal from von Bernstorff in which he emphasized the dangers of resort

[64] George Edward Cockayne, ed., *Complete Peerage of England, Scotland, Ireland, Great Britain, and the United Kingdom* (London, 1893), V, 17–19.

[65] Gatzke, *Germany's Drive to the West*, pp. 139–140, 142–144, 148.

to all-out submarine warfare, if no accord was reached.[66] After Wilson's reëlection in November, these earlier moves were followed by a speech by the German Chancellor in the Reichstag Budget Committee in which, after defending Germany's part in the war's outbreak, he stated that "Germany is at all times prepared to join a union of peoples to hold disturbers of peace in check." He further emphasized that the annexationist war aims of Germany's enemies precluded the possibility of a league of that sort, and concluded that he "had never indicated that the annexation of Belgium had been the Government's aim."[67] In an interview with Joseph Grew, the American Chargé, on November 22, the Chancellor informally discussed the question of peace and emphasized Germany's long desire for it.[68] Grew did not doubt the Chancellor's sincerity and also was convinced that the Germans as a whole, with the exception of certain elements in the Army and the Navy and certain politicians, were ready to welcome steps in the direction of peace.[69]

Immediately after the election, Wilson corresponded and later conferred with House about the possibility of a peace move. House was at this time for delay, realizing probably more truly than Wilson how unfavorable articulate public opinion in England would be.[70] Wilson was encouraged by a letter from Charles Trevelyan, prime mover in the U.D.C., who wrote of the "yearning for a great solution" and that Wilson was the hope of this. A memorandum from Howard Whitehouse, one of the Liberal M.P.'s who favored a negotiated peace, had given an analysis of the political situation in Parliament which indicated some hope for action by the moderates.[71]

---

[66] Count Bernstorff, *My Three Years in America* (New York, 1920), pp. 293-294.

[67] Document 4889, November 10, 1916. *Papers Relating to the Foreign Relations of the United States, 1916* (Washington, 1929), Supplement, p. 64.

[68] Document 4636, November 22, 1916. *Foreign Relations, 1916*, Supplement, pp. 68-69.

[69] Document 4671, December 1, 1916. *Foreign Relations, 1916*, Supplement, pp. 77-78.

[70] Charles Seymour, ed., *The Intimate Papers of Colonel House* (Boston, 1926), II, 398.

[71] Baker, *Wilson*, VI, 394-395.

Confidential reports came to the President that war weariness was far advanced in France. On November 21 von Bernstorff cabled his government that Wilson would make a peace move before the new year.[72] When the German peace note was sent, Wilson feared that a brusque refusal from the Allies might end all hope of negotiation, and so sent his immediately. Whatever force this note might have had was probably destroyed by its appearance after the German note.

In the message Wilson pointed out that the neutrals had a great stake in peace, and called attention to the fact that, "as stated in general terms to their own people and to the world," the objects of the belligerents seemed the same.[73] Both wished security for the rights of small states and security for themselves, and each was ready to consider formation of a League of Nations after a settlement on terms which would "safeguard the independence, the territorial integrity, and the political and commercial freedom" of the nations involved. Since this was true, Wilson proposed, as an interchange of views which might clear the way to peace, that "soundings be taken." The first draft of the message which Wilson had drawn up had been a stronger and more explicit statement. Recollecting, perhaps, the reception which the statement "with its causes and objects we are not concerned" in his May speech had encountered, he omitted in his final draft his original phrase, "and yet the reasons for this upheaval of the world remain obscure."[74] In his first draft he made a definite suggestion of a conference, later omitted. Further, in his first draft, he had anticipated the "peace without victory" speech which he was to make five weeks later, in a sentence later deleted, which read, "Upon a triumph which overwhelms and humiliates cannot be laid the foundations of peace and equality and good will."[75]

The Allies replied promptly to the German note on December 30, stating that they "refuse to consider a proposal which is empty and

[72] Document 33, November 21, 1916. *German Documents*, II, 993–994.

[73] James Brown Scott, ed., *Official Statements of War Aims and Peace Proposals* (Washington, 1921), pp. 12–15.

[74] Baker, *Wilson*, VI, 382.

[75] Baker, *Wilson*, VI, 385.

insincere."[76] On January 10 came the Allies' reply to Wilson's proposals which, after protesting that Wilson had drawn no distinction in his note between the purposes and aims of the opposing powers and reaffirming German guilt and Allied innocence in the outbreak of war, stated their war aims in vague but harsh terms.[77] The terms included the "liberation" of a list of peoples which would have meant the dismemberment of the Austro-Hungarian Empire and of the Turkish Empire, accompanied by the restitution of territories earlier annexed from the Allies and by wide demands for reparations. They were impossible terms for acceptance by a nation in the favorable military position in which Germany found herself at the beginning of 1917. Nor could the Allies have accepted the German terms of peace, which were never publicly announced, although agreed to by the German General Staff in the autumn and communicated privately to Wilson by Count von Bernstorff on January 31 when it was too late.[78] Nevertheless, the hardening of the attitude of responsible officials in both Germany and Great Britain made impossible the solution of problems which in historical perspective appear to us to have been perhaps not intrinsically insoluble.[79]

[76] Scott, *Official Statements*, pp. 26–28.
[77] Scott, *Official Statements*, pp. 35–38.
[78] Document 72, January 29, 1917. *German Documents*, II, 1048–1050.
[79] This point is cogently urged by Forster, in *Failures of Peace*, pp. 142–152.

Chapter III

British War Aims and Disarmament, 1917–1918: New Theories of International Relations

Currents of Thought, 1917: Disarmament in the Background

In England, the great majority of people accepted the orthodox version of Germany's move as an insincere "peace offensive" and the belief that Wilson had been made the pawn of German purposes. Nevertheless, the fate of the attempt at peace negotiations at the end of 1916 demonstrated to the satisfaction of some moderates that an extension of Allied war aims had, in fact, taken place.[1] After the Allied answer to Wilson's December peace note, references by certain Englishmen to British "imperialism" became more frequent. The "liberation of Italians, of Slavs, of Roumanians, and of Czecho-Slovaks from foreign domination"[2] mentioned in the note had surely been no part of the original Allied purposes in commencing the war, but had appeared as the result of bargaining for the entrance of Italy and Rumania into the conflict. The demand for the disruption of the Austro-Hungarian Empire and for terms which would also have meant the disruption of the Turkish Empire, as well as the territorial transfers necessary to the creation of a new Poland, showed that the purpose of the Allies now turned toward

[1] See Snowden, *Autobiography*, I, 437–448.
[2] Scott, *Official Statements*, p. 37.

the total solution of all problems in a total victory. If, as a consequence of the Allied answer of January 10, any hopes arose that the officials had repudiated the jingo ideas of the extreme sections of the press—since nothing had been said of dethroning the Hohenzollerns, disarming Germany, making the Rhine the German boundary, or retaining the German colonies—utterances from responsible government sources which followed soon afterwards put strict limits on these hopes. For Sir Gordon Hewart, the Solicitor General, soon declared that the war aims of the January 10 note were minimum demands, and the Colonial Secretary, Walter Long, announced that Britain must keep the German colonies.[3]

In Germany, the statement of these terms caused a hardening of resistance. The Kaiser's proclamation of January 13 that "our enemies have dropped the mask" and "admitted their lust for conquest,"[4] was followed a few days later by a statement of the German trade unions that "the Entente's answer removes every doubt that Germany is waging a war of defence."[5]

In the face of the failure of his attempt to influence the officials through his peace note, Wilson determined to address an appeal to the peoples of the world. This he did in a speech in the Senate on January 22.[6] The theme of the address was declared to be the conditions under which the United States could take part in a "League of Peace" to follow the ending of the war. Basic to the achievement of such a League was to be a "peace without victory," and it was by this phrase that the speech was remembered. Along with this idea, Wilson, in contrast to the public silence of responsible leaders in all countries on the subject, stated that "the question of armaments, whether on land or sea, is the most immediately and intensely practical question connected with the future fortunes of nations and of mankind."

The context into which the President wished to fit specific

[3] *The Times*, January 24, 1917, p. 8, and February 1, 1917, p. 6.
[4] Text in Scott, *Official Statements*, p. 45.
[5] R. H. Lutz, ed., *Fall of the German Empire* (Stanford, Calif., 1932), I, 401–402.
[6] Text in Scott, *Official Statements*, pp. 49–55.

programs of arms limitation presumed the existence of some international organization to keep the peace. While he had used the phrase "League of Nations" in his peace note of December, he spoke more vaguely in this address of "some definite concert of power which will make it virtually impossible that any such catastrophe should ever overwhelm us again." Later on, he used the phrase "community of power." As bolstering principles for such a concert, he stressed equality of rights among nations, in which he apparently included self-determination and freedom of the seas. He said of the latter:

It is a problem closely connected with the limitation of naval armaments and the cooperation of the navies of the world in keeping the seas at once free and safe, and the question of limiting armaments opens the wider and perhaps more difficult question of the limitation of armies and of all programs of military preparation.

Wilson's speech marks a divide in the history of thinking on international relations. In it was crystallized the point at which liberal ideas had arrived. Wilson himself was fully convinced that he was speaking for a "silent mass" of world opinion. "I hope and believe that I am in effect speaking for liberals and friends of humanity in every nation and of every program of liberty," he said. The main thesis of the speech may be expressed in three phrases: "peace without victory," the need for a "concert of power," and the imperative principle of "limitation of armaments." Wilson was voicing the hope of many inarticulate people in all the belligerent countries when he called for a "peace without victory." Throughout 1917, in all the warring countries, war weariness and disillusionment were expressed in various ways. The sentiment for a "peace of accord" rather than a "peace of victory" grew among the people. Throughout the year peace feelers through official, semi-official, and non-official channels, most of them not known about until later, were numerous.

As far as "concert of power" was concerned, Wilson was developing an idea which had already been voiced in various forms in England. A few days after the outbreak of the war, in an oft-quoted speech made in Dublin, Asquith had said that the force of arms in international affairs must give way to the force of right.[7] Later he had expressed his view more concretely in the form of approval of the idea of a League, which Sir Edward Grey had also already advocated. As has been noted, the Fabian Society and the U.D.C. had published plans for a League, and in 1915 the League of Nations Society had been formed in England, although as yet it had not presented definite plans. The Labour Party Conference, held in Manchester from January 23 to January 25, 1917, had also voted approval of a League,[8] and various Socialist and leftist groups had endorsed it. While no minister who had remained in the British Cabinet on the formation of Lloyd George's government had up to this time voiced any specific approval of a League, it had been discussed in the Cabinet, and already a commission had secretly been set up to study the idea.[9] Now it received what was apparently its first official nod of approval from the Lloyd George government when Bonar Law said in the House of Commons on February 20: "I shall be glad to see such a League."[10] After Wilson's speech of January 22 and after America's entry into the war, the interest in the question increased rapidly.

The idea of limitation of armaments as a specific end in itself had received no official approval in England up to this time. Even Grey, who before the war had expressed himself in favor of arms limitation, had said nothing about it during the war and had revealed privately to Colonel House doubts about the possibility of its achievement.[11] None of the groups, either in America or England, who were really important in influencing general opinion on questions of the peace, such as the League to Enforce Peace, the League of Nations Society, or the Fabian Society, had publicly discussed it. Except for a few left-wing Socialist societies and international

---

[7] Asquith, *Memories and Reflections*, II, 46–47.
[8] Brand, *British Labour's Rise to Power*, pp. 89–90. Compare *Report of the Sixteenth Annual Conference of the Labour Party* (London, 1917).
[9] The Phillimore Committee, set up in January 1917. See p. 68.
[10] *H.C. Debates*, 5th series, XC, col. 1233. February 20, 1917.
[11] Seymour, *House Papers*, II, 282–283.

Socialist gatherings, only the U.D.C. in England had made definite statements in favor of limitation of armaments. A few individuals, and *The Nation* and *The Economist* among the generally read periodicals, had sponsored it. Other groups, including the Fabian Society, had thought that it might come about as a result of the success of some great international organization, but had not advocated it as a specific program.

Both President Wilson and Colonel House were, however, thoroughly committed to the idea of disarmament as a specific end in itself. Their approach early in 1914 had been toward limitation of armaments as a means of relieving the tension in Europe, and, with the outbreak of the war, such plans gained in importance in their minds, as did the idea of the prohibition of private manufacture of arms. In combination with the principle of strengthening the force of international law, particularly through a mutual guarantee of independence and territorial integrity by some association of nations, disarmament had become the basis of any plans which Wilson and House expressed in private for the maintenance of peace after the war. To these views on disarmament Wilson held firmly. Ironically enough, at the same time that he spoke to the world as a kind of "voice of the people" for "peace without victory," decisions whose results would make this idea impossible of realization had already been taken.

On January 9, in spite of Bethmann-Hollweg's opposition, the renewal of unrestricted German submarine warfare had been decided upon.[12] On January 31, it was announced to begin the next day,[13] and on February 3 the United States severed diplomatic relations with Germany. In addition to this, the German intrigues in Mexico, revealed in the Zimmermann Note,[14] pushed Wilson close to the acceptance of the British and French thesis on the origins of the war.

The path for this shift in Wilson's views was made easier by the

[12] Gatzke, *Germany's Drive to the West*, p. 162.
[13] Scott, *Official Statements*, pp. 61–66.
[14] *Papers Relating to the Foreign Relations of the United States, 1917. Supplement I. The World War* (Washington, 1922), p. 147.

news of the Russian Revolution, which reached England and the United States on March 15. Already, a few months earlier, in October 1916, Wilson had stated in a press interview his conviction that only governments and never peoples initiate wars and that, therefore, "democracy is the best preventative of such jealousies and suspicions and secret intrigues as produce wars among nations where small groups control rather than the great body of public opinion." [15] Throughout the war the anomaly of the alliance with Czarist Russia by those fighting a war proclaimed to be for democracy had been difficult to explain. Now the way was cleared for the triumph of the slogan of the war of "democracy against autocracy." In his speech of April 2, asking for a declaration of war, Wilson characterized the autocratic Prussian government as one productive of intrigues leading to war and emphasized the democratic nature of the coalition against it. This now included a Russia which, he said, "was known by those who knew it best to have been always in fact democratic at heart." [16] From this time on, there was no obstacle in America to the triumph of those same myths and slogans which had captured most articulate opinion in England: they fell on the fertile soil of a highly suggestive people.

"No Annexations, No Indemnities"

At the same time that these changes were taking place in the United States, in England the groups who hoped for a peace of negotiation were becoming more articulate. In the last months of 1916, Francis Hirst, who had resigned as editor of *The Economist* the previous spring, had started a new periodical, *Common Sense*, which, though of small circulation, served as their organ. In February 1917, a debate took place in the House of Commons on the war policies.[17] In March, various groups, working for a moderate peace under the leadership of Noel Buxton, Lord Parmoor, and others, held a meeting at Central Hall, Westminster, with a

---

[15] Harley Notter, *The Origins of the Foreign Policy of Woodrow Wilson* (Baltimore, 1937), pp. 568–569.
[16] Text in Scott, *Official Statements*, pp. 85–93.
[17] *H.C. Debates*, 5th series, XC, cols. 1177–1302. February 20, 1917.

large attendance, at which a peace of accord was urged.[18] About this time, some leaders of the U.D.C. addressed to Wilson, through Colonel House, an appeal to demand negotiations on the basis of his January 22 "peace without victory" speech.[19]

A focus was given to the efforts of those who wished for a moderate peace by the slogan of "no annexations, no indemnities" as a peace basis which became current as a result of the peace demands which the Russian Provisional Government proclaimed on April 10.[20] Moderate groups in Parliament attempted to make capital of this in a debate on a resolution by Snowden, calling for a similar declaration by the British government. On this resolution, the first division on any debate on war aims, the motion received thirty-two votes.[21] In this debate, Snowden made one of the few references to the disarmament question which had been heard in Parliament during the war and returned to the theme he had stressed in the years before the war's outbreak—that of the dangers of the private manufacture of armaments.

In addition to the groups interested in a peace of negotiation, the groups interested in a future organization to preserve the peace also stepped up their efforts. Lord Bryce took the moment of America's entry into the war to publish in the *Manchester Guardian* his plan for a League.[22] This was followed up in May by another meeting at Central Hall, with Lord Bryce in the chair, to promote the interests of the League of Nations Society and launch the Bryce League Plan. Besides certain of the eminent Liberals who had been prominent in peace movements, such as Lord Buckmaster, Lord Parmoor, G. Lowes Dickinson, and others, many prominent M.P.s and others not associated with the negotiated peace movement were present. On this occasion, the connection of the disarmament idea to the idea of a League to keep the peace was emphasized in a speech by

[18] Thomas P. Conwell-Evans, *Foreign Policy from a Back Bench, 1904-1918* (London, 1932), pp. 138-141.
[19] Swanwick, *Builders of Peace*, p. 80.
[20] Scott, *Official Statements*, pp. 95-96.
[21] *H.C. Debates*, 5th series, XCIII, cols. 1625-1637. May 16, 1917. Compare Snowden, *Autobiography*, I, 449.
[22] *Manchester Guardian*, April 12, 1917.

General Smuts, who had come to England in the winter. After calling attention to the difficulties involved, he remarked that "it was no use trying to prevent wars if nations continued to be armed to the teeth." More significant than this was his remark that "the time had come when an Anglo-American Committee should be appointed to go thoroughly into the whole matter." [23]

The increasing interest in a moderate peace settlement and in future international organization to keep the peace was closely related to the growth of war weariness which was apparent everywhere in the first part of 1917. In England, this is recorded by many observers and is apparent from the periodical press.[24] In Germany throughout the spring, there were serious strikes. In France, the danger of mutiny in the Army was averted for the moment by the leadership of Marshal Pétain, who went himself among the troops asking them to tell him their grievances.[25]

On the surface no hint was given from any officials in power in the Allied countries of any tendency to modify terms. Wilson in June in a note to the Russian Provisional Government emphasized that no peace on the basis of the *status quo ante* was possible,[26] and there was no change in the pronouncements of the responsible leaders in Britain. However, behind the scenes there was evidence that officials were recognizing that certain official attitudes were being modified, particularly in France. A confidential memo which Balfour presented to the Cabinet sometime before the middle of May acknowledged that France might now be content with a peace which did not give her Alsace-Lorraine; but at the same time he pointed out the advantages to the British strategic position of its transfer from Germany to France.[27] In the summer Lord Bertie recorded that Lloyd George was worried over the situation in France,[28]

[23] *The Times*, May 15, 1917, p. 10.
[24] See "Ethics of International Punishment," *The Spectator*, CXVI, no. 4629, 327–328 (March 17, 1917).
[25] B. H. Liddell Hart, *The Real War, 1914–1918* (Boston, 1930), p. 301.
[26] Scott, *Official Statements*, pp. 104–106.
[27] *Papers Relating to the Foreign Relations of the United States. The Lansing Papers, 1914–1920* (Washington, 1939), II, 31–32.
[28] *Lord Bertie's Diary*, II, 161. July 27, 1917.

and confidential memos to House and Wilson also reported that France would probably make a peace without obtaining sovereignty over Alsace-Lorraine.[29]

During these spring months, not only was there evidence of a tendency behind the scenes for some modification of the Allied terms, but also there were clear signs that some of the professed objects in regard to Germany might be gained. The growth of liberal sentiment in Germany during the months just passed had been reported by all observers,[30] and now in April a declaration was made by Chancellor Bethmann-Hollweg of forthcoming basic reforms in the electoral system.[31] In view of the stress which President Wilson, in particular, was putting upon the need for a democratic Germany and his distinction between the German government and the German people, it might have been expected that all this would predispose the Allies to favorable consideration of moves giving evidence of conciliatory steps stemming from the German people. And, in fact, such a move was forthcoming in July.

The Reichstag Resolution and the Pope's Proposals

On July 19, 1917, the German Reichstag, by a vote of 212 to 126, declared itself "for peace and a mutual understanding and lasting reconciliation among the nations." [32] The majority for the resolution was composed of the Social Democrats, the Progressive Party, and the Catholic Center Party. Two weeks earlier, Erzberger, the Center leader, had revealed to a Reichstag Committee the virtual failure of the submarine campaign.[33] He had decided that peace must be sought by returning to the August 1914 formula of a war of defense. "Germany," the resolution read, "took up arms in defense of its liberty and independence and for the integrity of its territories." With the kind of peace for which the resolution called, "forced

[29] *Foreign Relations. The Lansing Papers*, II, 41.
[30] *Foreign Relations, 1917. Supplement I. The World War*, pp. 66–75.
[31] Gatzke, *Germany's Drive to the West*, p. 173. The famous "Easter Message" of April 7, 1917.
[32] Scott, *Official Statements*, pp. 114–115.
[33] A. J. Berlau, *The German Social Democratic Party, 1914–1918* (New York, 1949), p. 132.

acquisitions of territory, and political, economic, and financial violations are incompatible." In the course of the disturbed weeks between Erzberger's first announcement of the move and its passage, the Chancellor, Bethmann-Hollweg, against whom the military command had been waging a campaign for several months, was forced to resign. Ironically enough, he was in sympathy with the aims, if not the timing and form, of the resolution. As in England in December, when Lord Lansdowne left the Cabinet, his fall marked the overthrow of the hopes for moderate policies. By the interpretation put upon the peace resolution by his successor, Michaelis, its possible usefulness was destroyed.

In contrast to this vote of 212 in the Reichstag for such a resolution, the British Independent Labour Party could get only 19 votes in an attempt to have the same resolution endorsed by the House of Commons.[34] The British press in general soft-pedaled it, and only a few papers stated what the resolution was. Ramsay MacDonald on the floor of the House of Commons stated without challenge that "one afternoon, about three o'clock, certain evening newspapers appeared with this Resolution in a prominent position. The same papers, I believe, a little later on . . . had relegated the Resolution to a very obscure corner of their column."[35] MacDonald was of the opinion that many well-informed people in the country did not know of the resolution at all. The propaganda current in England about the undemocratic German government as the cause of all Europe's miseries had prepared the way for the interpretation which was put upon the resolution. For it was widely contended that the Reichstag was of no significance since the German people could not control their government. As an alternative to this idea, *The Times* was fond of hinting that all the parliamentary difficulty centering around the resolution was a theatrical display staged by the German government itself.[36] There was no official action in Britain on the resolution.

The Reichstag resolution was followed on August 1 by an appeal

[34] *H.C. Debates*, 5th series, XCVI, cols. 1479-1480. July 26, 1917.
[35] *H.C. Debates*, 5th series, XCVI, col. 1421. July 26, 1917.
[36] *The Times*, July 23, 1917, p. 7.

addressed by Pope Benedict XV to each of the belligerent powers.[37] For the first time, the principle of disarmament was presented as the keystone of a settlement and, by implication, the connection of its possible achievement with the conclusion of a peace of negotiation was made clear. He wrote:

> First, the fundamental point must be that the material force of arms shall give way to the moral force of right, whence shall proceed a just agreement of all upon the simultaneous and reciprocal decrease of armaments according to rule and guarantees to be established in necessary and sufficient measure for the maintenance of public order in every state.

Arbitration, having taken the place of arms, was to make possible a conciliatory approach to territorial and other questions and a peace settlement without reparations. The implications of his appeal, not so specifically stated, were that territorial and related questions would be settled largely on the basis of the *status quo ante bellum*.

In the press, the foundation of the whole structure of the Pope's proposal—that is, the acceptance of the ideas of disarmament and arbitration—was completely ignored. *The Times*'s leading article made no mention whatever of disarmament and claimed that the peace advocated by the Pope would be a German peace: that his "wide and ambiguous suggestions" could be interpreted by the Germans as they liked.[38] Furthermore, the general belief in the Allied countries was that the Pope's note was definitely instigated by Germany. The truth appears to be quite different from this. The Pope was, of course, aware of the strong desire of Emperor Karl of Austria for peace, a desire which had been pursued through private channels and which the moderation of the speeches of the Emperor's Foreign Minister Czernin had suggested. With this as a basis, the Pope had sounded out both Germany and Austria. With the help of a favorable general statement of probable terms from Bethmann-Hollweg and the Reichstag resolution, the Pontiff's note had been drafted.[39]

[37] Text in Scott, *Official Statements*, pp. 129–131.
[38] *The Times*, August 16, 1917, p. 7.
[39] For the most complete discussion of this point, see Forster, *Failures of Peace*, p. 128, and Gatzke, *Germany's Drive to the West*, p. 183.

The alarmed reaction in many quarters in both England and America is indicated by the telegram which the highly sponsored American organization known as the League to Enforce Peace sent to President Wilson three days after the publication of the papal note. It began:

> The League to Enforce Peace feels that a League of Nations which will guard the future peace of the world should be made effective only by the abolition of the Prussian military autocracy at whatever cost. Peace made with such a government could not, as President Wilson has clearly pointed out, establish conditions of mutual trust and security.[40]

The League, therefore, urged vigorous prosecution of the war. As might have been expected by the political developments in July, the reception in a large part of the German press was favorable. Even the *Vossische Zeitung* went so far as to hint at possible concessions to France on the question of Alsace-Lorraine. The *Berliner Tageblatt* published a series of articles on the necessity of disarmament proposals as the basis of peace.[41]

In the United States, the revolution in the highest official opinion since the "peace without victory" speech of January became clear from the fact that now Wilson was more belligerent than his adviser, House, and even considered not replying at all to the Pope's appeal.[42] However, on August 27 a reply was dispatched which reflected the same point of view as that of *The Times*'s leader and the telegram of the League to Enforce Peace. Lansing, speaking for Wilson, interpreted the Pope's proposal as implying that the *status quo ante bellum* must form the basis for a peace. This would be impossible of acceptance, since it would keep power in the hands of the old rulers of Germany. These he could not accept as guarantors of anything enduring, "unless explicitly supported by such conclusive evidence of the will and purpose of the German people themselves

---

[40] General Staff, War Office, *Daily Review of the Foreign Press*, series 4, no. 17, 158 (August 21, 1917: London, 1917).

[41] *Daily Review of the Foreign Press*, Enemy Press Supplement, II, no. 18, 514 (August 30, 1917), and *ibid*, II, no. 18, 518–519 (August 30, 1917).

[42] Seymour, *House Papers*, III, 154.

as the other peoples of the world would be justified in accepting."[43]

Both the Austrian and German replies to the Pope were sent on September 21. While the German note from the new government headed by Chancellor Michaelis paid lip-service to the Pope's disarmament proposals, the tone of the note was ambiguous regarding them. It stated: "The Imperial Government will in this respect support every proposal compatible with the vital interests of the German Empire and people." The Austrian reply expressed unqualified approval of the Pope's disarmament and arbitration proposals, and the ideas were further developed in a speech by Foreign Minister Czernin on October 2.[44] The idea of disarmament was as basic to this speech as it was to Pope Benedict's note. After expressing complete approval of "this new conception which has forced its way into the world," he added: "It is superfluous to state that this measure of disarmament must never be directed against any particular state, or any particular group of Powers, and that it must of course comprise land, sea, and air in the same degree." Echoing a phrase of Clausewitz which was to have an interesting history in the 1920's, he added: "War as an instrument of policy must be combated."[45]

A few days after Czernin's speech, the Pope's disarmament ideas were further developed in a note sent to Lloyd George the contents of which were not officially revealed. An unofficial but substantially accurate summary of the Pope's note was, however, printed in *The Times*.[46] The note suggested proposals for the abolition of compulsory military service and the institution of a commercial boycott against any violators of peace. An international tribunal was to determine whether a violation had been committed. The writer of *The Times* leader the next day was not impressed by these proposals and could only echo in the strongest terms the "knockout blow"

---

[43] Scott, *Official Statements*, pp. 133-135.
[44] The texts of the German and Austrian notes and of Czernin's speech may be found in Scott, *Official Statements*, pp. 139-141, pp. 137-139, and pp. 152-156, respectively.
[45] Compare *The Living Thought of Clausewitz* (Philadelphia, 1942), p. 171.
[46] *The Times*, October 3, 1917, p. 5.

idea. "There is no place for compromise . . . The choice for both sides is surrender or defeat. There can be no halfway house."[47] In its editorial the following day on the Czernin speech, *The Times* made its almost sole specific reference during the war to the question of disarmament when it said: "We all look forward to disarmament and arbitration and other specific schemes, which he [Czernin] advocates with the fire of a convert, as ideals which the world may hope to attain. But we are not so simple as to think that their present realization can be made a condition of peace."[48] The tone of this article and the temper of a large section of the British nation at that time was reflected in its quotation from a recent speech of Churchill's: "This is not the time to talk of peace."[49]

In spite of the unfavorable reception given to the Pope's appeal, his emphasis upon disarmament came just at the time when it was really beginning to achieve some prominence in public discussion. The tone as well as the letter of some of the Pope's proposals was echoed in a speech by General Smuts on October 24 before a meeting organized by the National War Aims Committee at Sheffield.[50] He said:

When we talk about our war aims, to my mind there is one great dominant war aim, the end of militarism and the end of standing armies. So long as the burden of militarism is resting on Europe, so long as our young manhood from year to year has to be sacrificed to this moloch of war, it has not yet solved the economic, industrial and social questions which are ahead of us.

No one in authority in the Allied countries had before this time emphasized the idea of the end of standing armies. General Smuts did not wish to continue war until we got rid of all evils. "Give us," he said, "a good and fair peace and we need not solve the other problems which concern the universe." To make it clear, however, that his speech conformed with British policy, he added that at

[47] *The Times*, October 4, 1917, p. 9.
[48] *The Times*, October 5, 1917, p. 9.
[49] *The Times*, October 4, 1917, p. 3.
[50] *The Times*, October 25, 1917, p. 6.

present a negotiated peace would be dangerous and that certain issues must be settled before we go to the conference table.

While this speech did not depart in any specific way from the official viewpoint of the British Cabinet, nevertheless it breathed quite a different tone from the "knockout blow" utterances of Lloyd George and of Winston Churchill. Also, it gave neither hope nor expectation that the peace would solve all problems.

At the same time, however, that the idea of disarmament was gaining greater prominence and acceptance, signs were appearing of the expectation of total solutions for all problems in the peace settlement. A speech by Asquith, now out of office but in the guise of elder statesman, reflected this attitude when he spoke of "just claims, long overdue" in the territorial settlement. "You must proceed," he said, "on the lines of racial affinity, of historic traditions, above all of the actual wishes and aspirations of the inhabitants." In addition to wishing the peace settlement to provide solutions for all the old problems of Europe, he wished for an all-embracing organization to keep the settlement made.[51]

Lord Lansdowne's Letter

Both the pressure for a war *à outrance* and the notion of a peace treaty furnishing total solutions were met head on by the letter of Lord Lansdowne, published in the *Daily Telegraph* on November 29, 1917.[52] It represented the culmination of the efforts of the moderates in England for a negotiated peace and reflected the opinions expressed by Lord Lansdowne in his memorandum to the Cabinet a year earlier. He emphasized the horror and destructiveness of the war and concluded that the British aim was that of security and the prevention of future wars. To this end, he suggested some system of arbitration and pointed out the fact that Wilson, Bethmann-Hollweg, the papal note, and the Austrian government had all welcomed such an idea. Lord Lansdowne regretted that the statement of Allied territorial aims in the note of January 10, 1917, had not been more precise. He then suggested that, in order to draw

[51] *The Times*, September 27, 1917, pp. 7-8.
[52] Text in *International Conciliation*, no. 122, pp. 5-10 (January 1918).

from Germany a more definite statement of her aims, the Allied governments declare that they did not desire to annihilate Germany as a great power, nor impose any government upon her, nor, "except as a legitimate war measure," to deny her a place among the great trading nations. Further, the Allies should state that they would examine the question of freedom of the seas and that of a pact for the settlement of the international disputes.

It would be difficult to exaggerate the abuse heaped on Lord Lansdowne for presenting these moderate proposals. *The Times*, which had refused to print the letter, condemned it in violent terms.[53] The music halls rang with "Hands down to Lansdowne." The Old Etonians refused to elect Lord Lansdowne as their president, although his name had been scheduled for the honor. The *Daily Express*, which devoted much space to the matter, after remarking that in some quarters it had been taken as a sign that Great Britain might be growing reasonable, concluded firmly: "Great Britain is not growing 'reasonable.' "[54] Among the more widely circulated journals, only *The Nation* and the *Manchester Guardian* defended it. Such approval as it received from a few M.P.s such as Ponsonby and Philip Morrell was played down in the press. In the French press the letter was scarcely mentioned.[55]

A few weeks later the government was to deny in the House of Commons that it had been consulted on the letter.[56] Later evidence, however, has shown that while technically true, this was misleading. Lord Lansdowne had sought a meeting with Balfour and explained his views to him and his intention of publishing them. Balfour was leaving for America and instructed him to show the letter to Sir

[53] *The Times*, November 30, 1917, p. 9.
[54] Osbert Sitwell, *Those Were the Days* (London, 1938), pp. 399–400.
[55] "Events of the Week," *The Nation*, XXII, no. 9, 289 (December 1, 1917). Compare Second Section, U.S. General Staff, G.H.Q.A.E.F., (*Confidential*) *Press Review*, no. 1, 1–2 (December 12, 1917). See also *Daily Review of the Press*, Allied Supplement, pp. 160–161 (December 12, 1917). An exception is Austin Harrison, "Lord Lansdowne's Interrogation," *English Review*, XXVI, 76–92 (January 1918).
[56] *The Times*, December 1, 1917, p. 9. See also Snowden, *Autobiography*, I, 440.

Charles Hardinge, Permanent Secretary of the Foreign Office, who, as Balfour said, "knows my views." This Lord Lansdowne did. Hardinge later claimed, however, that his assistance had been invoked "simply as a technical expert," that he had made a few technical criticisms, and expressed disapproval of the tone of the letter. After the refusal of *The Times* to publish it, Lord Burnham of the *Telegraph*, a personal friend of Lansdowne's, agreed to do so. According to Hardinge, Lord Burnham was under the impression that the Foreign Office approved publication and was greatly disturbed by the later reaction to the letter.[57]

After the violently abusive reception of the Lansdowne letter in England, all hope for a negotiated peace was gone. The year, 1917, had been the period during which a possibility for such a peace had existed. Besides the moves known to the public, such as the Reichstag resolution and the Pope's appeal, many moves for peace, not known till later, had been going on behind the scenes. In April, Czernin had warned Berlin of the necessity for peace,[58] and at the same time talks were held between Lloyd George, Ribot, then French Foreign Minister, and Baron Sonnino, the Italian Foreign Minister, about the possibility of an Italian-Austrian peace.[59] In September and early October, secret diplomatic moves growing out of the papal appeal were continuing: negotiation between Briand, then out of office, and von der Lancken, a German staff officer in Belgium. Ribot was soon informed of the talks, but the French Cabinet was not favorable.[60] After the failure of the Pope's appeal, the German Foreign Minister, von Kühlmann, sent out feelers by way of the German Embassy in Spain.[61] In the late autumn, however, after the Italian disaster at Caporetto in October and the armistice between Russia and Germany in November, German feelers no longer

[57] Lord Hardinge of Penshurst, *Old Diplomacy* (London, 1947), pp. 223-224. The whole question is discussed in the Marquess of Lansdowne's article, "The Peace Letter of 1917," *Nineteenth Century*, CXV, no. 685, 370-384 (March 1934).

[58] Gatzke, *Germany's Drive to the West*, pp. 176-177.

[59] Forster, *Failures of Peace*, pp. 98-101.

[60] See Forster, *Failures of Peace*, chapter VII.

[61] Forster, *Failures of Peace*, pp. 134-139.

appeared. On the basis of the Central Powers' changes of temper due to the altered military situation, as well as the hostile reaction in Great Britain to Lord Lansdowne's proposals, it was clear that by the end of the year the possibility of negotiation had disappeared.

Labour's Aims, Lloyd George's Concessions, and Wilson's Fourteen Points

While these moves for a negotiated peace had been commenced and lost within the ranks of officialdom, the movement in the country for a moderate peace continued to grow in strength until the beginning of the German drive in March 1918. The growth in sentiment during 1917 for a negotiated peace is well illustrated by what was happening in the Labour Party. At the Party Conference in January 1917, the delegates had ignored a motion to insist upon a more definite declaration of peace terms.[62] By the end of that year, however, the Trade Union center of the Labour Party had shifted toward a position on the peace close to agreement with that which the left wing, as represented by the Independent Labour Party, had always held.[63] At the same time, the drive of the Independent Labour Party for a declaration of peace aims had strengthened.

The activities of branches of the Labour Party for a peace of moderation, active since 1915, had been stepped up in May 1916 by the organization of the Peace Negotiations Committee with representatives of the I.L.P., the British Socialist Party, and the Women's Labour League. They held a number of meetings throughout the country, distributed pamphlets, and collected signatures for a memorial urging the government to explore the possibilities for securing peace by negotiation. Signed by 221,617 people and endorsed by local Labour parties with a membership of 900,000, it was presented to the Prime Minister in May 1917. All this had been accomplished without any aid from the press, save that controlled by Labour, for other newspapers refused to print the memorial even as a paid advertisement.

[62] *Report of the Sixteenth Annual Conference of the Labour Party*, p. 28.
[63] Compare Brand, *British Labour's Rise to Power*, p. 43.

During the spring and summer of 1917, opinion in the Labour Party had risen to a high pitch on the question of granting passports to representatives of British Socialism to attend the proposed Stockholm Conference at which representatives of not only Allied but belligerent Socialist parties would be present. The final decision of the government not to grant passports resulted in the resignation of Henderson from the Cabinet and his replacement by George Barnes as Labour representative.

After this, Henderson devoted himself to the preparation of a Labour Party program on war aims, and MacDonald and Sidney Webb collaborated with him in the memorandum.[64] The plan, made public in August, was presented in its final form to a special Party Conference in December, where it was accepted in substance as the program of the Party.[65] This Labour statement of war aims called for complete democratization of all countries, abolition of compulsory military service, limitation of armaments, and abolition of private arms manufacture. Its scheme for the establishment of a League of Nations with an International Court and an International Legislature was substantially the Fabian scheme which had been set forth in the *New Statesman* in July 1915. The principle of self-determination was accepted, as was also the Fabian advocacy of plebiscites for all disputed territorial questions, including Alsace-Lorraine. Federation in a customs union was advocated in the Balkans, as well as administration of colonial areas under the League for the benefit of the natives.

While this memorandum incorporated a good deal of the 1915 Fabian plan for a future League, its stress upon limitation of armaments and abolition of private arms manufacturing were principles associated with the Independent Labour Party's program. It reflected, then, the ideas of the Socialist societies on war aims and a moderate peace. It was followed in June 1918 by the adoption of the Labour Party's reconstruction manifesto, *Labour and the New Social Order*, embodying the Fabian blueprints for future domestic policy.

[64] Beatrice Webb refers to it as "Sidney's memorandum." *Beatrice Webb's Diaries*, p. 93.
[65] Text in *International Conciliation*, no. 123, pp. 23–34 (February 1918).

At a conference in February, meanwhile, the Party accepted a new constitution which molded the Party into a fighting instrument, transforming it from a federation of affiliated societies into a national party with individual members and with a local party in every Parliamentary constituency.[66] The Labour Party was well on the way to being, first, His Majesty's Loyal Opposition and, later, His Majesty's Government. Toward the preparation of the Party for power, the war aims question had played a vital part.

In February 1918, a meeting of the Inter-Allied Labour and Socialist Parties in London adopted the points of the British Labour Party's war aims memorandum,[67] which would serve as the basis for their approach to the Central Powers Socialists and for a joint conference to be held later in the year in Switzerland. Nevertheless, censorship prevented the Inter-Allied memorandum from reaching the German Socialists, and it was not until May that Ebert, the Social Democrat leader, announced indirect receipt of the text. The international conference, however, never took place. The German Socialists were in favor of the general principles of the memorandum, including disarmament, but balked at some of the territorial proposals which were disadvantageous to the Central Powers, and a direct response to the Allied text was never received.[68]

In the meantime, some features of the program had found expression from the highest official sources in England. After the declaration of Labour war aims in December, Lloyd George, realizing the necessity of conciliating the Labour groups, agreed to address the Trade Union Congress on January 5. In his speech he made the most definite statement of war aims which had come up to that time from any responsible Allied statesman. Just a little earlier he had made two speeches on war aims, the first mainly on the subject

---

[66] See Brand, *British Labour's Rise to Power*, pp. 54–60, and Cole, *History of the Labour Party*, p. 45.

[67] The text of the British memorandum was accepted with a few minor changes. See Charles A. McCurdy, *A Clean Peace: The War Aims of British Labour* (New York, 1918), for the complete text of the memorandum of the Inter-Allied Socialist Conference.

[68] Brand, *British Labour's Rise to Power*, pp. 191–193.

of the Lansdowne letter, but their tone had been much more vague than that of his speech of January 5.[69]

In it he summarized three conditions for permanent peace: the establishment of sanctity of treaties; recognition of the principle of self-determination; and "the creation of some international organization to limit the burden of armaments and diminish the probability of war."[70] While in this summary statement of conditions the idea of limitation of armaments is not stated as a specific aim in itself, Lloyd George for the first time began to talk of armaments in a way similar to Sir Edward Grey's earlier pronouncements. "The crushing weight of modern armaments," he said, "the increasing evil of compulsory military service, the vast waste of wealth and effort involved in warlike preparation—these are blots on our civilization of which every thinking individual must be ashamed."

Wilson's epoch-making speech three days later, which included the statement of the famous Fourteen Points, was prepared quite independently of the British Prime Minister's speech. As was Lloyd George's speech, so was Wilson's an attempt to keep alive the hopes of Liberal and Labour circles in the Allied countries, especially in France.[71] Wilson, however, went much further to meet their point of view. At the Inter-Allied Conference in Paris at the end of November 1917, Colonel House had attempted to get a declaration of war aims which would make certain the Allies were not "waging war for the purpose of aggression or indemnity."[72] It was the failure of this attempt, combined with the increasing demands of liberal circles for a statement of war aims and the demands of the Bolshevik government in Russia for a peace of "No Annexations and No Indemnities," that formed the background to the Fourteen Points speech. The accord of the general position of the Fourteen Points with the British Labour manifesto was clear. The *New Statesman*

---

[69] Lloyd George's speeches of December 14 and December 20, 1917. Texts in Scott, *Official Statements*, pp. 210–215, 216–220.

[70] Text of the January 5 speech in Scott, *Official Statements*, pp. 225–223.

[71] Seymour, *House Papers*, III, 317. Compare Walter Lippmann, *Public Opinion* (New York, 1922), pp. 208–217.

[72] Seymour, *House Papers*, III, 281–282.

a few months later spoke of the Fourteen Points as "plagiarism" from the manifesto.[73] The principles of open diplomacy, no trade barriers, self-determination, limitation of armaments, and a league to keep the peace were common to both.

Wilson's statement in regard to limitation of armaments, which constituted his Fourth Point,[74] read:

> Adequate guarantees given and taken that national armaments will be reduced to the lowest point consistent with domestic safety.

This statement of purpose by the head of a leading Allied state marked a turning-point in the consideration of the disarmament question. Thus, a plain statement expressed the purpose of making specific plans for the limitation of armaments an integral part of the postwar settlement.

While Wilson's speech was hailed in Great Britain with the greatest acclaim, official and non-official silence on the Fourth Point was the rule. *The Times*'s leader on the Fourteen Points did not mention either the subject of disarmament or the Fourth Point. On the Fourteenth Point, that is, the formation of "a general association of nations," it warned: "The chief criticism which cautious leaders may be supposed to make upon it is that in its lofty flight to the ideal, it seems not to take sufficient account of certain hard realities and situations."[75] Even in the House of Commons debate on the war, just after the resolution of the Allied Conference in Versailles which reaffirmed the "knockout blow" policy,[76] the Fourteen Points were discussed at length, but the debate almost entirely ignored the Fourth Point.[77] Even Snowden made no reference to it.[78] Colonel Collins, an old Liberal and an officer of the line, called attention to the fact that the government had made no reply to Wilson's Fourth Point.[79] His argument hinged largely on the dangers of insolvency

[73] *New Statesman*, XI, no. 286, 502 (September 28, 1918).
[74] Text of Wilson's speech in Scott, *Official Statements*, pp. 234–239.
[75] *The Times*, January 10, 1918, p. 7.
[76] See *H.C. Debates*, 5th series, CIII, cols. 148–149. February 13, 1918.
[77] *H.C. Debates*, cols. 148–232. February 13, 1918.
[78] *H.C. Debates*, cols. 184–198. February 13, 1918.
[79] *H.C. Debates*, cols. 205–207. February 13, 1918.

in continental countries if there were not a limitation of armaments and the dangers to England of such a situation. He pointed out that the removal of the fear of Russia on the Continent would make the achievement in regard to arms limitation more possible. The only other mention of the Fourth Point was by Sir Willoughby Dickinson, President of the British League of Nations Society, who spoke of limitation of armaments as one purpose for which an international organization should exist.[80] The most significant omission in the debate was, however, in the speech by Lord Robert Cecil, the Minister of Blockade, who summed up for the government.[81] Like *The Times* editorial, he discussed all the points in order, omitting only any discussion of the Fourth. President Wilson and his advisers would have been better prepared for the realities of the situation they were to encounter in Paris just a year later if they had pondered well the signs so clearly pointed out by the omission of any mention of the Fourth Point, first by the well-informed *Times*, second, by Lord Robert Cecil, the representative of official opinion, who, as President Wilson at that time knew, had been the main instigator of the preparation of the British official plan for a League of Nations.

Party Alignments and Britain's War Aims

During the early months of 1918, when discussions of war aims were taking place in Parliament and in the country, the political grouping on the subject became clear. On the extreme right was the group whose views were reflected in periodicals like the *National Review* and in the Northcliffe press. These interests had been earliest in the field with the "Delenda est Germania" slogan. They believed it possible to secure power and prosperity for England through the imposition of harsh reparation measures against Germany and the continuation of the war by economic means after the shooting war had ended. Almost indistinguishable from this group as far as war aims were concerned was that section of the Liberal Party, now represented by Lloyd George and his friends in the Cabinet, a frac-

[80] *H.C. Debates*, cols. 214–217. February 13, 1918.
[81] *H.C. Debates*, cols. 223–232. February 13, 1918.

tion which had grown out of the Liberal Imperialist group of the early years of the century. Those members of the group who held public office paid occasional lip service at least to the idea of a League of Nations. On the question of disarmament, except on the idea of unilateral disarmament for Germany, they were silent.

There were, moreover, special interests with special axes to grind whose views were, for the most part, similar to those of the Conservatives and Lloyd George's Liberal group. Among these was that group led by intellectuals and composed of persons with special interests in east-central Europe, who desired a break-up of the Austro-Hungarian Empire and the rise of independent Slavic states upon its ruins. Mouthpiece of this group was *The New Europe*, a periodical which first appeared in October 1916. Another special interest group, led by Lionel Curtis, published the quarterly review called *The Round Table*. Its nucleus was the handful of young men who had gathered around Lord Milner in the Boer War. Their object was the binding of the British Empire more firmly together, the maintenance of its dominant position in the world, and, as a corollary to these ideas, the development of the principle of federalism everywhere. In justification of their view that the power of Germany must be destroyed, they argued that it was lack of sufficiently advanced development of democracy in Germany which was the basis of all the prewar international difficulties. They differed sharply from *The New Europe* group on the settlement of the question of eastern Europe, since, in accordance with their federal principles, they opposed further creation of small sovereign states.

The larger and more influential divisions in the House of Commons indicated an affinity in war aims among the Asquith-Grey Liberals, such groups as *The Round Table* contributors, and the groups on the left, including the Labour Party and the Fabians. The Fabian *New Statesman*, like *The Round Table*, put an early emphasis upon the dangers from an "undemocratic Germany." The Fabian plan for a League of Nations, as it developed in the pages of the *New Statesman*, did not include any provision for disarmament. In accordance with what might have been expected from Fabian circles, it went beyond the idea of a League which would be mainly a mechanism for ensuring against wars, and envisaged the setting up of an international bureaucracy and provisions for the beginning of international legislation.[82] With these ideas, as developed in the *New Statesman*, the so-called "War" Labour Party members were in more or less general agreement.

One section of the left became, indeed, as jingo as any group in the country. That was the section of the British Socialist Party, the prewar Marxist organization, which under the leadership of Hyndman split off from the main body in the spring of 1916 on the question of war aims. Calling itself, curiously enough, the "National Socialist Party," it controlled labor unions which prevented ships from sailing which were to carry Labour delegates to the wartime International Socialist conferences.

Apart from these Conservatives and Liberals of jingo tendencies, and the "War" Labour people, there was another group of Liberals who were not enthusiastic followers of Lloyd George. Asquith himself voted only once against the Government during the war period,[83] although in private he was reported to have at certain periods hoped for a negotiated peace. About one-third of his followers in the House of Commons at some time cast a vote for the principle of seeking peace by diplomatic means. From Asquith had come early support for the Wilsonian principles and for the idea of a League of Nations, and most of the members of this group were more prone to favor both this idea and that of disarmament than was that section of the Liberal Party now in control.

In the interval between the Lansdowne letter and the beginning of the new German offensive in March 1918, the moderate peace movement reached its height in England. The aims which the earliest defenders of the movement had announced early in the war

---

[82] See "The Duty of the Allies," *New Statesman*, V, no. 110, 124–125 (May 15, 1915); "Suggestions for the Prevention of War," *ibid*, V, nos. 118–119, Special Supplements (July 10 and July 17, 1915); "An Allied Peace," *ibid*, VII, nos. 179, 180, 181, 183, 184 (September 9, September 16, September 23, October 7, October 14, 1916); "A League of Nations," *ibid*, IX, nos. 223–227 (July 14–August 11, 1917).

[83] See this Chapter, p. 65, the debate on the Maurice motion. *H.C. Debates*, 5th series, CV, cols. 2347–2406. May 9, 1918.

British War Aims and Disarmament, 1917-1918

—the Union of Democratic Control in the autumn of 1914, the Independent Labour Party in the spring of 1915, and the Inter-Allied Socialist Conference in February 1915—had found vindication during these months in the close relation of the Fourteen Points to their aims.

While the Labour Party was the only one of the groups which, as an organization, gave aid and comfort to the movement for a moderate peace, the voting on the resolutions introduced by the moderate peace section of the House of Commons received far more support from a group of old Liberal members. The fact that most of the Labour members owed their return largely to Trade Union organizations and some of them to Liberal support, as well as the greater party discipline within the Labour Party itself, made it a less likely field for independent voting.

Between May 1917 and February 1918, there were five divisions in the House of Commons on resolutions concerned with the problem of peace terms.[84] Altogether, 37 Liberals and 9 Labour members voted on one or more of these measures in the minority opposing the government.[85] Support for such resolutions from these sources reached its height on November 6, 1917, in a vote of 31 for a motion by Lees-Smith favoring moves for a peace settlement, provided guarantees concerning Belgium were given and a solution of the problem of Alsace-Lorraine was forthcoming.[86] This was the period in which war weariness was at its height in England. The division marks a turning-point in Liberal support for a negotiated peace. Before this only a little more than half of the Liberals who finally

[84] H.C. Debates, 5th series: XCIII, cols. 1731–1734. May 16, 1917; XCVI, cols. 1587–1590. July 26, 1917; XCVII, cols. 1549–1550. August 16, 1917; XCVIII, cols. 2051–2056. November 6, 1917; CIII, cols. 231–234. February 13, 1918.

[85] On the first of these resolutions, May 16, 1917, nineteen Irish Nationalist members voted in opposition. They did not appear in later divisions, and their position is not relevant to the purposes of this study. However, this means that actually 65 M.P.s in all voted in opposition on these resolutions. A list of the Liberal and Labour members who voted in opposition is included in Appendix A.

[86] H.C. Debates, 5th series, XCVIII, cols. 2007–2052. November 6, 1917.

came out for a negotiated peace had voted in opposition. On this division, and on one in February 1918, the rest were added.

The opposition voters in the House of Commons reflect, of course, the different components of the moderate peace movement in the country. The leaders of the Independent Labour Party, Ramsay MacDonald and Philip Snowden, were constant in their opposition, the latter giving a most active leadership to the movement in his speeches in the House. Their colleagues in the Union of Democratic Control, Trevelyan and Ponsonby, still members of the Liberal Party, joined them in speeches and in discussions. The support which MacDonald and Snowden received in the House from Labour members was small, only five of them appearing in any of these minorities, and most of these only once.

Several different groups among the Liberals lent support to the movement in the House of Commons. Noel Buxton, who had been associated with Ponsonby, Philip Morrell, and others in 1912 in the formation of the Foreign Affairs Group of the Liberal Party—an organization for the improvement both of the general relation of Parliament to foreign affairs and of Anglo-German relations in particular—had not gone in with his earlier co-workers to the U.D.C. In 1916, however, after a visit to the United States and a conference with Colonel House, Buxton began to ask for a negotiated peace. His connections in the House of Commons joined the Liberal group for a moderate peace.[87] Other groups, such as that led by Francis Hirst, editor of *The Economist* until 1915, had representatives in the Commons.[88] Particularly by the autumn of 1917, certain industrialists and financiers began to see the importance of a moderate peace movement. There were seventeen M.P.s who were industrialists, merchants, or bankers among the Liberals who appeared on these discussions.[89] Practically all of these sat for constituencies in the north of England.

The future politics of many of these men was to be very significant. While, for several reasons, Labour members added little

[87] Conwell-Evans, *Foreign Policy*, pp. 80–84, 119.
[88] Richard Durning Holt, who was a nephew of Mrs. Sidney Webb.
[89] A list of these members is included in Appendix B.

strength to these opposition votes in Parliament, nevertheless the two Labour M.P.s who were most prominent in the movement during the war, MacDonald and Snowden, became soon after the war the Party's acknowledged leaders. Also, several of the leaders of the then-Liberals in this movement at the end of the war or soon thereafter joined the Labour Party.[90] Of course, it would be expected that the Liberals in this group would prove to be of the old Gladstonians, who now would follow Asquith rather than Lloyd George. A large number of them were elderly men; this was particularly true of the industrialists and barristers. They had been in the Liberal Party in the days of Gladstone, had adhered to the non-Imperialist section of the Party under Sir Henry Campbell-Bannerman and were now opposed to the Lloyd George policies. In March 1918, on the question of General Sir Frederick Maurice's letter challenging Lloyd George's statements on the comparative number of troops in France in January of 1918 with those of a year earlier and the General's subsequent relief from active duty, Asquith moved for an investigation commission.[91] Asquith had never up to that time voted in opposition to the Lloyd George government. In private, however, during the early months of 1918, he had been speaking favorably of the Lansdowne letter and voicing hopes for a moderate peace.[92] Now in his challenge to the government on the General Maurice matter, he forced a division in which 98 Liberals supported him. Since almost all of the Liberal opposition members we have been considering were of that 98, they formed about a third of the group. The vote on this division was taken as a test in the election of 1918 for the sponsoring of candidates by the Lloyd George Coalition,[93] and many of the 98 went down to defeat as a result. Since many were elderly men, a number of them did not again appear in politics.

There was, therefore, a close connection between the war aims

[90] These included Trevelyan, Ponsonby, Buxton, Lees-Smith, and E. T. John.

[91] *H.C. Debates*, 5th series, CV, cols. 2347-2406. May 9, 1918. Compare Major General Sir Frederick Maurice, *Intrigues of War* (London, 1922).

[92] Snowden, *Autobiography*, I, 443-444.

[93] Keith Hutchison, *The Decline and Fall of British Capitalism* (New York, 1950), p. 149. See p. 91 below.

controversy and the subsequent strengthening of the Labour Party, after the break-up and decline of the Liberal Party in the postwar years. Many Liberals who supported the idea of a moderate peace later moved over to the Labour Party, and it was from this group that many of the Labour Party's leaders in the postwar disarmament movement were drawn.

The Growth of the League Idea and Its Relation to Limitation of Armaments

Many of those who had long favored a negotiated peace were also active in the much larger movement for a League of Nations after the war which received new impetus at the time of the Fourteen Points speech. The idea had been sponsored by small private groups from the very beginning of the war, and the spring of 1915 had seen the organization of more general associations with this aim, both in England and in the United States. One by one they had released plans: the Fabian Society in the summer of 1916; the League to Enforce Peace in that same year in America; and just after the United States' entry into the war, Bryce had released the plan of his small group, now grown into the League of Nations Society.[94]

In the meantime, several responsible officials had expressed themselves in favor of an organization to keep the peace. Wilson had first publicly stated in May 1916 that he favored a League. Asquith and Grey had during their terms in office indicated acceptance of the idea. Not long after the Lloyd George Cabinet came into office, Bonar Law, then Chancellor of the Exchequer, had said that he would be glad to see such a League; and, finally, in his speech which just preceded the Fourteen Points speech, Lloyd George declared himself in favor of a League.

It was the Fourteen Points speech which marked the beginning of general acceptance of the League idea. Soon afterward, Wilson

[94] The texts of these plans are published in Leonard S. Woolf, ed., *The Framework of a Lasting Peace* (London, 1917), pp. 91-123 (Fabian Society); pp. 61-62 (League to Enforce Peace); and pp. 65-66 (the Bryce Group). For a complete discussion of the subject, see Henry R. Winkler, *The League of Nations Movement in Great Britain, 1914-1919* (New Brunswick, N.J., 1952).

began seriously to attempt to influence public opinion in its favor, and the growth of public interest and support was apparent in both America and England from then until the Peace Treaty. By March 1918, opinion in the United States in favor of a League had advanced so far that Colonel House, on the ground of public demand, was advising the appointment of an official commission to study the League question.[95] During the spring many important speeches and pamphlets on the subject of the League appeared, particularly in England, and a pattern which was gaining widespread agreement began to emerge. Most of the plans provided that certain kinds of disputes, conceded to be justiciable, should be determined by some international tribunal whose decision would be binding. Nearly all the plans provided that there should be some organization, called a "court" or a "conference," to which such disputes of a nonjusticiable character would be submitted. The very fact of submission of the dispute would involve a kind of moratorium or cooling-off period during which the good offices of the international organization would have time to function. If these deliberations were unsuccessful, then certain kinds of sanctions were to operate: in some plans, economic boycott; in others, provision for an ultimate recourse to armed force.

By almost all writers on the general subject of a League, limitation of armaments was considered a desirable end toward which to work. However, when precise plans of different organizations for a League appeared, the idea of arms limitation was omitted. The exception was in plans submitted by members of the Union of Democratic Control. However, the idea persisted that disarmament might be attained as a kind of by-product of a successful League of Nations, and much greater stress began, however, to be put upon disarmament as a specific aim in the early months of 1918. When Sir Willoughby Dickinson, President of the League of Nations Society, whose plans had not included any provision for disarmament, spoke on the League in the House of Commons, he said: "We are fighting for the creation of some international organization to limit the

[95] Seymour, *House Papers*, IV, 3-4, 8, 9-10.

burden of armaments and diminish the possibility of war."[96] Lord Shaw, President of the League of Nations Union, spoke in a similar vein in the House of Lords a month later.[97]

While these privately sponsored plans had been appearing, and while private groups had been attempting to influence public opinion, the British Cabinet had commenced the study of plans for a League. The first step had been a memorandum prepared by the Foreign Office in the autumn of 1916 at the time of the first peace feelers.[98] The document drew up a suggested basis for territorial settlement, which went far toward recognizing the principle of self-determination. After discussing the prepared settlement, it continued:

We have tried to work out a scheme that promises permanency; we have aimed at a reconstruction of the map of Europe intended to secure a lasting peace. We have been guided by the consideration that peace remains the greatest British interest. The most direct way to this end is, of course, to arrest the race in armaments which has gone on increasing the last forty years. This object can be best achieved by means of general arbitration treaties and consequent reduction of standing armies and navies.

This Foreign Office memorandum, prepared while the Asquith government was in office, was followed early in 1917 by the appointment by the new Cabinet of a commission to study the question of an international organization to keep the peace. Under the chairmanship of Lord Phillimore, the committee consisted of three representatives of the Foreign Office and three well-known historians.[99]

---

[96] *H.C. Debates*, 5th series, CIII, col. 215. February 13, 1918.

[97] *H.L. Debates*, 5th series, XXX, cols. 412–419. June 26, 1918.

[98] Text in David Lloyd George, *The Truth about the Peace Treaties* (London, 1938), I, 31–50.

[99] David Hunter Miller, *The Drafting of the Covenant* (New York, 1928), I, 3. The members of the Committee were, in addition to Sir Walter G. F. Phillimore (later Lord Phillimore): Professor A. F. Pollard, Dr. J. Holland Rose, Sir Eyre Crowe, Sir William Tyrrell, Sir Julian S. Corbett, C. J. B. Hurst, and A. R. Kennedy (Secretary). The text of the Phillimore Committee Report of March 20, 1918, is in *ibid*, II, 3–6, and its Interim Report in *ibid*, I, 4–8.

Its interim and final reports were submitted to the War Cabinet on March 20 and July 3, 1918. It provided for the establishment of a conference between the Allied states through which disputes which could not be settled by an international tribunal could be submitted. A moratorium was to follow, and finally a recommendation which, however, was to have no sanctions behind it. The plan was never accepted as the official plan of the British Cabinet and was not made public until much later. The principles which it contained were, however, put before the public, as they were reflected in Lord Curzon's speech in the House of Lords in June 1918.[100]

In spite of the interest shown in the earlier Foreign Office memorandum in regard to limitation of armaments, the report of the Phillimore Committee was entirely silent on this question. It was, perhaps, the disapproval of Sir Maurice Hankey, the Secretary of the Committee on Imperial Defence, which prevented any discussion of the question. During 1916, Hankey took over the newly established post of Secretary to the Cabinet in addition to his other post. A few months later, Lord Bertie recorded in his diary that Hankey's influence with Lloyd George was increasing.[101] Hankey, as can be seen in his essays published much later, believed that limitation of armaments would be not only a menace to the security of his country, but probably a cause of degeneracy as well.[102] In other branches of the government the Civil Servants were soon to prepare memoranda directed against the possibility of arms limitation. Apparently no branch of the government during these years made any study of the technical problems involved in any scheme of disarmament.

In contrast to the ideas current in British official circles, Wilson's ideas on disarmament developed early and had become very definite before America's entrance into the war. Even before August 1914, during Colonel House's mission to Europe in the spring of that year, he had put great stress on the necessity of arms limitation

[100] *H.L. Debates*, 5th series, XXX, cols. 393-407. June 26, 1918.
[101] *Lord Bertie's Diary*, II, 127.
[102] Lord Hankey, "The Study of Disarmament," in *Diplomacy by Conference* (London, 1946), pp. 105-119.

agreements. As soon as war broke out in the summer, President Wilson at once began to put out feelers regarding possible peace negotiations and peace terms; consequently his own ideas on these subjects began to crystallize at that time. In an exchange of views between himself and Secretary of State Bryan and his personal adviser, Colonel House, not only was emphasis put upon the idea of reduction and limitation of armaments, but a strong predilection fastened itself on Wilson's mind for the abolition of the private manufacture of armaments.[103] The origins of this conviction may be traced to several sources. Before the war, there had been a good deal of attention given in all countries of Western Europe as well as in the United States to the danger inherent in private manufacture. Wilson's domestic as well as foreign policy was based on the assumption that private interest in trade must be subordinated to general interest and that the influence of special interests in the government must be guarded against. His opinions regarding the abolition of private munitions manufacture followed from these premises. As a contributing factor, his experience with the difficulties made by private armament firms in the Latin American troubles was important. As we have seen, in his public speeches Wilson emphasized far more, far earlier, and far more explicitly than had any of the English statesmen the question of the importance of arms limitation.

In the autumn of 1917, Wilson had turned over to House the task of setting up an organization to study the problems of the peace. This resulted in the establishment of the group known as "The Inquiry." Walter Lippmann, then a young man, acted as its Executive Secretary.[104] In this capacity he wrote to the Secretary of War, Newton D. Baker, in October 1917, suggesting a special study of the question of reducing armaments. In a paragraph of great insight, Lippmann pointed out that what the whole question needed at that

---

[103] Notter, *Foreign Policy of Wilson*, pp. 330, 344-353, 356.

[104] Two prominent members of The Inquiry were Professor Isaiah Bowman (Executive Officer), the geographer, and Professor Charles H. Haskins, the historian. Other members of The Inquiry included President Mezes of C.C.N.Y. (Director), Professor J. T. Shotwell, and David Hunter Miller. Seymour, *House Papers*, III, 169-172.

stage was "creative study of the question by a group of men who thoroughly understand military science." Baker replied enthusiastically that he would "turn General Bliss' mind loose on the subject."[105] While General Bliss soon afterward became Chief of Staff and therefore had no time to give detailed study to the problem of peace, nevertheless, by the time of the Armistice he had become one of the most convinced proponents of the necessity of agreements in regard to the limitation of armaments.

While no detailed technical studies of disarmament appear to have been made by this group, some of the staff studies probably contributed to the draft of the article on arms limitation which Colonel House included in his draft for a League Covenant which he submitted to the President in July 1918. The article provided that the Council of Delegates should be directed to formulate plans for bringing about the reduction of armaments contemplated in Wilson's Fourth Point. The plan would not be binding until approved by all the governments signing the Covenant. Further, private manufacture of armaments was to be abolished and publicity of armament programs guaranteed.[106] This article formed the basis of the various drafts which resulted in Article VIII of the League Covenant.

In contrast to those of the British statesmen, Wilson's ideas for a League were far less specifically developed than his plans for disarmament. Following up the ideas which he and House had held before the war on arms limitation, Wilson gave careful attention to the correspondence between Grey and House in 1915.[107] He had much earlier hoped for some means of giving some sort of sanction to international law. Grey had also developed this idea, and he considered the refusal of a conference of powers at the start of the war as a disastrous step.[108] When Wilson prepared his speech to the League to Enforce Peace in May 1916, in which he voiced public

[105] *Papers Relating to the Foreign Relations of the United States, 1919. The Paris Peace Conference* (Washington, 1942), I, 12–13, 13–14.

[106] For the text of House's draft of July, 1918, of Article VIII, see Appendix C.

[107] Seymour, *House Papers*, IV, 3.

[108] Grey's interview with Bell of the Chicago *Daily News*, reported in *The Economist*, LXXXII, no. 3795, 886–887 (May 20, 1916).

approval of the League idea, he called for the Grey–House correspondence. He was also supplied at this time by material from Norman Angell, one of the leaders of the U.D.C., and later in the autumn House corresponded with Trevelyan and still later with Whitehouse.[109] Wilson's ideas on the subject of a League seemed to have developed very little before 1917, although he had mentioned it in his campaign speeches in the autumn of 1916, and the Democratic platform had included a statement in favor of it. The "peace without victory" speech in January 1917 also approved the idea of a League. In February 1917 he handed Lansing a memorandum on Bases of Power with four headings, including "Mutual guarantees of political independence" and "Mutual guarantees of territorial integrity."[110] These two points represented a more specific statement of the idea of a guarantee for basic international law.

After the Fourteen Points speech in January 1918, both Wilson and House made some attempts to influence public opinion in favor of a League, and House conferred with both English and American leaders who favored the principle.

Throughout the war period, Wilson contended that "the administrative constitution of the League must grow and not be made, that we must *begin* with solemn covenants, covering mutual guarantees of political independence and territorial integrity."[111] As a follow-up of this idea, he was against publishing the plan for a League which House had developed in the summer of 1918 and later amended.

This plan originated in correspondence between Lord Robert Cecil and House in the early summer. Cecil had wished for a conference on British and American views on the League before the Phillimore plan should be published.[112] A few weeks later on July 8, Wilson concerned himself with the project. It appears that he had not read the Phillimore report at this time, although he had been

---

[109] Baker, *Wilson*, VI, 218n; VIII, 43–44.
[110] *Foreign Relations. The Lansing Papers*, I, 19–20. The other two points were: guarantees against the continuation of economic warfare; and limitation of armaments.
[111] Baker, *Wilson*, VIII, 43–44. March 22, 1918.
[112] Seymour, *House Papers*, IV, 8–9.

sent a copy of it. Now, however, he instructed House to draw up the draft of a covenant. David Hunter Miller of The Inquiry group assisted House. The House plan was more extensive than the British plan, where a kind of diplomatic alliance had been set up which should prevent war by assuring the use of arbitration. To this, House made four important additions: first, a permanent secretariat; second, a permanent court; third, guarantees of territory; and fourth, provision for assuring agreements on limitation of armaments. The document became, with very few changes, the draft which Wilson took to Paris with him in 1919. Wilson made only two important changes in the House plan. He omitted the provision for an international court and included the use of force as well as economic sanctions for assuring resort to arbitration.[113]

While the creation of a League organization seemed to everyone, including Wilson, the necessary condition for achieving arms limitation, the effects of a rather general acceptance of the League had curious results. Most persons who accepted the idea of a League appeared to be convinced that if only such an organization were once set up, open diplomacy, popular control of foreign policy and the preservation of peace would follow. This view was best summed up in a sentence from a speech by Sir Edward Grey in May 1918: "The establishment and maintenance of a League of Nations is more important and essential to a secure peace than any of the actual terms of peace that may conclude the war."[114]

Basically this notion had its roots in a wholly oversimplified view of the origins of the war. As moderate a man and as good a humanitarian as the classicist, Professor Gilbert Murray, stated in 1918 that the whole question of the origins of the war was completely decided.[115] That its outbreak was due solely to Germany's lust for conquest was surely the view generally held in the Allied countries. The acceptance of this notion closed people's minds, however, to what really needed to be done to ensure for Europe a peaceful

[113] Seymour, *House Papers*, pp. 21-39.
[114] *The Times*, June 20, 1918, p. 5.
[115] Gilbert Murray, "The League of Nations and the Democratic Idea," reviewed in *The Times*, July 25, 1918, p. 351 (Literary Supplement).

evolution; in fact, closed their minds to the problems that a League, if established, must face. It paved the way for a continuation of psychological warfare after the shooting war was over. The history of these ideas makes clear that nothing is so essential to sound political development as an intelligent interpretation of recent history. It was not until nearly ten years after the war that understanding of the idea of general responsibility for its outbreak began to win acceptance.[116]

Another member of the Phillimore Committee, Professor A. F. Pollard, has defined a conqueror as one who believes that peace will come through the imposition of his own will.[117] But no one saw that something very close to this was going on in the minds of many persons who talked about a League. For each one saw the League as accomplishing what he himself most desired. Arthur Henderson looked upon it as a means of saving expenditure and therefore expediting social reform. The U.D.C., as well as Henderson, looked upon the League as the means of bringing about popular control of foreign policy. Members of *The Round Table* group, who saw federalism as the key to all solutions, looked upon the League as the means to further this end. Some of the higher Civil Servants, Sir Maurice Hankey, for example, were reconciled to the idea of a League because they realized that after the war a closer connection between public opinion and foreign policy would be necessary. The periodic meetings of the highest political officials, contemplated in the League, would facilitate this new task which would face those who guided policy. The French hoped that the League would provide the framework for an International General Staff which would preserve the European hegemony which France intended to achieve for herself through the peace settlement. The President of the United States saw the League as the means of preserving international peace. However humanitarian Wilson's aim might have been, it also was

---

[116] The most important step in the acceptance was the publication of Professor Sidney B. Fay's *The Origins of the World War* (New York, 1928).

[117] Albert Frederick Pollard, *The League of Nations: a Historical Argument* (London, 1918), p. 3.

surely in the best interests of the United States, whose prosperity depended to a large extent on a flourishing international trade.

These plans for a League of Nations, now well advanced in unofficial if not official circles, were the result of the development of ideas of international organization, of arbitration and arbitration treaties, and of sanction for international law, all brought together by the impact of the war and by the necessity of giving the people hope of avoiding future conflicts. However, along with the peace terms which would accompany the establishment of a League, such an organization came to be looked on as a "total solution." It was with the idea of "total solution" that disarmament became linked, although it was at first advocated by those who counseled moderation and a negotiated peace, a "peace without victory." Nevertheless, the ideas of a negotiated peace had been discarded. Wilson himself cast aside the concept when America entered the war. Limitation of armaments was a rational idea which could thrive only in an atmosphere of moderation. "Total war," "total victory," and "total solutions" alike created an atmosphere in which the achievement of agreements on arms limitation proved impossible.

Chapter IV

The Disarmament Idea from the Armistice to the Peace Conference

Negotiations for an Armistice

The German appeal for an armistice in the fall of 1918 came as a surprise to the Allied military and political leaders. Nevertheless, wthin five weeks the Allies' vague and uncoördinated war aims and principles of peace had been converted into practical and detailed armistice terms, terms which set the framework for the final military, naval, and air conditions of the Versailles Treaty under which Germany was to be disarmed. More was accomplished during these few weeks toward clarifying the joint war aims of the Allies and the United States than in any other similar period, but the attempted coördination of these aims also brought to light the serious points of difference between the Allies. The conflicting national interests and attitudes which appeared in these pre-Armistice negotiations suggested the more important struggles of the coming peace conference. While the Fourteen Points with stated reservations were accepted as the basis of the future peace, certain officially undeclared Allied war aims influenced the construction of the Armistice terms. The purely military terms secured certain political results quite unrelated to the Fourteen Points. Drawn up by the Allied General Staffs, they seemed to be designed rather to realize the general aims of Marshal Foch.[1]

After the battle of Amiens in mid-August, the increasing serious-

[1] F. S. Marston, *The Peace Conference of 1919* (London, 1944), p. 231.

ness of the German military situation became apparent to the German High Command, particularly Generals Ludendorff and Hindenburg, who began to press their government for an immediate peace. It was not, however, until October 3 that a note was sent to President Wilson by the newly appointed Chancellor, Prince Max of Baden, asking for an immediate armistice and for the initiation of peace negotiations based on the acceptance of the Fourteen Points and Wilson's subsequent pronouncements.[2] The German note, sent by way of Switzerland, did not reach Wilson until three days later, although it was intercepted by the French Intelligence on October 5 and its content was known to the Allied Premiers who were at that time meeting in Paris.[3] If the German government, in appealing to Wilson alone, had hoped to create dissension between the Allied and Associated Powers, there were some grounds for its aspirations. Both the French and British governments feared that Wilson might act independently in these negotiations, forcing the Allies to accept certain points of his program to which they would not otherwise have agreed. The Fourteen Points, announced in an address to the Congress of the United States, had never in fact been officially communicated to the Allies. Nor had the British or French governments made any attempt to resolve the important differences in the stated war aims of the Allied and Associated Powers. The German appeal for an armistice was unexpected, but the French and British Premiers, forewarned of its existence, were able to settle between themselves the general principles upon which they would grant it.[4] They also agreed to send a note to Wilson explaining their position on the question of an armistice.[5] Marshal Foch at Clemenceau's request began work on the military terms as early as October 5, and a day later Admiral Wester Wemyss had been instructed to prepare suggestions for the naval terms. General Bliss, the American Military

---

[2] Text in *Papers Relating to the Foreign Relations of the United States, 1918. Supplement I. The World War* (Washington, 1933), I, 337–338.

[3] Harry R. Rudin, *Armistice, 1918* (New Haven, Conn., 1944), p. 89.

[4] See Major General Sir Frederick Maurice, *The Armistices of 1918* (London, 1943), pp. 28–30.

[5] Text in Seymour, *House Papers*, IV, 87.

Representative at Paris, was informed on October 7 of the meeting of the Prime Ministers of the previous day and of the principles of the armistice decided upon. The detailed terms were to be considered the following morning by a meeting of the Representatives of the Allied Armies, but Bliss decided not to attend, having had no specific instructions for such a conference.[6] It was becoming apparent that an American representative possessing the full confidence of President Wilson was needed in Paris. The lack of coördination between the Allies and the United States was presenting serious difficulties. And on October 8 Wilson sent a reply to Germany without consulting the Allies, a reply which indeed appeared in the press before it had reached the Premiers through official channels.

When the exchange of notes between Prince Max and President Wilson began, it appears that Wilson was inclined to expect a negotiated peace rather than an unconditional surrender, but strong pressure from many sides soon forced him to abandon this idea. Excited American press comments appeared, demanding the removal of the Kaiser before an armistice be considered. Republican Senators indicated their opposition to a moderate settlement. Senator Henry Cabot Lodge in particular feared that Wilson would not demand unconditional surrender.[7] In addition to this pressure at home, reports of the foreign press, as well as strong hints from the Allied Premiers, helped to convince Wilson that a real surrender must be demanded. His reply of October 8, however, was mild in tone.[8] He stated that he would not approach the Allies on the question of an armistice unless Germany agreed to evacuate Allied soil and asked whether the Chancellor was speaking "merely for the constituted authorities who have so far conducted the war." Nevertheless, Wilson's second note, six days later, made it clear that the Allies would demand terms which would assure complete and continued military superiority and that unrestricted submarine warfare must end at once. Further, he called attention to his own speech of

[6] Rudin, *Armistice*, pp. 90–91, 93–94.
[7] *Selections from the Correspondence of Theodore Roosevelt and Henry Cabot Lodge, 1884–1918* (Boston, 1925), II, 539–540.
[8] Text in *Foreign Relations, 1918. Supplement I*, I, 353.

the preceding July 4, in which he demanded "the destruction of every arbitrary power anywhere that can disturb the peace of the world." This note was received in Germany with disillusionment and shock. It seemed to Prince Max that Wilson had yielded to the spirit of Foch and had abandoned "the high office of arbitrator" that the American President had professed even after entering the war. There was even discussion in some quarters whether negotiations for an armistice should be continued at all. The German High Command, especially General Ludendorff, wished the government to reply in strong terms to Wilson's demands and opposed the suggestion that Germany be deprived of the submarine weapon. Without more positive assurance of Wilson's ability to carry out his intentions of a just armistice, Ludendorff even advocated a *levée en masse* and a fight to the finish.[9] Prince Max, however, fearing that a brusque reply might be answered by a refusal to continue negotiations, brushed aside the objections of the High Command, and on October 20 accepted Wilson's demands, including the cessation of unrestricted submarine warfare.[10]

While the German government had been shocked by the tone of Wilson's second note, it was received with comparative enthusiasm in Allied official circles and by the Conservative press who assumed that Wilson had given up the idea of a bargained peace.[11] In spite of this favorable reaction, there remained among certain officials a feeling of resentment at the manner of Wilson's negotiations. It was felt that, in the course of his exchange of notes with Prince Max, he was imposing conditions preliminary to an armistice without first consulting his Allies.[12] Foch was of the opinion that the Allied Commanders-in-Chief alone should make the armistice terms, although Clemenceau, who realized the immense political questions involved, had rebuffed this suggestion. The German note of October 20, however, alarmed the Marshal, who believed that Berlin was endeavoring to set a trap for the Allies and that Wilson's position

[9] Rudin, *Armistice*, pp. 134-136.
[10] Text of Prince Max's note in *Foreign Relations, 1918. Supplement I*, I, 380-381.
[11] *The Times*, October 16, 1918, p. 9.   [12] Maurice, *The Armistices*, p. 32.

as arbiter was very undesirable.[13] Moreover, the question of Allied acceptance of the Fourteen Points had not yet been settled, and Lloyd George suspected with good reason that one of Prince Max's objects during the negotiations was to commit the Allies to Wilson's peace program to which they had many yet unstated reservations.

On October 23 Wilson sent a note to Germany stating that he would take up the question of the armistice with the Allied governments since Germany had assured acceptance of his conditions of peace.[14] The note further emphasized the necessity of democratic German government and of armistice terms which would make impossible the renewal of hostilities. The fact that Wilson now officially informed the Allied governments of his negotiations with Germany cleared the air in England and France, and the military and naval advisers were able to put their armistice proposals into final shape. Furthermore, Colonel House was due to arrive in Paris three days later, and as Wilson's plenipotentiary, he would be able to confer with the Allied Premiers on the principles of the armistice and to settle outstanding differences concerning the Fourteen Points.

Wilson's latest reply had meanwhile produced a crisis in Germany, and the struggle between the government and the High Command came to an open breach. Ludendorff and Hindenburg, who originally had urged the initiation of negotiations for an armistice, now again protested against continuing negotiations with an enemy who desired to destroy them. Wilson's note, said Hindenburg, was proof "that our enemies use the term 'peace of Justice' only to deceive us and to break our will to resist."[15] Ludendorff resigned on October 27. Prince Max took matters into his own hands and on behalf of the German government decided to proceed with the negotiations.

While the Allied and United States Commanders-in-Chief were considering the military terms and the Allied Naval Council the naval terms in the last week in October, House's arrival in Paris enabled the Allied Premiers to begin discussion of Wilson's pro-

[13] Rudin, *Armistice*, p. 167.
[14] Text in *Foreign Relations, 1918. Supplement I*, I, 381–383.
[15] Maurice, *The Armistices*, p. 44.

Disarmament Idea from Armistice to Peace Conference

gram. The primary purpose of House's mission was to make certain of Allied acceptance of the Fourteen Points as the basis for the peace settlement. But before he met with Lloyd George and Clemenceau and the other Premiers, House had to meet the plausible criticism that the Fourteen Points were "too indefinite in specific application."[16] A commentary was therefore prepared in Paris by Walter Lippmann and Frank Cobb of The Inquiry, which was approved by Wilson on October 30 as "a satisfactory interpretation" of his principles.[17] This memorandum was always before the Peace Conference and was referred to constantly.

When the meetings of the Premiers and House began on October 29, the point immediately raised was the question which had been bothering Lloyd George and Clemenceau since the armistice negotiations had started: if the Allies agreed to the terms of the armistice as they now stood, would they not be committeed to the Fourteen Points in their entirety, to which they had never agreed? In the ensuing discussions, which lasted until November 4, it became apparent to House that the British would not accept the principle of "freedom of the seas" and that a reservation must also be made concerning reparations, if a decision on the Fourteen Points was to be made at this time. And House was determined that an agreement should not now be postponed.[18] The reluctance of the French, British, Italian, and Belgian representatives to accept Wilson's principles, however, forced House to threaten that the President might be compelled to resort to further and more embarrassing "open diplomacy."[19] When the Allies had at length agreed to the Fourteen Points with reservations only on the two points above, House was jubilant. "I am glad," he recorded in his diary, "the exceptions were made, for it emphasizes the acceptance of the Fourteen Points." Walter Lippmann wrote to House, congratulating him on a triumph

[16] Robert Lansing, *The Peace Negotiations, A Personal Narrative* (Boston, 1921), p. 191.

[17] *Foreign Relations, 1918. Supplement I*, I, 421. Text of the Cobb-Lippmann memorandum is in Rudin, *Armistice*, pp. 412–421.

[18] Rudin, *Armistice*, p. 269.

[19] George Bernard Noble, *Policies and Opinions at Paris, 1919* (New York, 1935), p. 57.

he would not have thought possible.[20] Most curiously, Colonel House appears to have considered any lack of complete understanding an advantage. For he wrote to the President clearly with satisfaction on November 5: "I doubt whether any other heads of the governments with whom we have been dealing realize how far they are now committed to the American peace programme."[21]

The Fourth Point of these fourteen:

... adequate guarantees given and taken that national armaments will be reduced to the lowest point consistent with domestic safety ...

had been the first definite statement in favor of disarmament by a responsible official of the belligerent powers. After Wilson's speech the hope of general disarmament had been widely discussed. Now, with the conclusion of the Armistice, limitation of armaments became part of the basis for the peace settlement agreed on by the Allied powers, the United States, and Germany. Although arms limitation was generally thought of as a desirable object to be accomplished in connection with the future League, few people had thought seriously how to implement this ideal. The Cobb–Lippmann memorandum, which the negotiators in Paris considered the accepted commentary on the Fourteen Points, had not added much to the understanding of the Fourth Point. It defined "domestic safety" as including protection of territory against invasion, an important distinction which was later stressed by opponents of disarmament during the formation of the League Covenant.[22] Beyond that, it stated only that the principle of arms limitation be adopted and that an international commission of investigation be appointed to prepare detailed projects for its execution.[23]

The extremely important position which the purpose of limitation of armaments held in Wilson's ideas for a peace settlement was made clear in a cable which he sent to House on October 30, during the height of the negotiations with the Allies on the Fourteen Points. He could not participate in a settlement, he said, "which does not

[20] Seymour, *House Papers*, IV, 188–189. [21] Baker, *Wilson*, VIII, 554.
[22] See Chapter VI, pp. 133–134. [23] Seymour, *House Papers*, IV, 194.

include a League of Nations because peace would be without any guarantee except universal armament which would be intolerable."[24]

The Armistice Terms

The military and naval terms of the Armistice, drawn up by the Allied High Commands, laid the basic framework for the final terms imposed on Germany by the Treaty of Versailles. Since the disarmament of Germany was intended to make possible general disarmament, these terms were to have a profound effect on the future of the movement for arms limitation. The territorial and military provisions, as finally approved by the Supreme War Council on November 4, were substantially the same as those originally drawn up by Marshal Foch and discussed at a meeting of Generals Pétain, Pershing, and Haig on October 25 at Senlis. In brief, these final provisions were: the immediate evacuation of the invaded countries—France, Belgium, Luxembourg, and Alsace-Lorraine—as well as evacuation of the districts on the left bank of the Rhine, with the subsequent occupation of these territories by Allied and United States forces.[25] Control of the Rhineland would be ensured by Allied garrisons holding the principal crossings at Mainz, Coblenz, and Cologne, together with bridgeheads at these points of a 30-kilometer radius on the right bank and a 10-kilometer neutral zone from the Netherlands to the Swiss frontier. A large amount of military equipment was to be surrendered: 5,000 heavy and field guns, 25,000 machine guns, 3,000 trench mortars, and 1,700 aeroplanes. To render large-scale transportation of military forces impossible, as well as to ease the French transport situation, a large amount of railroad rolling stock and motor lorries were to be turned over to the Allies.

The naval terms of the Armistice, on the other hand, were based on the original proposals of Admiral Wester Wemyss of the British Admiralty. These proposals were discussed at a meeting of the Allied Naval Council on October 28 and, with some minor modifications, were sent on to the Supreme War Council for final approval. The final terms asked that all existing submarines, as well as six

[24] *Foreign Relations, 1918. Supplement I*, I, 423.
[25] Text of the Armistice terms in Maurice, *The Armistices*, pp. 91–100.

battle cruisers, eight light cruisers, ten battleships, and fifty destroyers, be disarmed and interned in the designated neutral ports, or, failing them, in Allied ports. All naval aircraft were to be immobilized and concentrated in specified German bases. Furthermore, the Allied blockade was to remain in effect. The great German Navy ceased for the moment, practically speaking, to exist.

In the history of armistices, these terms were harsh ones. In the past, an armistice had been regarded as a truce in which an effort was made to maintain the opposing forces in the same relative position. The Armistice of 1871 more nearly approximated this concept. The Armistice of 1918 was, however, so designed as to make impossible Germany's renewal of hostilities and may therefore be regarded as a kind of preliminary peace treaty, save that it did not establish peace. Besides the strictly military terms, there were several clauses of a sort not ordinarily included in armistices: for example, statements in regard to reparations and financial provisions designed to facilitate the later collection of reparations. The fact that the Armistice terms would inevitably condition the final peace treaty was generally recognized, since a number of the questions involved in the Armistice were obviously political in nature. Foch pointed this out to Clemenceau in a letter on October 16, remarking that the Allied High Command, who would have to sign the Armistice and discuss its conditions with the enemy, should be in close collaboration with the Allied governments.[26] This was no ordinary armistice concerned only with a suspension of hostilities. Nevertheless, the fact that the terms were originally drawn up by the military advisers necessarily influenced their content. Marshal Foch, for instance, believed that the most important single condition of the Armistice was Allied control of the right bank of the Rhine which would ensure consolidation of the Allied victory and would make possible the imposition of the desired peace terms, particularly reparations.[27] Furthermore, the bridgeheads at Cologne, Coblenz, and Mainz established a base for a possible advance into the heart of Germany. The bridgehead at Cologne overshadowed the industrial heart of Germany. Foch therefore opposed any other harsh

[26] Maurice, *The Armistices*, pp. 34–35.   [27] Maurice, *The Armistices*, p. 39.

proposals, especially the British naval terms, which might induce Germany to refuse the Armistice and thus imperil his own suggestions.

The conditions and extent of the military clauses also accomplished other Allied political aims. The differences between the provisions for Alsace-Lorraine and those for the other Rhine provinces indicated that France would later keep Alsace-Lorraine. It was included under the heading "invaded territories" along with Belgium, France, and Luxembourg. The rolling stock of Alsace-Lorraine was to be turned over to the French Army. Moreover, this territory was excluded from the clauses regarding the costs of Allied occupation to be paid by Germany. When Clemenceau read the Armistice terms to the French Senate, the return of Alsace-Lorraine was hailed in an emotional scene.

However, French ideas as to the future of the western borders of Germany had advanced much beyond this. The French government intended to demand the frontier line of 1814, which would include the rich Saar Basin.[28] They also hoped for the creation of a buffer state, politically independent of Germany, out of the districts west of the Rhine. These French ambitions had been agreed to in principle by the Czar's government in March 1917,[29] and the British were not officially informed of these aims until much later. While Lloyd George had publicly accepted the validity of the French claims to Alsace-Lorraine, Balfour had denied in the House of Commons that the British had ever encouraged the "bigger Alsace" idea or the idea of a Rhenish buffer state.[30]

As far as the naval clauses were concerned, the Supreme War Council was in agreement that the terms were necessary in order to define the extent of the postwar German navy.[31] However, when the naval terms were discussed by Colonel House and the Premiers on

[28] Noble, *Policies and Opinions*, pp. 205–208.
[29] F. Seymour Cocks, *The Secret Treaties and Understandings* (London, 1918), p. 67.
[30] *H.C. Debates*, 5th series, C, col. 2017. December 19, 1917.
[31] See Lady Wester Wemyss, *The Life and Letters of Lord Wester Wemyss* (London, 1935), pp. 386–387.

November 4, there was general admission that they were too severe. On the suggestion of Lloyd George, a compromise was adopted: that the submarines only would be "surrendered" while the surface fleet should be "interned."[32] It was understood within the Supreme War Council that the ships would never be returned to Germany,[33] but the question of their ultimate disposal was left for the Peace Conference.

By the military and naval terms of the Armistice, the military disarmament of Germany which became a part of the Versailles Treaty was already foreshadowed and the naval disarmament clearly outlined. While Lloyd George had at first thought the Foch military terms too harsh, the French Marshal considered the British Admiralty's naval terms equally severe, a judgment with which Lloyd George was himself inclined to agree.[34] Both sets of terms, however, were finally adopted with little change. The Armistice of 1918, so different in character from previous armistices, was but another illustration of the developing tendency toward total war and total victory.

The Khaki Election

Against this background, Lloyd George announced the day after the Armistice that there would be a general election at once. The date of the dissolution of Parliament was set for November 25 and the election for December 14. Because of the feeling that there should not be an election during the course of the war, the life of the House of Commons had been prolonged by Act of Parliament, so that the election of 1918 was the first since 1910.

The effect of the "Khaki Election," as it was called, on the Peace Conference has received a good deal of commentary,[35] and it is possible to say that the storm of public passion in Great Britain

---

[32] Seymour, *House Papers*, IV, 133–134.   [33] Rudin, *Armistice*, p. 303.
[34] Wemyss, *Wemyss*, pp. 386–387.
[35] See R. B. McCallum, *Public Opinion and the Last Peace* (London, 1944), Chapter I; also J. M. Keynes, *Economic Consequences of the Peace* (London, 1919), and G. P. Gooch, *History of Modern Europe, 1878–1919* (New York 1923).

whipped up by the election could not have failed to influence the attitude of the British delegation in some degree. The question yet remains, however, to what extent the election affected public sentiment and swept away all elements of moderation. One may argue that after four years of war the nation as a whole, election or no election, wanted a hard peace and that the candidates' lack of moderation during the campaign was more an effect of the popular temper than a cause. It is more likely, however, that the campaign speeches only served to intensify the already strong tendencies of the British public. Limitation of armaments was not a major issue in the election, except insofar as it meant "getting the boys home" as soon as possible and disarming the enemy. Nevertheless, the disarmament movement as a moderate and a rational idea was affected indirectly by the immoderate and irrational atmosphere created by the election, an atmosphere which was to condition British politics for a long time after the polls had closed.

The leaders of the Coalition wished, of course, to take advantage of the emotion of victory to secure themselves a good majority, and Lloyd George himself desired the authority of a new Parliament behind him at the Peace Conference. However, the Prime Minister probably underestimated the turbulent forces behind the British electorate at the time. His addresses just after the Armistice were moderate enough; he attempted to focus attention on domestic reconstruction and on foreign policy, aims which suggested his desire for a "just peace." Yet the most striking fact about Lloyd George's speeches was his optimism in regard to what could be accomplished by a League of Nations. There was little discussion in this period of the details of the organization of a League, but it was believed that an international organization must be established and that with such a League all things, including disarmament, could be achieved. "A League of Nations," said Lloyd George on the day after the Armistice, "guarantees peace and guarantees an all-round reduction of armaments, and that reduction is a guarantee that you can get rid of conscription here."[36] There was more of a note of realism in the pronouncement of Winston Churchill, then Minister of

[36] Text in Scott, *Official Statements*, pp. 472–473.

Munitions, at about the same time, that the "League of Nations is no substitute for the supremacy of the British fleet."[37] Curiously enough, the one note of caution on over-optimism with regard to disarmament was struck by Lord Robert Cecil, who later became its most diligent and most hopeful advocate.[38]

Signs soon began to appear among Lloyd George's supporters of a breaking away from the earlier moderation of the election campaign. Again, rumblings came from Churchill, speaking to his constituents at Dundee on November 26. In this speech, he declared himself for punishment of the so-called war criminals and stressed the theme of payment of the expenses of the war by Germany.[39] These twin themes of war criminals and indemnities, first heard by election candidates from hecklers, were to become the most widely stressed themes of the anti-moderates. Soon the *Daily Mail* and the Northcliffe press were asking daily for assurance on these points. During the week following Churchill's speech public passion became aroused: everywhere there were demands for hanging the Kaiser and for making the Germans pay. From none of the political groups campaigning in the election was there any real opposition to what had become a universal cry. The Asquith Liberals were surely as emphatic on these points as the extreme Conservatives.[40] Labour members were only a little more moderate. G. M. Barnes, the Labour representative in the Cabinet, announced: "Well, I'm for hanging the Kaiser," and others stated the same thing in more temperate language.[41]

Up to this time, it had been the policy of Lloyd George in his own speeches to stress as much as possible domestic reconstruction and making Britain "a nation fit for heroes." On the eve of the election, however, he made a hasty decision to speak at Bristol. He reiterated the right to demand the whole cost of the war from Germany, but

[37] *The Times*, November 27, 1918, p. 10.
[38] *The Times*, November 13, 1918, p. 6.
[39] *The Times*, November 27, 1918, p. 10.
[40] See the statement of General Page-Croft, a Conservative, that the National Party puts in the forefront of all issues at the election the demand that the criminal enemy shall pay the bill. *The Times*, November 29, 1918, p. 10.
[41] *The Times*, December 2, 1918, p. 10.

was cautious enough to add that reparations must be effected in such a way that they would not do more harm to the recipient country than to the country paying them. He further said: "There is no doubt at all as to the demand which will be put forward on the part of all the European Allies to make the Kaiser and his accomplices responsible for this terrible crime." [42] Beyond this, however, he did not go. Therefore, he probably rightly denied later in his memoirs that he had ever advocated the hanging of the Kaiser.[43]

However moderate Lloyd George's speeches may have been in comparison with those of some of his supporters, the whole atmosphere of the election was to remain a conditioning force in British politics for some time to come. British ministers were to become the prisoners of this atmosphere, as in the election campaign itself they had been the prisoners of the hate propaganda which had been stirred up by the war aims.

Pressure had been put upon Lloyd George from all sides to desert his earlier moderate views. The powerful Northcliffe press interests, which since 1909 had control of *The Times*, had throughout the war been supporters of Lloyd George. The activities of Lord Northcliffe in the intrigues which resulted in the resignation of Asquith and Lloyd George's assumption of the premiership are all well known.

By the beginning of December, however, pressure from that source was being applied to the Prime Minister. An editorial in the *Daily Mail*, another Northcliffe paper, almost threatened to forsake him, unless he gave satisfactory pledges in regard to two points: hanging the Kaiser and making the Germans pay, which the Northcliffe press sensationalized to the very best of their considerable ability.[44] Had the Northcliffe press deserted Lloyd George during the election campaign, the only important newspapers left to support him would have been the *London Chronicle* and the *Daily Telegraph*, neither of large circulation. The *London Chronicle* had recently been bought by a few personal friends of the Prime

[42] *The Times*, December 12, 1918, p. 6.
[43] Lloyd George, *Truth about the Peace Treaties*, I, 177.
[44] *Foreign Relations, 1919*, I, 409–412.

Minister, but had developed no great influence. The *Daily Telegraph* had always been of a pronounced conservative trend.

The part which the Northcliffe press played in this campaign is perhaps easy to exaggerate. Confidential reports of American diplomatic officials on British politics in these months put great weight upon it.[45] Its vehemence appeared particularly in the policy of the *Daily Mail*, for *The Times* was far more moderate in these months than later when Wickham Steed became its editor in February 1919. Although Lloyd George would have been left in serious straits if the Northcliffe press had deserted him during the election campaign, we should emphasize that the demands of the British electorate resulted from the atmosphere already created by the war propaganda and were only intensified by sensational journalism at the time of the election. It is usual for the ordinary man to interpret history in terms of personalities and to seek a villain when anything goes wrong. In view of this fact, a public outcry for the punishment of the Kaiser was not surprising. The demand for heavy indemnities was likewise a natural popular reaction to the consequences of the war and was based on naïve ideas about the economic effects of reparations. The Northcliffe press played in with and intensified a popular demand already created by the consequences of the war and by earlier press and propaganda campaigns, in the creation of which it had played a large part.

In the atmosphere created by the final days of this election, the first preliminary conference between the Allies on the organization of the Peace Conference took place in London. President Wilson arrived in Paris on the day the election was held.

The polling took place on December 14, and when the results were announced they showed an overwhelming victory for the Coalition.[46] In form, the Khaki election gave the Prime Minister an assurance of support—one could not question the representative status of his delegation as one might question President Wilson's—but in fact the election was detrimental to Lloyd George's ultimate

---

[45] *Foreign Relations, 1919*, I, 409-412.
[46] The Coalition received 526 seats, Labour 63 seats, Asquith Liberals 33 seats, and Irish Nationalists 73 seats which they refused to occupy.

freedom of action at the Conference. The electorate had cleared the House of Commons of its more moderate elements, and, in giving the Conservatives and Unionists more than twice the number of seats as the Liberals within the Coalition itself, the election had subjected Lloyd George to the views of an extremely jingoist House. However, the Prime Minister himself was in no small way to blame for his curious and embarrassing position, when at the Conference he became once more the statesman and pleaded for moderation while his Parliament at home chided him and demanded that he fulfill his election pledges to the country and make Germany pay in full.

If Lloyd George had done little in a positive way to restrain the emotional forces stirred up during the war and let loose during the election campaign, perhaps he believed that the ferment was but a passing one which he would be able to control once the election was over. He was, however, bound by his position in the Coalition, and his independence was hampered by his necessary reliance upon the Conservatives for his political life. The only groups in opposition to the Coalition in the election had been, first, those Liberals who had followed Asquith and who had had no part in the government, and second, the Labour Party, which had now declared itself independent of the Coalition and had fought the election as an opposition party. Those Liberals, including Asquith, who had voted against the government on the Maurice motion[47] were marked for defeat by the Coalition in this "Coupon Election." Thus Lloyd George lost the sections of Parliament most strongly committed to a moderate and a just peace treaty.

The House of Commons of 1919 has been described as one of "the wealthiest, the stupidest, and the least representative since the Great Reform Bill of 1832." [48] It is interesting to note that this was the first general election since the new electoral laws were passed in the early months of 1918, which allowed universal manhood suffrage and gave the vote to women over 30 years of age. Nevertheless when the election took place, only 50 per cent of the eligible voters came to

[47] See Chapter III, p. 65.
[48] D. C. Somervell, *British Politics since 1900* (New York, 1950), pp. 122–123.

the polls. What influence this fact had upon the final outcome we cannot say; however, the result was a House of Commons which Stanley Baldwin described as "a lot of hard-faced men who look as if they had done very well out of the war."[49] We must point out that, election or no election, the most violent jingoes in this Parliament would have been there in any case and would have held the opinions they did hold: for the men who carried on the debates and who pressed for prosecuting the Kaiser and for demanding the full cost of the war from Germany had nearly all been in the previous House of Commons.[50]

With such a Parliament in the background, Lloyd George attempted to play the part of the statesman at the Peace Conference, a part made difficult enough under the growing tensions in Paris.

Interlude

Since both British and American political leaders had given continued public assurances that at the end of the war plans for avoiding future conflicts would become their first concern, and since the Fourteen Points had in the Armistice negotiations been accepted as a basis for the settlement, many persons in Great Britain and the United States believed that specific agreements on arms limitation would follow shortly on the conclusion of the war. During the weeks which elapsed between the Armistice and the opening of the Peace Conference in January, however, political signs less dramatic than those of the British election indicated the probable atmosphere of the Conference. In view of these signs, limitation of armaments clearly was not to be as easily accomplished as many people optimistically believed.

In the first weeks following the Armistice there were already hints that the Allied acceptance of the Fourteen Points had not been as "glorious" a victory as House had supposed. On November 23, a

[49] Quoted in Somervell, *British Politics*, p. 123.
[50] These men were: Brig.-Gen. Page-Croft, Col. Guinness (Lord Moyne), Col. Burn, Mr. McMaster, Col. Claude Lowther, Mr. R. McNeill (Lord Cushendun), Col. Grieg, and Col. Gretton. McCallum, *Public Opinion and the Last Peace*, p. 41.

Times leading article had remarked: "These Fourteen Points of President Wilson's were never intended as the table of a new law brought down from an American Sinai."[51] Moreover, official opinion continued to resent the manner in which Wilson had maneuvered the Allies into accepting his program. A French memorandum, dated November 21, even went so far as to reject the Fourteen Points as the bases of negotiations. Instead, it declared that the only bases of peace would be those contained in the Allied note of January 10, 1917, which was the Allied reply to President Wilson's peace note.[52] Later, commenting on this memorandum, David Hunter Miller of the American Peace Commission staff pointed out that the French statements could in no event be supported. In the first place, the United States had never agreed to the Allied declaration of January 10, 1917, and, secondly, the Fourteen Points with stated reservations had been accepted as the bases of peace negotiations not only by Great Britain, France, and Italy, but also by the Central Powers.[53] The validity of Miller's comments cannot, of course, be denied; however, the existence of the French memorandum suggested that the situation in Paris was not as favorable to American plans as might have been hoped. The French government had evidently not given up certain original war aims. Indeed, in December, Lippmann wrote Professor Mezes, Chief of Intelligence of the American Commission, that in the last few weeks the extension of the boundaries of Lorraine to include the frontiers of 1814 had become "a very serious political question."[54]

As a part of this lack of support in official Allied circles for the general conception of the treaty terms and of future international relations envisioned in the Fourteen Points, a great divergence of views existed specifically on the Fourth Point. Between American and British official pronouncements regarding it, there was a great contrast. The President of the United States had made it one of the

[51] *The Times*, November 23, 1918, p. 7.
[52] David Hunter Miller, *My Diary at the Conference of Paris* (New York, 1924), II, 4–16.
[53] *Foreign Relations, 1919*, I, 359–360. Also see Miller, *Diary*, II, 28–42.
[54] *Foreign Relations, 1919*, I, 287–288.

bases of peace. The Prime Minister of Great Britain, when he had found it necessary to conciliate opinion in the Labour Party, had conceded that "we must seek by the creation of some international organization to limit the burden of armaments and diminish the probability of war." [55] As we have noted, however, official and semi-official commentaries on the occasion of the Fourteen Points speech made no mention of arms limitation. Such was the situation as it might have been understood by the British public, but the public did not realize the extent to which their government was hostile to the ideal of disarmament. So widespread was the notion that limitation of armaments would shortly follow the Armistice that *The Times*, in January 1919, thought it desirable to warn its readers that disarmament plans would probably *not* be a part of the peace treaty, but would be left to be accomplished later by the League.[56] This forecast was optimistic in view of what was happening behind the scenes, where an even greater gulf existed between American and British ideas on disarmament.

Wilson's interest in the question went back to the months before the outbreak of the war and had steadily developed during the course of the war. He had been influenced by unofficial circles in Great Britain—the leaders of the U.D.C. and others—as well as by his general political and economic philosophy and his experience with the Latin American states. Not only was he determined to bring about arms limitation in accordance with his public pronouncements, but he wished also to establish government ownership of the munitions industry. His adviser, Colonel House, was equally enthusiastic for the disarmament plans. His "Inquiry" appears to have planned to carry out technical studies of the question, but these had not advanced when the Armistice came in November.

Another American proponent of arms limitation was General Tasker Bliss, Chief of Staff during the war and one of the Commissioners to the Peace Conference. In December, David Hunter Miller sent Bliss a memorandum on the disarmament question which revealed the attitude of the advisers to the American delegation on the problem and outlined the attempts which had been made

[55] Scott, *Official Statements*, p. 233.   [56] *The Times*, January 11, 1919, p. 9.

in regard to disarmament.[57] The full proceedings of the Hague Conferences had just been published and were dispatched to Bliss. The memorandum also called attention to the successful Rush–Bagot agreement between the United States and Great Britain in 1817 concerning armaments on the Great Lakes; to the prewar British attempts at a naval holiday; and to the Hensley Rider to the United States Appropriation Bill of 1915, which authorized the President to call a disarmament conference at the conclusion of the war. Of the official utterances during the war, the memorandum mentioned, of course, President Wilson's statements and the German and Austrian replies to the papal appeal of 1917. It then quoted at length from Sir Edward Fry's article in *The Nation* in November 1915, and suggested six books on disarmament which General Bliss might find useful.[58] The majority of these books were the products of prewar Liberal and Socialist thinking and were concerned with the wastefulness of war expenditure and the evils of the private armament firms. In this respect, the memorandum reflected prewar attitudes on disarmament rather than emphasizing the developments which had taken place during the war: that is, the Liberal and Socialist concept of disarmament as a part of the over-all substitution of law for force in international relations, an idea which was more in the public mind than ideas of high armament costs and the dangers of private manufacturing.

To the military men, the high cost of armaments, present and future, was perhaps more vivid since they understood the tremendous increase in the importance of matériel in war. Also, because of the importance of the military timetable in the days just preceding the war's outbreak, military men had come to realize the vital part played by the existence of large armaments in bringing on war. This factor was most clearly present in General Bliss's mind.

Bliss later became one of the foremost advocates of arms limitation

---

[57] Miller, *Diary*, II, 219–222.
[58] These were: R. L. Bridgman, *First Book of World Law*; D. S. Jordan, *The Drain of Armaments*; A. T. Mahan, *Armaments and Arbitration*; G. H. Perris, *The War Traders*; Norman Angell, *The World's Highway*; and J. T. W. Newbold, *The War Trust Exposed*.

plans, but he never evinced any sympathy with the tone of the prewar publications. Instead, he talked of "rational disarmament." Convinced of the evils of war, fearful that another would mean the end of European civilization, and mindful of the part which the existence of large armaments play in making the onset of a struggle more probable, he wished to keep armaments within bounds.[59]

While the American officials were convinced of the necessity of disarmament, the situation in Great Britain was quite different. Not only had the British politicians been publicly silent on the question, but they had been subjected to great pressure from the higher Civil Servants against any plans for arms limitation. Lord Robert Cecil had warned Colonel House of this. Plans for a future League of Nations which were being developed by the British government did not include disarmament. The Phillimore plan, as we have seen, omitted it entirely. During the first half of November 1918, a memorandum had been prepared in the Foreign Office by Sir Alfred Zimmern which outlined the bases of a League, but was hostile to limitation of armaments. Although it was circulated within official circles as a departmental document, its main features were presented to the public in an article by Zimmern in the December number of *The Round Table*; here the question of disarmament was, however, not discussed.[60]

The proposals outlined in the memorandum itself would have ruled out most possibilities for implementing disarmament. Zimmern suggested that all treaty obligations between nations should be explicit and "capable of control and scrutiny," concluding that this would rule out limitation according to an agreed scale, "since the term armament defies accurate analysis and the development of commercial aircraft in the near future will still further blur the distinction between implements of war and instruments of peaceful intercourse." Moreover, Zimmern opposed limitation of armaments by prohibiting certain weapons or methods of war which, he said,

[59] See Tasker H. Bliss, "The Problem of Disarmament," in Edward M. House and Charles Seymour, eds., *What Really Happened at Paris* (New York, 1921), pp. 370–391.
[60] *The Round Table*, IX, no. 33, 80–113 (December 1918).

would only tend "to favor unscrupulous Powers as against their opponents."[61] These provisions were doubtless drawn up to lay the foundations for a case against the disarmament clauses which appeared in the American draft of the League Covenant. Further opposition to the American plans was to come from the British Admiralty, which in December completed a memorandum designed to show the necessity of a private munitions industry.[62] American officials were, however, unaware of the attitude of the British government and particularly of the Civil Servants. The fact that the Phillimore plan had omitted provisions for disarmament was, of course, known to Wilson and House, but the only inkling of the real aims of the British Civil Servants was Cecil's hint to House.

Meanwhile, efforts from many sources were beginning to converge on the study of the problem of an international organization which was linked in the public mind with the question of disarmament. In the United States, in July, House had drawn up a draft of the Covenant at Wilson's request,[63] but at the President's insistence neither the Phillimore plan nor the House draft with Wilson's additions were made public. Wilson feared dissension in the United States if concrete plans were officially presented and debated, and he considered it better strategy to support the idea of a League in vague terms.[64] Nor had any suggestions of what the House–Wilson plans contained been given to the public. In England, however, Lord Curzon's speech in the House of Lords, in June 1918, had reflected the Phillimore draft and British official opinion. Plans for a League developed by private groups in England and the United States had, of course, been made public: notably those of the Fabian Research Group and the so-called "Bryce Group" in England and that of the League to Enforce Peace in the United States.

British official pronouncements in favor of a League, particularly

---

[61] Sir Alfred Zimmern, *The League of Nations and the Rule of Law* (London, 1936), p. 197.
[62] Text in Miller, *Covenant*, I, 286–289. See also Chapter VI, p. 136.
[63] See Chapter III, pp. 72–73.
[64] F. P. Walters, *A History of the League of Nations* (London, 1952), I, 23.

Lord Curzon's speech, had revealed the British Cabinet as committed to attempt the formation of an international organization to keep the peace after the war.[65] Unlike the question of arms limitation, they did not here encounter the same kind of opposition from the higher Civil Servants. The development during the war of the inter-Allied councils, particularly the Supreme War Council, had demonstrated what achievements were possible with such coöperation. It was the function of the British Civil Servants to keep an ear to the ground and sense future political trends. Many Civil Servants at the end of the war saw clearly that a revolution was taking place in the relation between public opinion and foreign policy. Also becoming apparent was the utility of the participation of the politically responsible officials in conference with their opposite numbers in other countries. This idea of "diplomacy by conference" fostered the League and was itself later strengthened by the existence of the League.

In the days following the Armistice, the Foreign Office was at work on plans for a future League of Nations which would be considered at the Peace Conference. The Zimmern Memorandum, which had been hostile to the disarmament idea, outlined the bases of an international organization. Much influenced by the earlier Fabian schemes, the memorandum strengthened some of the provisions of the Phillimore plan. While the latter had provided for meetings of representatives of League members when peace was threatened, Zimmern suggested regular meetings of all members and more frequent meetings of the Foreign Ministers of the great powers who would act as an executive committee for the whole body. The plan also provided for the establishment of a permanent secretariat.[66]

Soon after the completion of this memorandum, Lord Robert Cecil, who had been in the Cabinet since 1916, resigned over the Welsh Church Bill and was offered the leadership of the newly established League of Nations section in the Foreign Office. Using

[65] See Winkler, *League of Nations Movement*, chapter IX, "The British Government and the League."

[66] Zimmern, *League of Nations*, pp. 196–206.

both the Phillimore plan and Zimmern's memorandum, Cecil worked out a further League plan which closely resembled its predecessor in its provisions for periodic meetings and a permanent secretariat. After further defining these suggestions, he added many of the Phillimore proposals concerned with the prevention of war. Significantly no mention of arms limitation was included in Cecil's plan, nor was it mentioned in any subsequent officially inspired British League plans. Cecil's draft was submitted to the War Cabinet on December 17 and was later taken to Paris where it was shown on January 1 to Miller of the American Peace Commission staff.[67]

While the Cecil plan was not strictly an official suggestion put forward by the British government, its influence on the official British attitude toward the League was significant. Moreover, it served as the basis for the pre-Conference Anglo-American compromises, and its author became one of the foremost British proponents of the League of Nations, both at the Peace Conference where he was a delegate on the League Commission and in later years.

Almost simultaneously, another draft outline of the League of Nations, also strictly unofficial, was put forward for the consideration of the War Cabinet. This was General Jan Smuts's plan, entitled "The League of Nations: A Practical Suggestion," which was to have a profound effect upon the drafting of the Covenant.[68] It was the first League plan, among all the other drafts proposed in official or semi-official circles, to be made public. It is also said to have influenced Wilson's own views to a great extent, particularly in regard to disarmament.[69] In substance, the plan outlined a scheme for an international organization which followed the general pattern of previous British proposals. There was to be a council which would act as executive committee for the League, with representatives from the great powers and a smaller number of representatives drawn in rotation from two panels of the middle and minor states. This council would meet periodically, hold annual meetings of the Prime Ministers or Foreign Secretaries, appoint a permanent secretariat,

[67] Text in Miller, *Covenant*, II, 61–64.
[68] Text in Miller, *Covenant*, II, 23–60. [69] Miller, *Covenant*, I, 34.

set up joint committees on certain subjects, and refer questions for debate to a general conference of all League members. The council would also hear nonjusticiable disputes, formulate measures of international law, and bring the machinery of international compulsion into effect when necessary. Smuts's council indicated his frank recognition of great power control in the League, but this council was far less exclusively a great power organ than Zimmern's or Cecil's executive committees.

General Smuts believed that the primary task of the Peace Conference was to set up a League of Nations,[70] an opinion with which President Wilson was highly sympathetic. Smuts put forward his plan in an effort to convince public opinion both of the necessity and the practicability of a League. He wished to counteract the impression that the League was a utopian ideal, and that it would be established only as a means of preventing wars. Instead, he envisioned it as "an organic change" and as the natural and necessary development of the political institutions of civilized life.[71] It should not be designed as a super-state, but rather along the lines of the conference system used successfully in the British Empire.

General Smuts did not avoid discussion of the question of disarmament; indeed he acutely analyzed the grave problems which it involved. He pointed out the totality of modern war: that the recent war had been fought not "only by the usual military weapons in the narrow sense, but by the whole economic, industrial, and financial systems of the belligerent Powers." If limitation were confined to direct instruments of war, however, how would one instrument be valued against another: tank against aeroplane? And if a system of comparative values were established, new inventions would upset such a system. Recognizing these technical difficulties, Smuts went on to propose a system of relative disarmament under the Council of the League. Conscription should be abolished, and each state would be allowed armaments in proportion to the militia required for the state's defense. He also advocated nationalization of armament factories, inspection of these factories by the Council, and

[70] Miller, *Covenant*, I, 35.
[71] See Walters, *History of the League*, I, 27–30.

notification to the Council of imports and exports of armaments. In connection with this provision for nationalization, he noted the fact that unless the League were allowed full rights of inspection, it would not be difficult to convert private factories to the production of munitions. Although he believed limitation of armaments to be a necessary function of the League, General Smuts also forecast the difficulties which the practical applications of the principle were to encounter in later years.

The plan was handed to Miller at the same time that he received the Cecil plan. In President Wilson's first Paris draft of the Covenant, dated January 10, 1919, the effect of Smuts's suggestions, particularly in regard to disarmament, was evident. Wilson's earlier Washington draft, modeled on the House plan of July, had included in the disarmament article: recognition of the principle of arms limitation by all members, formulation by the Delegates of plans toward that end, and agreement on abolition of private manufacturing of armaments and on publicity of national armaments.[72] In the draft of January 10, the President added to the list Smuts's proposal to abolish conscription and compulsory military service.[73]

The American delegation in Paris therefore had definite proposals lined up for consideration in regard to limitation of armaments and the League before the Conference opened. Indeed, Wilson appeared to look upon limitation as one of the main purposes for which a League would be set up. The British delegation came to Paris, on the other hand, with no one plan for a League which had the official stamp of approval, and, with the exception of Smuts's proposals, little encouragement had been given to the disarmament idea. The Italians and French had referred the question of arms limitation for later consideration in their League drafts.[74] Already there were hints that the French would consider disarmament feasible only if their cherished idea of an international general staff under the League were brought about. They expected that this would make possible

[72] Text in Miller, *Covenant*, II, 12–15.
[73] Text in Miller, *Covenant*, II, 65–93. See Appendix C.
[74] Text of the Bourgeois Plan in Miller, *Covenant*, II, 238–246. Text of the Italian draft in Miller, *Covenant*, II, 246–255.

the maintenance of French hegemony over Europe which they hoped to set up through the terms of the Peace Treaty.

These different plans for a League of Nations and for disarmament would be considered by the Peace Conference which was to open in Paris in mid-January. Nevertheless, by the end of December, there were already indications of the conflicting views of the different countries on arms limitation. The plans for the disarmament of Germany had been outlined in the Armistice, which had also been designed to make certain the enforcement of French demands. Furthermore, the Conference would be held against a background of immoderate opinions, the results of war propaganda and slogans, whose strength became clear when the British election returns were announced on December 28. President Wilson was coming to Paris to establish a "just and lasting peace," but the contrast between his vague ideals and the various European attitudes toward a settlement would stand forth vividly.

Chapter V

Disarmament in the Peace Treaty

The Paris Peace Conference and Disarmament

The Treaty of Peace, drawn up in Paris between January 18 and May 6, 1919, and signed at Versailles on June 28, did not include general arms limitation agreements. However, Part V of the Treaty provided for the disarmament of Germany, in order, so said the preamble, "to render possible the initiation of a general limitation of armaments of all nations."[1] The League Covenant, made part of the Treaty, set up the framework within which this stated purpose of the preamble might be implemented, for Article VIII of the Covenant provided that the League Council should formulate plans for reduction "for the consideration and action of the several Governments."[2] Further, the Council was to advise on the means of preventing the evil effects of private manufacture of armaments, and League members undertook to exchange information as to the scale of their armament. By these clauses the stated purposes of a general limitation of armaments became part of the public law of Europe.

Both of these sections of the Treaty concerned with disarmament were drawn up in substantially their final form early in the negotiations. The League Covenant was given officially to the press on February 15, and the negotiations which went on during February on the military terms of the disarmament of Germany were reported

[1] *Foreign Relations, 1919*, XIII, 309.   [2] *Foreign Relations, 1919*, XIII, 82.

unofficially but substantially correctly in the press soon after they were discussed.[3] While they were not at that time as complete as the wording of the Covenant, the main outlines of the military settlement had taken shape by the time President Wilson left on February 14 for a four weeks' trip to the United States. The few main points of contention were settled immediately following his return in March.

Not only did both the military terms and the Covenant receive priority in point of time, but the military terms were drawn up by a method unique in the procedure of the Conference: they were formulated under the guidance of the Council of Ten during the period in which that body was the directing force of the Conference. This council was merely a continuance of the Supreme War Council, which had been the directing body of the war for the Allies since its organization in the winter of 1917. The military section of the Treaty was, therefore, drawn up by the same organized group of men who had supervised the war against the Central Powers and had drawn up the Armistice terms.[4]

The effects of the Peace Conference on the disarmament idea were far-reaching. For the first time technical questions of disarmament were seriously attacked by a group of the most highly qualified military experts. The two Hague Conferences had been lacking in technical advice, but in the discussion which led to the drafting of the military terms of the Versailles Treaty, every essential problem connected with military power and armaments was covered in detail, including the question of conscription, the size of armies and navies, the problems of communication and blockade, the use of new instrumentalities of war, such as aeroplanes, wireless telegraph, poison gases, and submarines, as well as the principles of executing arms limitation. The provisions for disarmament, developed at Paris,

---

[3] See *The Times*, February 15, 1919, p. 10.

[4] To avoid confusion, note that the "Council of Ten," when considering the terms of German disarmament, officially reverted to its former title, the "Supreme War Council." For a detailed discussion of the procedures followed during the Peace Conference, see F. S. Marston, *The Peace Conference of 1919* (London, 1944).

served as a basis for technical discussions of disarmament in the years following. More important still, the military terms of the Treaty were the basis for the program for general disarmament submitted by the German delegation at the beginning of the Disarmament Conference of 1932. These German proposals came nearer to acceptance by the great powers than any other set of proposals for disarmament has ever done.

In contrast to the unique position of the military terms, the League Covenant was drawn up in one of the so-called "Commissions" of the Conference. These bodies constituted the normal means through which the work was carried on. On these commissions the smaller powers were represented, along with the Big Five, and it was the practice of the small powers to consider problems with an eye to the future.

The military sections of the Treaty had, then, limited German armaments, stating that this was to make possible a general limitation and, beyond that, had offered possible technical outlines for such a plan. The Covenant had also declared the purpose of making such a plan a reality and set up the machinery for drawing up a scheme. At the same time, however, the obstacles to an achievement of this magnitude became apparent. In the course of the discussion within the Council of Ten and in the League Commission, the French as well as the British theses in regard to disarmament emerged clearly, and the course which disarmament discussions were to take in the succeeding fifteen years was foreshadowed.

From the history of the war aims question in England, which we have traced, had emerged the atmosphere in which the Peace Treaty was to be drawn up. As we shall see, this atmosphere was nurtured during the Peace Conference by a well-planned press campaign in both England and France. The Treaty came forth a product of such a climate of opinion. The provisions of the Treaty beyond the disarmament clauses, particularly those in regard to reparations, created the political and economic conditions under which the conflicting national viewpoints toward the problem of limitation of armaments would be thrashed out.

The Drafting of the Military Terms

The question of disarmament was first broached before the Council of Ten by the British Foreign Minister. On January 21, just three days after the First Plenary Meeting of the Conference, Balfour suggested that a commission be appointed to consider disarmament.[5] There had already been agreement in principle that commissions should be set up to deal with the League of Nations, the question of indemnities, and international labor questions, and he suggested this as a fourth. Had the question of disarmament been placed so prominently before the Conference as a specific problem for solution parallel in importance to these other three, and before a body on which the small powers would have been represented, the history of its fortunes at the Conference might well have been changed. Serious consideration might have been given to specific plans for immediate agreements on limitation of armaments.

Balfour's remarks emphasized the vital place which the question of disarmament held in relation to the great problems of the peace. He mentioned it as "closely related to the question of strategic frontier" and said that a League of Nations would be a sham if there were no disarmament. Further, he touched upon what must have been very prominent in the minds of the British Cabinet just at that time, when he said that "it was most important in this connection to come to some agreement as to what arms Germany was to be allowed to have." For reports were then reaching the British that Foch considered it necessary to retain a British army of 1,700,000 men on the Western Front,[6] and such figures gave pause to the British politicians, pressed as they were for quick demobilization. Also, the military and naval estimates were due to be introduced in the House of Commons in a few weeks. Should German arms be reduced, reduction in troops in Europe and in future arms expenditure could follow. Furthermore, just at this time, Balfour's nephew, Lord Robert Cecil, was carrying on discussions with David Hunter Miller of the American Delegation in an attempt to reconcile the

---

[5] *Foreign Relations, 1919*, III, 669.   [6] *Foreign Relations, 1919*, III, 694.

American and British draft plans for a League, which, as we have seen, differed so sharply on disarmament.

The formal motion which embodied Balfour's suggestion was presented two days later by Lloyd George.[7] His resolution had two parts: that the Disarmament Commission to be set up was first to advise on an immediate reduction of the German forces, and second, to prepare plans in connection with the League for a permanent general arms reduction. The first part of this resolution set in motion the discussions in the Council of Ten and the succession of *ad hoc* committee reports which resulted in the drawing up of the military terms, comprising Part V of the final Peace Treaty. Lloyd George, himself, at once suggested that the renewal of the Armistice, due in the middle of February, be the occasion to demand of the Germans a drastic reduction in forces. Later, as will be seen, this plan was abandoned in favor of the idea of presenting terms of a Preliminary Peace Treaty to the Germans, of which the military terms should be a part. By the time the idea of a Preliminary Peace Treaty had been tacitly abandoned, the original plan, a reduction in German forces to ensure the security of Europe during the drawing up of the Treaty, had developed into the permanent military conditions to be demanded of Germany in the final Treaty.

The whole of the procedure which resulted in the drawing up of these terms remained in the hands of the Council of Ten, and no disarmament commission was ever appointed. Within a few weeks after the introduction of Lloyd George's motion in the Council of Ten, discussions began in the Commission for the League on the drafting of Article VIII of the Covenant, which set the basis for the later disarmament attempts by the League. The consideration of the second part of Lloyd George's motion, which he said at the time might be reserved for discussion at a future date, passed out of the hands of the Council of Ten into those of the Commission on the League. Thus, the question of general disarmament of all the powers was never discussed in the Council of Ten.

[7] *Foreign Relations, 1919*, III, 694-697. Text of the draft resolution in *ibid*, III, 702.

Lloyd George accompanied his motion by a vigorous speech in which he made clear the political importance in Britain of the conscription issue. Unless the numbers of troops envisaged by Foch as necessary to maintain on the Western Front could be reduced, the British would be forced to attempt to continue their draft. Lloyd George gave notice that it would be impossible to maintain the force which Marshal Foch demanded, and he proposed that when in a month's time a renewal of the Armistice was due, demands should be then made for a drastic reduction of German forces. It soon became clear that the presence of military experts was necessary, and the question was postponed until the following day when a committee of the military advisers, headed by Marshal Foch, should attend and report on the number of troops necessary to be stationed on the Western Front.

In the Council meeting the following day, January 24, the Foch report called for even larger numbers than had earlier been reported to Lloyd George, for the Marshal demanded 1,820,000 men as a minimum for safety.[8] Foch's insistence on the difficulty of enforcing provisions for reducing the German forces if such proposals were made part of a renewed Armistice opened up a discussion of the whole question of German power. On this occasion it was only considered in the Council of Ten in relation to the maintenance of security during the Peace Conference. As the discussion on the question developed, Clemenceau sent for Louis Loucheur, an expert on the munitions industry, to answer questions regarding production of German munitions. Loucheur advanced the opinion that since the production of Germany depended on the basin of Westphalia, if Essen and its neighborhood were seized, the Germans could in no circumstances go on fighting.[9]

The result of the deliberations was the creation of a committee, headed by Loucheur, which was to report on the strength of the armies which should be maintained by the Allies on the Western Front, and secondly, on the demobilization of the German Army

[8] Text of the Foch memorandum in *Foreign Relations, 1919*, III, 705–706.
[9] *Foreign Relations, 1919*, III, 713.

and guarantees regarding seizure of weapons and ammunition factories.[10]

In the course of the discussions, the essentials of both the British and French positions became clear. The discussion had shown the strength of the political pressures in Britain for reduction of armed forces, as well as the French concern for greater preponderance over the German strength and for control of the Ruhr district, the heart of the German industrial life, as a simple means of maintaining French supremacy.

Both President Wilson and General Bliss firmly insisted on the American view that it was not in accordance with the Armistice to make additional demands upon the Germans as a condition of its renewal.[11] General Bliss urged that such additional conditions should be included in the Peace Treaty and stressed the need to hasten the drawing-up of its terms. When, on February 7, the Loucheur report was finally presented, Bliss submitted a memorandum formulating these views.[12]

While crucial debates in the Council of Ten on certain of the issues raised in the Loucheur report were yet to come, the report as presented to the Supreme Council outlined the military terms in the final Treaty presented to the Germans in May.[13] It was based on four principles: limitation of the size of the German Army; limitation to a fixed amount of German armament; control of munitions manufacture; and the establishment of a commission of control, composed of technical experts and officers to impose these provisions. Further, the list of war materials necessary to be restricted, which was drawn up by a sub-committee of the Loucheur committee, comprised the items which were actually limited or forbidden in the final terms of

[10] *Foreign Relations, 1919*, III, 713. The other members of Loucheur's Committee were Marshal Foch, General Bliss, Winston Churchill, and General Diaz, Chief of Staff of the Italian Army. Churchill never actually sat as a member of the committee, since General Sir Henry Wilson sat for him. The result was that the presiding officer, Loucheur, was the only civilian member.

[11] *Foreign Relations, 1919*, III, 901.

[12] Text of the memorandum in *Foreign Relations, 1919*, III, 920–921.

[13] Text of the Loucheur report in *Foreign Relations, 1919*, III, 910–912.

the Treaty.[14] For the period of the Armistice, figures of these German armaments demanded for surrender were given, and they were stated by Loucheur in the Supreme Council to be based on figures supplied by the Intelligence Services of the different Allied armies. The surrender of three-fourths of the quantities believed to be in existence was called for.[15]

The most essential elements of the final military terms appeared in this report. It was, however, suggested in the report that one method of enforcing the provisions would be a military occupation east of the Rhine to a depth of almost 50 kilometers from Cologne to 15 kilometers north of Duisburg, to embrace Essen and the principal Krupp establishments, the greater part of the Rhenish-Westphalian coal fields and the metallic industries which depended on them. This plan did not become a part of the final Peace Treaty, but first the threat and later the accomplishment of this project became a part of French policy.

The outlines of the pattern for German disarmament which now emerged had been foreshadowed in the Armistice terms drawn up by the military advisers to the Supreme Council headed by Marshal Foch. Now they were extended by a committee under the leadership of Foch and of Loucheur, having as members the same military advisers. It reflected a well thought-out French plan for the disarmament of Germany. In the Supreme Council, however, at this stage the discussion still centered around the plan as a means of preventing the danger of disturbances or actual renewal of hostilities during the Armistice period, while the Peace Treaty was being drawn up. The idea of these provisions as terms to be imposed upon Germany as a continuing prohibition was not at this point clear in the minds of many of the participants in the proceedings. This was made clear, for instance, in the sub-committee, which stated that:

... on the understanding that control of war manufacture in Germany will only last for a limited period (under eight months), the Sub-

[14] Heavy guns, field guns, machine guns, trench mortars, automatic rifles, and rifles, tanks, asphyxiating gas, and gas masks. *Foreign Relations, 1919*, III, 913.
[15] *Foreign Relations, 1919*, III, 900.

Committee considers that it would be of no particular advantage to control explosive factories owing to the large stocks which exist.[16]

Lloyd George, however, looked forward to these terms as the basis for a permanent settlement, for speaking of the supposition that the disarmament of Germany was to be made one of the conditions of peace, he remarked that "he could not conceive the omission of such a condition."[17] However, since he had asked Loucheur how long a period of time would be necessary for Germany to replace the equipment required to be surrendered, it would seem that, at this stage, he did not look forward to a long-continuing period of control of the factories.

At any rate, President Wilson surely envisaged no extended period of control. While he thought the Germans should surrender the big guns, he objected to provisions for control of detail of German factory management, and he was in favor of controlling factories only by regulating the raw material which went into them.[18] Since Wilson's frequently expressed views would have precluded any such control of trade continuing for an indefinite period of time, clearly he was thinking in terms of the control necessary for the period of drafting the Treaty.

The objections of the American delegation to the Loucheur report were not confined to Wilson's belief that the Allies were under obligation not to insert new conditions when renewing the Armistice and to General Bliss's memorandum on that same point, nor to Wilson's objection to control of the details of German manufacturing. Wilson was wholly unprepared for the severity of the plans now shaping up for the disarmament of Germany and characterized the whole report as a "panic program."[19] Wilson at once put the question to Foch whether the Germans would agree to the imposition of such additional terms, and Foch admitted that they would do so only under pressure.[20] Pressure meant at this stage to the French the military occupation of the Ruhr. As a way out of the dangers

---

[16] *Foreign Relations, 1919*, III, 918.   [17] *Foreign Relations, 1919*, III, 899.
[18] *Foreign Relations, 1919*, III, 908.   [19] *Foreign Relations, 1919*, III, 908.
[20] *Foreign Relations, 1919*, III, 897–898.

of such a situation, Wilson proposed the appointment of a civilian commission to treat with a similar German commission, which would offer concessions in the way of food and raw material, if the Germans would agree to the renewal of the Armistice under harsher terms.[21] Clemenceau was, however, opposed to negotiating in any way with the Germans and objected in a violent speech. He said that the Germans were becoming insolent and would become more so, and that the French Chamber would throw him out if he assented to Wilson's suggestion.[22]

Lloyd George finally suggested that a small committee be appointed to report the next day, which would "examine and determine the items of war material to be surrendered by Germany with a view to her disarmament." This was finally agreed: Robert Lansing and Lord Milner, with André Tardieu as chairman, were to compose the membership.

On the next afternoon, February 10, the Tardieu committee presented its report to the Supreme War Council.[23] It called for a statement from Germany within two weeks on the war matériel in her possession in the two most important categories—guns and aircraft. In order to reduce German strength at once, a specified quantity of matériel was to be surrendered immediately.[24] After the amounts of armaments had been determined, all war matériel not necessary for the maintenance of a stipulated number of divisions was to be surrendered. Even though the figure for the divisions was not given in the report, discussions in the committee meeting had placed it at thirty divisions,[25] and this figure appeared from the discussion in the Supreme Council to have been generally agreed on. However, in the committee, Tardieu had shown that he regarded thirty divisions as a minimum to be stated now, with the idea that a final minimum should be decided on later. It was, perhaps, because this was known

[21] *Foreign Relations, 1919*, III, 901.
[22] *Foreign Relations, 1919*, III, 903–904.
[23] Text of the report in *Foreign Relations, 1919*, III, 937–938.
[24] 20,000 machine guns; 4,000 field guns; 1,000 heavy guns; 5,000 aeroplane engines; 250 machines for naval aviation.
[25] *Foreign Relations, 1919*, XI, 24–25.

to President Wilson that he uttered on this occasion such vigorous protests against making successive restrictive demands upon the Germans. He said that he had hoped "that we should be able to make a final demand once and for all in fixed numbers." In this discussion, then, began the idea of submitting final military terms as a preliminary peace. As a temporary expedient, it was finally agreed to demand the stated amounts of war matériel from the Germans on the ground that this was necessary in view of their refusal to stop hostilities in Poland.[26]

The idea of a preliminary peace treaty was further advanced that same afternoon when the Naval Committee report on the disarmament of Germany was presented. In introducing the report Admiral Wemyss said that the Allies "had come to the conclusion that they would now fix what should be the state of the German Fleet in time of peace."[27] The initiative for preparing the report had apparently been taken by Admiral Wemyss, who had persuaded his colleagues, Admirals de Bon and Benson, to seek along with him authorization for its preparation.[28]

The draft was very close to the final treaty settlement. The list of warships to be surrendered was included, as well as provision for the surrender or destruction of warships in neutral ports and for the break-up of all submarines. No further naval construction was to be permitted until after the signature of the final Peace Treaty. The report did not suggest final figures of the future strength of the German Navy, but left them to be fitted in. Further recommendations went beyond strictly naval terms. These included a recommendation that no German colonies be returned to her; terms of reparations for merchant vessels destroyed and Allied vessels condemned by German prize courts; and provisions in regard to fortifications of Heligoland and the Baltic and control of the Kiel Canal. Particularly on the ground that these last terms could not be part of an Armistice agreement, but must wait for the final Treaty, both Balfour and Wilson objected to Admiral Wemyss's idea that the

[26] *Foreign Relations, 1919*, III, 929, 932.
[27] *Foreign Relations, 1919*, III, 933. Text of the report in *ibid*, III, 938-944.
[28] *Foreign Relations, 1919*, XI, 4. Compare Wemyss, *Wemyss*, pp. 414-416.

naval terms should be settled at the next renewal of the Armistice.[29]

Thus, the idea of a preliminary peace settlement, including the military, naval, and air terms, at the time of the Armistice renewal received another setback.

The whole problem of the renewal of the Armistice was not yet solved, and its expiration date was only nine days away. The Supreme Council was to face still more complications on February 10 when evidence was presented of difficulties in enforcing some of the financial as well as some of the naval clauses of the Armistice. This led to the appointment of a joint military and economic committee to recommend solutions. Two days later this committee reported, advising renewal of the Armistice unchanged but further recommending that military and naval terms be drawn up at once and imposed on the enemy.[30]

The easy solution of renewing the Armistice unchanged was agreed to. The French objected, however, to the idea of presenting separate military terms.[31] For, connected with the idea of a preliminary treaty of any kind, was the presumption that the remaining terms—political and economic—would be negotiated with German delegates present. Clemenceau in the Supreme Council, however, based his objections on two grounds. First, that military terms depended on other terms; for example, if the League of Nations gave the guarantees expected of it, the military terms would be different. Second, if preliminary terms were imposed, demobilization might have progressed so far by the time of the final peace that it would be impossible to impose it. The German newspapers, he said, were breathing threats. President Ebert had said: "We will not accept terms which are too hard." The result of the discussion was a final resolution in regard to renewal of the Armistice which appeared to give success to the American view.[32] The resolution stated that as a

[29] *Foreign Relations, 1919,* III, 934.

[30] Text of the report in *Foreign Relations, 1919,* III, 980–986. The members of the committee were: Mr. Norman Davis and General Bliss (U.S.); Lord Robert Cecil and General Thwaites (Great Britain); Mr. Clementel and General Degoutte (France); and Mr. Crespi and General Cavallero (Italy).

[31] *Foreign Relations, 1919,* III, 974–979.

[32] Final text of the resolution in *Foreign Relations, 1919,* III, 1005.

condition of the renewal of the Armistice, the Germans should agree to "desist from all offensive operations against the Poles." The Armistice, so renewed, was to be terminable by the Allies at three days' notice. The Germans were to be informed that "final military, naval and air conditions of the preliminaries of peace" were to be drawn up and to be presented for signature to them. The further point in the resolution, that after the signature of such preliminaries there was to be a controlled lifting of the blockade, was not to be communicated to the Germans.

At the same time, the Council provided that the Military, Naval, and Air committees should sit as one committee under Marshal Foch to draw up these terms. "It was," said Clemenceau, "essential that the military experts should lay down what was to be Germany's military law. It might, further, be necessary to control those operations by means of High Commissions appointed by the Allies."[33] Balfour added that a similar provision must be made concerning munitions. The basic principles, then, of the Loucheur report had been accepted, and the Foch committee was to draw up the plans.

However, as yet, there was no clear agreement in what form these terms would be presented to the Germans. Some members of the Supreme Council still appeared to be thinking in terms of an Armistice agreement, but one fixing military terms. The idea of a preliminary peace treaty which should include bases of settlement beyond the military terms was favored, particularly by Colonel House and Lansing. The French feared that the conclusion of such terms would mean the hastening of Allied demobilization and that before final terms were agreed on, German arms might have recovered strength. During the last week of February, Lloyd George, Wilson, and Clemenceau were all absent from the Supreme Council. Balfour, after a conference with Clemenceau, presented on February 22 a motion to speed up consideration of other peace

[33] *Foreign Relations, 1919*, III, 1006. Foch's joint committee included General Bliss, Admiral Benson, General Patrick (U.S.); General Sir Henry Wilson, Admiral Wemyss, General Sykes (Great Britain); General Degoutte, Admiral de Bon, General Duval (France); General Cavallero, Admiral Grassi (Italy). *Ibid*, III, 1009.

terms.[34] It was resolved that these preliminary terms should include the territorial, financial, and economic conditions to be imposed and a statement of German responsibility for breaches of the laws of war. Lord Milner made it clear that the British did not wish to shut out entirely the idea of separate military terms.[35] The question was therefore left open to await the final report of the military committee. Between the time of the presentation of the report on March 3 and the final approval of the terms on March 17, the idea of a preliminary peace had quietly disappeared, although it never seems to have been abandoned in a formal resolution.

The Press Campaign

The last fortnight in February, during which the Foch Committee was working on its final report, was a period of interlude in the work of the Supreme Council. President Wilson had left on the 14th for nearly a month's absence to be present at the opening of Congress; Lloyd George was absent for a time for the opening of a new Parliament; and on February 19 Clemenceau was temporarily disabled by an attempted assassination.

By this time, the numerous problems of a peace treaty had begun to emerge. Not only had the discussion in the Supreme Council over the Armistice renewal and the Loucheur report taken place just before Wilson's departure, but also the struggle over the League had reached its height, and the issues involved in the territorial clauses were just appearing. With this background, a press campaign had begun about the second week in February in both England and France, stressing Allied insecurity in the face of continued German strength. The ultimate aims of this campaign coincided with the ultimate aims of French official opinion: that, through the terms of the Treaty, the German military establishment and economic system must be thoroughly crushed if Europe were to be assured any real sense of security in the postwar years.

[34] *Foreign Relations, 1919*, IV, 85. Text of Balfour's resolution in *ibid*, IV, 108–109. See the discussion of the question of a preliminary peace in this chapter, pp. 129–130.
[35] *Foreign Relations, 1919*, IV, 102–103.

On February 10, Clemenceau granted an interview to the American press which was much featured in French and British papers.[36] The French Premier maintained that the present period was only a lull in the storm. He pointed out the military dangers of the present situation: Russia was in chaos, and reports were being received of a big German army being organized in the east.

There were signs that the press campaign in France was officially inspired. Ray Stannard Baker reported that "one day in February 'President Wilson had shown him' a memorandum from unimpeachable sources" giving instructions sent out by the French government to the government-influenced press concerning three points which they wished to stress: first, the strength of Republican opposition to the President in the United States; second, the chaotic conditions in Russia; and third, the willingness and ability of Germany to renew the struggle.[37] Whether or not the memorandum was authentic, it is certain that such a press campaign flourished in France and was echoed by the Northcliffe press in England and by such Conservative organs as the *Morning Post*. The point of view of the French press and of French officials was to be reflected in these Conservative British newspapers for several years.[38]

Various news sections as well as leaders and special features in *The Times* contributed to the total effect. Dispatches from a special correspondent in Germany on February 10 reported that Germany was full of rumors of the rapid dissolution of the Allied forces and

[36] *The Times*, February 11, 1919, p. 11.
[37] R. S. Baker, *Woodrow Wilson and World Settlement* (New York, 1923), I, 153. Already there were fears appearing in France that the United States Congress would not support the League of Nations. As France saw the League as the bulwark of French security, she found frightening any suggestions that the League might not be all-powerful. Her thoughts then naturally turned to immediate, practical, and certain guarantees, one of which was a weak Germany.
[38] See the article in *The Times* by the Paris Correspondent who reported that the French General Staff said that Germany could, in a short space of time, mobilize armies bigger than those then in occupation on the Rhine. *The Times*, February 10, 1919, p. 9.

"the result is that the people begin to believe that the Entente cannot enforce terms which Germany passively declines."[39]

To back up rumors of German strength and Allied weakness and German recognition of this fact, the summaries of the German press, printed during the next fortnight in *The Times* under the heading "Through German Eyes," quoted from the German reactionary press statements which tended to bear out this thesis.[40] *The Times* also reprinted articles of Frank Simonds, which were syndicated in the American press and which took a most alarmist view of German ambitions.[41]

On February 12, Lloyd George met Parliament and gave the members new assurances on the war guilt trials and that the Germans would be made to pay.[42] Two days later a *Times* leader explained that a "large number of Germans are as arrogant and unrepentant as ever . . . It should help to keep before our minds the undoubted fact that the new Germany is the old Germany again."[43] On that same date the special correspondent reported an interview with Ebert, then newly elected President of the Reich, in which he was quoted as saying that the German delegation expected to take a lively part in the negotiations and would not allow themselves to be subject to dictation.[44]

Reports from *The Times*'s political correspondent in Paris during this period showed that the discussions of the Loucheur report in the Supreme Council must have been completely known to the press although they were not reported as such. Moreover, the political correspondent wrote as if the Armistice would be renewed on the basis of that report.[45] Up to the time of the renewal of the Armistice,

[39] *The Times*, February 11, 1919, p. 10.
[40] *The Times*, February 7, 1919, p. 7; February 10, p. 7; February 12, p. 9; February 14, p. 7; February 19, p. 7; March 7, p. 9.
[41] *The Times*, January 25, 1919, p. 7; February 10, p. 6; February 11, p. 8; February 12, p. 8; February 26, p. 8; March 8, p. 9.
[42] *H.C. Debates*, 5th series, CXII, col. 183. February 12, 1919. Reported in *The Times*, February 13, 1919, p. 9.
[43] *The Times*, February 14, 1919, p. 9.
[44] *The Times*, February 14, 1919, p. 8.
[45] *The Times*, February 13, 1919, p. 10; February 14, p. 8.

this seemed to have been generally believed. When it became known a little later that there had been no further military stipulations, the disappointment in France and in certain circles in England was great. For a long time, however, it was still expected that military terms would soon be imposed as a preliminary peace.

The naval terms, as developed in close to their final form by the Naval Committee in the report presented on February 8, were published substantially correctly in the English newspapers on February 28.[46] The press was eager to learn the terms of the report of the Foch Committee which was submitted to the Supreme Council on the 1st of March and discussed on the 3rd and 6th.[47] Two days later *The Times* remarked that "the main lines have already been indicated in these columns," and added, "no doubt we shall in the fullness of time get the complete details by way of Germany, which always knows about these things before we do." [48]

During the early spring months the British Conservative press continued to warn of Germany's aspirations and purposes: that she intended to separate the United States from the Allies, to refuse a dictated peace, and to avoid reparations payments. The Northcliffe press expressed fear that Germany was now endeavouring in effect to win the war she lost by arms.

The effect of this press campaign upon the attitudes and aims of the delegations then negotiating the terms of peace in Paris is difficult to determine; nevertheless, it did tend to surround the Peace Conference with an atmosphere of high excitement. At home, at least, the campaign served to take the pressure off Lloyd George in one respect. It reconciled the British people to the fact that conscription would temporarily be maintained and that high military expenditures must be maintained.[49] All this occurred on the eve of the introduction of the defense estimates in Parliament.

[46] *The Times*, February 28, p. 10.
[47] Text of Foch report in *Foreign Relations, 1919*, IV, 183-184.
[48] *The Times*, March 3, 1919, p. 11.
[49] Churchill's "Mansion House" speech on February 19, 1919, also stressed the importance of conscription in order to maintain an army on the Rhine: to make certain that Germany could not reopen offensive warfare and to make Germany pay.

Final Decisions On The Military Terms

The report of the combined military, naval, and air commissions headed by Foch was first discussed in the Supreme Council on March 3. A revised draft of this report was finally accepted by the Supreme Council just a fortnight later, on March 17,[50] but in the meantime several long discussions had taken place. The report dealt with the maximum military strength to be allowed the German army, its staffing, and its recruiting; the numbers and kind of armaments which Germany might keep and manufacture; various limiting measures on German legislation; and finally, the system of Allied control. The naval terms followed the general provisions of the report of the admirals which had been submitted in February; the air terms were along similar lines.

The points which raised the greatest controversy in the Supreme Council were the method of recruitment of the German forces and the question of methods and duration of Allied control.

As presented in the report of March 3, the strength of the army was to be 200,000 men and 9,000 officers, staffed in fifteen infantry divisions and five cavalry divisions, five Army Corps Headquarters, and one Army Headquarters. The officers were to be recruited on the voluntary basis and must serve 25 years, while the noncommissioned officers were to be recruited on the voluntary basis and must serve 15 years. The men were to be recruited by conscription by any method the Germans might determine and were to serve on the basis of one year's continuous service. The numbers of trained men in each class of yearly recruits could not exceed 180,000.

The differences of opinion which produced the big debate in the Supreme Council were foreshadowed in the Foch Committee in the reservation by the British delegation to the report in favor of a German army based on voluntary service on a long-term basis rather than on conscription.[51] The British representative had accepted the report with its provision for conscription only to make some decision possible.

Foch made a strong defense before the Supreme Council of the

[50] Text of this draft in *Foreign Relations, 1919*, IV, 385-403.
[51] *Foreign Relations, 1919*, IV, 185.

French insistence on continuing the policy of conscription. According to the Marshal, a highly trained voluntary, long-term service army in Germany which could serve as a training ground for a reserve force of officers would be a far greater danger to the peace of Europe than an army conscripted on the basis of a year's service. The backbone of the strength of the old German Army had consisted, he said, of the 120,000 trained, noncommissioned officers. All the members of a voluntary long-term service army might be considered as potential officers to serve as a nucleus in rapidly building up a large trained army. Doubtless, in the minds of both the French military men and statesmen was the fear that, if conscription were abolished in Germany, pressure might be great for the abolition of conscription in other continental countries, including France.[52] This idea was wholly untenable to the French, both on military and on other grounds often misunderstood in other countries. The idea of the duty of every citizen to render military service was a vital part of the democratic egalitarian idea of post-revolution France.

Opposed to the political background of the question in France was the great pressure during this period in Britain for the abolition of conscription everywhere. In the minds of many Englishmen, the presence of large conscripted armies in continental Europe had made war unavoidable. At any rate, in answer to Foch's argument, Lloyd George's contention that the question was not wholly military, but partly political as well, was hard to refute.[53] In the discussion on March 7 the British Prime Minister made clear that the status of the German army was a matter for the decision of the governments and not the military advisers. He further stated that he was in favor of a small, long-term, voluntary army and proposed that the Military Committee draft a scheme on that basis.[54] The revised report, presented on March 10, called for a long-term service army for Germany, but with a strength of only 140,000 men.[55] This compromise

---

[52] *Foreign Relations, 1919*, IV, 218. For Foch's attitude on this matter, see Lloyd George, *Truth about the Peace Treaties*, I, 586–587.

[53] *Foreign Relations, 1919*, IV, 219.

[54] *Foreign Relations, 1919*, IV, 263–265.

[55] Text of the report in *Foreign Relations, 1919*, IV, 305.

could not, however, secure complete agreement in the Military Committee, for a statement was appended by Foch, stating that from the French point of view, if the principle of a voluntary long-term service army were to be adhered to, a reduction to 100,000 men was indispensable. Before the Council, Clemenceau defended this point of view, while General Bliss said that he "felt that safety could not be assured with less than 140,000." [56]

In the final resolution by the Supreme Council, the army of 100,000 men advocated by Foch triumphed, but not without vigorous protests from the American and British delegates. Balfour said that if the army of Germany should be reduced to a police force, and that a small one, Germany must be secured against invasion. "If the Germans were to be told that they would have only 100,000 armed men, while France, Poland, or Bohemia could have as many as they wished, they would say that the Allied Powers were leaving them at the mercy even of their small neighbors." In view of the fact that there was no plan at present before the Conference for general disarmament, Balfour maintained that some form of guarantee against invasion should be found for Germany, but he made no specific suggestions. Clemenceau said, perhaps with malice, that the solution should be left to the League of Nations. Balfour replied that "if this was the solution, it should be communicated to Germany." At this Council meeting, however, the figure for the new German voluntary army was accepted at 100,000.[57]

On March 15, Wilson had returned to Paris and attended a Supreme War Council meeting again on March 17. Agreement in principle had been reached in the Council on March 10 on the issue of conscription versus voluntary army and on the numbers of the future German army, both House and Lansing attending the Council. The final decision was to have taken place on March 15, but, according to General Sir Henry Wilson, the President on the day of

---

[56] *Foreign Relations, 1919*, IV, 295–296.

[57] *Foreign Relations, 1919*, IV, 298. During the course of the discussions since February, the strength of the German army had been reduced from the thirty divisions estimated by the Tardieu Committee to this final figure of 100,000 men.

his return conferred with the other Prime Ministers and wished to change the military terms and impose conscription.[58]

At any rate, final approval of the terms was postponed until March 17.[59] Sir Henry reports another conference between Wilson and Lloyd George just before the Supreme Council meeting, at which Lloyd George threatened withdrawal of his support from the League Covenant unless Wilson agreed to the British views on a voluntary army.[60] In the face of this opposition, Wilson retreated; and, later in the Council meeting, he did not directly raise the issue of conscription.

No explanation is given in Sir Henry's diary for the President's stand. However, in the discussions in the Council meeting, the President questioned the military experts very carefully as to whether the dangers which Germany must meet on her eastern frontier had been sufficiently considered in fixing the maximum for her armed forces.[61] It is probable, therefore, that, as General Bliss had always considered 100,000 men too small a number for safety, Wilson was willing to accept the principle of a conscripted rather than voluntary German army in order to win French support for a larger German force.

[58] "President Wilson and other Prime Ministers had a long meeting this afternoon and did absolutely no business. Wilson talking of League of Nations and other nonsense. Curiously enough, Wilson wants to change our military terms to the Boches and to impose conscription. If he brings this up tomorrow when we are to agree to the voluntary principle, it will be curious." C. E. Callwell, ed., *Field Marshal Sir Henry Wilson* (London, 1927), II, 174.

[59] Clemenceau announced in the Supreme Council on March 14 that he had received a request from Wilson to postpone the discussion of the terms until March 15. *Foreign Relations, 1919*, IV, 354.

[60] "Meeting at Quai d'Orsay at 3 p.m. Wilson came down with intention to challenge our voluntary-principle army for the Boches, on the ground that he had not been present when the decision was reached, although both House and Lansing were. Lloyd George at a private talk with Wilson made it clear that he would not tolerate this and said that if he persisted, he—Lloyd George —who was not present when the League of Nations was agreed to, would challenge that decision. Wilson collapsed. We discussed and passed our military terms and naval terms and nearly all our air terms." Callwell, *Sir Henry Wilson*, II, 174.

[61] *Foreign Relations, 1919*, IV, 356-357.

The second major question faced by the Supreme War Council was that of the supervision of the execution of the military clauses. Two difficulties arose: the question of the duration of control, and the problem of maintaining continued Allied enforcement. The French had apparently long realized both the American opposition to their desire to secure continued control in Germany and the American awareness of the difficulties of continued inter-Allied functioning in Germany. When, on February 12, Wilson had remarked that the disarmament of Germany was morally justified and that it was right "to subject her to a generation of thoughtfulness," Clemenceau at once expressed enthusiastic agreement.[62] It is clear from his constant references in later Council debates to Wilson's remark that Clemenceau thought that Wilson had now committed himself.

The question of control had first encountered difficulties in the Foch committee. General Bliss and General Pershing had blocked efforts of Foch to insert a clause which "gave the possibilities of perpetual control" and had agreed only to a commission which would exist for a limited period of time. General Bliss pointed out the probability that the United States Senate would object to participation of American officers in a commission for perpetual control.[63]

In the first draft of the military terms submitted to the Supreme Council by the Foch Committee on March 3, the work of execution of the clauses was to be carried out by an Inter-Allied Committee of Control, who would supervise "the reductions imposed upon Germany as regards her strength and armament within the prescribed period." Provisions for future supervision were to be continued "by such means and by such body as the League of Nations may deem necessary." [64]

This first draft was very far from solving the problem of the duration of control, since it was not consistent within itself. As Balfour at once pointed out, the air control clauses were to last till the

[62] *Foreign Relations, 1919*, III, 1002.
[63] *Foreign Relations, 1919*, XI, 80–81.
[64] Text of the draft in *Foreign Relations, 1919*, IV, 183–184.

conclusion of peace, the naval clauses till Germany had fulfilled all the terms of the Armistice, and the military ones "until the Day of Judgment." [65] Foch appeared to take the decision of February 12 to submit final terms as meaning terms in perpetuity. When Balfour and Milner challenged this interpretation, Clemenceau replied that he "was not content to tell Germany to limit her forces until Peace Terms were fulfilled, and to leave the future at the mercy of events." [66] The result of this discussion was that the second draft, presented on March 6, achieved uniformity in the duration of controls. However, as Balfour pointed out, agreement had been reached only "by omitting all reference to any period of time." [67] This left the matter for final decision in the big debate on the military terms until after Wilson's return.

The problem of the difficulty of continued Allied functioning in Germany was met in this first draft by the provision that the League of Nations should supervise after the initial carrying out of the clauses. To this, Lloyd George objected in the debate on March 10, pointing out that the League of Nations was not a body of police to enforce the execution of a treaty, and it was finally decided that the clauses should read: "by such means and by such organs as the Associated Powers may decide to employ or to create." [68]

When President Wilson returned to the Council on March 17, he spoke vigorously on the question of duration of control, saying:

> That while it was not specifically stated that any of the Commissions provided should have an indefinite duration, he thought it would be advisable to add a statement including the explanation made by Marshal Foch that these Commissions would not continue more than three months.[69]

Marshal Foch objected to undertaking any such contract with the Germans, saying that the Allies should agree to this among themselves. In response to Balfour's inquiry as to whether it would not be necessary to continue to exercise supervision over the German

---

[65] *Foreign Relations, 1919*, IV, 187.
[66] *Foreign Relations, 1919*, IV, 187–189.
[67] *Foreign Relations, 1919*, IV, 215. Text of the draft in *ibid*, IV, 230–251.
[68] *Foreign Relations, 1919*, IV, 303.   [69] *Foreign Relations, 1919*, IV, 375.

army and its armaments in order to ensure their maintenance in the status stipulated, President Wilson held that supervision would become endless. He thought that the Allies should agree among themselves that these Commissions would cease to function when the terms had once been carried out; for example, as soon as the army actually had been reduced to 100,000 men.[70]

The clauses regarding this, as finally decided upon, read:

> All Military, Naval, and Air Clauses contained in the present stipulations for which a time limit is fixed shall be executed by Germany under the control of Inter-Allied Commissions specially appointed for this purpose by the Allied and Associated Governments.[71]

Some weeks after the acceptance of the draft of March 17, with certain minor changes, the final wording of the control clauses was settled. In Article 213 of the final Treaty, both French pressure for continued control and British and American fears that a permanent right of control over German military institutions would affect her sovereignty were reconciled:

> So long as the present Treaty remains in force, Germany undertakes to give every facility for any investigation which the Council of the League of Nations, acting if need be by a majority vote, may consider necessary.[72]

There were other clauses of importance relating to the military terms which were discussed by the Council of Four, after the abandonment of the Council of Ten. One of these was the famous preamble to Part V which was suggested by President Wilson during a meeting with Lloyd George and Clemenceau on April 26. After a discussion of the form of the Treaty, where the decision was reached that the peace should be "agreed," rather than "imposed," Wilson pointed out that the military, naval, and air terms would be more acceptable to the enemy if they were presented as preparing the way for a general limitation of armaments.[73] With the backing of the British delegation, this proposal was finally accepted as the preamble, which read:

[70] *Foreign Relations, 1919*, IV, 375.
[71] *Foreign Relations, 1919*, IV, 376.
[72] *Foreign Relations, 1919*, XIII, 362.
[73] *Foreign Relations, 1919*, V, 299.

In order to render possible the initiation of a general limitation of armaments of all nations, Germany undertakes strictly to observe the military, naval, and air clauses which follow.

The insertion of this preamble and the later commentary on it in the Allied reply to the German counterproposals were of key importance in the later German claims that the Allies had also entered into an agreement to disarm.

The Naval Terms

The naval clauses called forth no such important debates as did the military clauses. The naval terms of the Armistice had temporarily put the German Navy out of commission and had placed the power in the hands of the Allies to continue this state of immobilization for an indefinite period.

By the end of January, continued Allied naval demobilization and some unrest among the naval personnel, combined with the necessity of keeping up the blockade as a final potential means of coercion, had alarmed some of the Allied admirals. Accordingly, Admiral Wemyss persuaded his colleagues on the Naval Committee to take the initiative in requesting that the Supreme Council instruct them to prepare naval terms to be submitted at once to the Germans.[74] The Supreme Council so instructed on February 2, and the report of the Naval Committee was first presented and discussed in the Supreme Council on February 8.[75] As we have seen, this report went beyond strictly naval terms in discussing the disposition of German colonies, the Kiel Canal, and ocean cables. These questions were later referred to other commissions of the Conference.

The real discussion of the naval terms in the Council did not take place, however, until March 6, after they had been integrated into the whole military plan by the Foch report.[76] When this was done, restrictions on personnel and armaments paralleling the restrictions on the army were inserted. These had not been a part of the

[74] Wemyss, *Wemyss*, pp. 406–408.
[75] *Foreign Relations, 1919*, III, 933–934. Text of the report in *ibid*, III, 938–944.
[76] Text of the naval conditions in *Foreign Relations, 1919*, IV, 242–251.

admirals' report. The Foch report provided that all the ships and submarines surrendered by the Germans should be sunk or broken up. The French objected,[77] and this problem occasioned the most important discussion on the naval terms in the Council. What might have proved to be big issues in the naval clauses—the question of recruitment of personnel and the question of enforcement—were settled by the general debates on those issues in connection with the military clauses.

As far as duration of control was concerned, the naval clauses of the first draft of the Foch report, presented on March 3, were intended to last until all agreed-on terms of the Armistice had been fulfilled,[78] but in the second draft, discussed three days later, the restrictive clauses were imposed with no limitation of time. To all these clauses Admiral Benson made reservations, saying that he would agree to the imposition of restrictions after the conclusion of peace, only if imposed by the League of Nations.[79] The final solution to the problem of duration of controls was the same for the naval clauses as for the military terms: omission of all references to time, which seemed to suggest that control was to be perpetuated. Similarly, the most controversial sections of the naval clauses, those providing for the sinking or destruction of the surrendered ships, were solved by providing only for surrender, leaving for the Allies to solve later the problem of what should be done with them.[80]

The Air Terms

No special provisions in regard to disarmament in the air were made by the Armistice, except, of course, that the Germans agreed to cease all their military aerial operations. The air clauses, drawn up by the Air Committee headed by French General Duval, were first considered by the Supreme Council on March 12, after they had been incorporated in the Foch report.

[77] *Foreign Relations, 1919*, IV, 220.   [78] *Foreign Relations, 1919*, IV, 187.
[79] *Foreign Relations, 1919*, IV, 243–251.
[80] It was Admiral de Bon who objected to scrapping the ships as he wished to add a share of them to the French Navy. See Baker, *Woodrow Wilson and World Settlement*, I, 388–389.

The terms provided that there should be no air force in the German military organization and that all planes, including their armaments and equipment, should be surrendered, as well as all material in process of manufacture for such purposes. All manufacture of aeroplanes was to be prohibited until the signature of the Peace Treaty. The clauses provided for a commission to carry out the provisions, which was to be withdrawn as soon as the work was done.[81]

While this settled the restrictions up to that time, the significant debate occurred on March 17 on the question of permitting the Germans to engage in commercial aviation after the Peace Treaty.[82] Although all were agreed that civil aviation should be forbidden until the conclusion of the Peace Conference, the French thought it might be prohibited for twenty to thirty years, and the British thought two to five years would be sufficient. The Americans, however, stood firmly against any restrictions on civil aviation after the signing of the Treaty, considering such restrictions neither wise nor practicable. All clauses related to it were accordingly stricken from the draft, but a restriction of six months following the coming into force of the Treaty was included in the final draft.[83]

The Supreme Council also discussed the final disposition of the surrendered air matériel. The question was settled on the same principles as was the problem of the disposition of naval matériels. Surrender only was provided for in the Treaty, and the Allies would decide later what should be done with it.[84]

The discussion of the duration of restrictions on civil aviation again raised the question of the status of the terms which were being

---

[81] Discussion of March 12 in *Foreign Relations, 1919*, IV, 334-344. Texts of the air clauses in *ibid*, IV, 239-242.

[82] *Foreign Relations, 1919*, IV, 370-372.

[83] *Foreign Relations, 1919*, XIII, 353. This was Article 201 of the Treaty. Miller comments that the clause was accepted on March 17 without amendment, reading "The manufacture of aeroplanes [etc.] . . . shall be forbidden in all German territory until the signature of the final Treaty of Peace." He notes that the specification of a time limit—"during the six months following the coming into force of the present Treaty"—was made later, but that he could find no record of a decision for this change. Miller, *Diary*, XIX, 239-240.

[84] *Foreign Relations, 1919*, IV, 372-373.

drawn up—whether they were to be included in a preliminary peace or in the final Treaty. As Lansing pointed out in the discussion on March 12, the clause prohibiting the manufacture of aeroplanes "until the signature of the definite Treaty of Peace" made no sense if the article was to be part of the final Treaty.[85] The Air Committee without guidance from the Supreme Council had assumed that the military, naval, and air terms would be included in a convention which would be presented to the Germans without delay. When the question was raised in the Supreme Council on March 17, it appeared that Wilson had also been thinking in terms of a "preliminary Convention," a "sort of exalted armistice" which would be reincluded in the formal Treaty of Peace.[86] This would have been legally feasible under the United States Constitution and would not have constituted a Preliminary Treaty of Peace requiring ratification by the Senate.[87] At this late date, however, the Supreme Council did not seem to have considered seriously the separate presentation of the military, naval, and air terms.

[85] *Foreign Relations, 1919*, IV, 340-341.
[86] *Foreign Relations, 1919*, IV, 374.
[87] If the "Convention," which would have included only military, naval, and air terms, had been a "Treaty of Peace," or even a "Preliminary Treaty of Peace," instead of an armistice, it would have ended the state of war and thus required ratification by the United States Senate. Then all other terms of peace, including the Covenant, boundaries, reparations, etc., would have been "out of the Treaty." Miller notes a "fog" in the minds of nearly everyone who was talking about the question of a preliminary treaty. And the phraseology which maintained the fiction that the Conference was engaged in the preparation of the "preliminaries of peace," even through March, confused everyone, including the Germans. See Alma Luckau, *The German Delegation at the Peace Conference* (New York, 1941), p. 43. For discussions of the question, see Miller, *Covenant*, I, 86-99, and Marston, *The Peace Conference of 1919*, pp. 137-157.

Chapter VI

General Disarmament and the Peace Treaty

Article VIII of the League Covenant

The military terms of the Treaty provided for the disarmament of Germany, thus disposing of the first part of Lloyd George's motion of January 23. The second part of this motion—the preparation of plans for a permanent general reduction of armaments—was the purpose of Article VIII of the Covenant of the League, which was drawn up in the League of Nations Commission in the same weeks that the Supreme Council was preparing the military terms. The moral, if not indeed the legal, obligations of the Allies to reduce their armaments in the postwar years rested in the main upon these two sections of the Treaty. The Preamble to Part V had stated that Germany was to disarm in order to make possible general disarmament, and this aim was to be realized through Article VIII. The position of Article VIII in the Covenant indeed showed its importance in the League structure, for it appeared immediately after the articles creating the constitutional structure of the League.

In its final form, Article VIII contained four main points: first, the reduction of national armaments to the lowest point consistent with national safety; second, that the Council of the League shall formulate plans for such reduction, subject to revision; third, that private manufacture of armaments is open to objections for which the Council shall advise remedies; and fourth, that the League members shall exchange full information as to the scale of their armaments.[1] These final terms were the results of many drafts and conflicting opinions, much discussion and compromise, both in and outside of the League Commission. The history of the drafting of Article VIII throws light upon the attitudes of the three major powers toward the idea of limitation of armaments.

As has already been suggested, the inclusion of Article VIII in the Covenant was mainly due to American efforts, although it reflected many of the ideas of British liberals. No mention had been made of disarmament in the drafts for a League which owed their source to the British Foreign Office during the last years of the war. Neither the Phillimore Commission reports nor Lord Robert Cecil's plan had suggested a general limitation of armaments, while both the Foreign Office memorandum of November and the Admiralty report of December were aimed at blocking American efforts toward reduction of armaments and prohibition of private manufacture. If British official plans were cool to the idea, there was nevertheless a movement in England which favored disarmament, led by such groups as the U.D.C., the League of Nations Society, the League of Nations Union, and the Labour Party itself. Former Foreign Secretary Sir Edward Grey had declared himself in favor of postwar disarmament in a letter to Colonel House in 1915,[2] and lately General Smuts's proposals had been given wide publicity.

It was, however, through the initiative of the American delegation to the Conference that Article VIII materialized. Only in the United States were any official drafts prepared or any serious study given to the question. The original draft of Article VIII, drawn up by Colonel House in July 1918, contained many of the phrases and was not so very far in spirit from the article as it finally appeared in the Covenant. In the meantime, however, the disarmament article underwent many vicissitudes. Examination of the changes from the first American drafts and of the points of serious difference during the months in which Article VIII took shape may reveal the conflicting views on the application of Wilson's Fourth Point and on the role of the League in peacetime.

[1] For the complete text of Article VIII in its final form, see p. 141 below.
[2] Seymour, *House Papers*, II, 89.

General Disarmament and the Peace Treaty

A decision on the actual scope of general postwar limitation was not undertaken in the various drafts of the article nor by the League Commission, but was left to be accomplished later by the League. Nevertheless, Article VIII did attempt to define the general principles upon which such a decision could later be based. Yet even upon such a general definition Wilson was obliged to make a compromise of some significance, long before the Peace Conference opened, in order to preserve the disarmament ideal as one of the bases of peace.

The first paragraph of House's draft of July had recognized that "national armaments shall be reduced to the lowest point consistent with safety."[3] Wilson, however, clearly intended that limitation of armaments be carried to the lowest point possible: to quote from his Second Inaugural Address, "limited to the necessities of national order and domestic safety."[4] In his first draft of the Covenant, he changed House's wording to include the word "domestic" before "safety."[5] Although it seems probable that Wilson was originally thinking in terms of maintenance of internal order rather than of national self-defense, one may question whether he believed that such an interpretation of disarmament could be acceptable to the European powers or even to his own Congress. The logic of Wilson's original interpretation cannot be denied, if limitation of armaments was to be carried out simultaneously with the establishment of a League. But compromise, often the foe of logic, set into operation in the final draft of Article VIII two conflicting principles: the idea of common action by international agreement in an association of nations and the ancient principle of absolute self-defense.

By the time of the Cobb–Lippmann commentary on the Fourteen Points, in October 1918, Wilson had compromised his original concept of the scope of disarmament, for the Cobb–Lippmann interpretation of the Fourth Point included the "protection of territory against invasion" within the term "domestic safety."[6] During the

---

[3] Miller, *Covenant*, II, 10. The text of House's July 1918 draft is in Appendix C.
[4] Quoted in Miller, *Covenant*, I, 15.   [5] Miller, *Covenant*, II, 13.
[6] Seymour, *House Papers*, IV, 194.

Fourth Meeting of the League Commission on February 6, when Article VIII was first considered, a Japanese proposal to substitute the words "national safety" for "domestic safety," which was immediately accepted, formally disposed of the issue and cleared up any doubts remaining as to the general scope of postwar disarmament. The change, as David Hunter Miller comments, is certainly of significance.[7]

Wilson's decision to compromise on the question of "domestic safety" had been made before the convocation of the Peace Conference. Most of the other important points of contention emerged and were dealt with either in the few weeks in Paris immediately preceding the Conference or during the sessions of the League Commission. There was, in particular, one proposal in Wilson's drafts of Article VIII which was to encounter stiff opposition from the British delegation and which was to be substantially altered in the final draft of the Covenant. This read:

The contracting Powers further agree that munitions and implements of war shall not be manufactured by private enterprise or for private profit.[8]

As we have seen, the British did not share the American concern over the subject of private manufacture of arms and its evil effects upon governmental policy, although there had been instances in prewar England of such pressure by armaments firms on the government. In unofficial circles, however, there was some discussion of munitions manufacture. In the Labour Party memorandum of December 1917 the abolition of private manufacture of armaments had been included among the proposals. The attitude of the Labour Party was further revealed in the speech by G. N. Barnes, a Labour member of the Coalition government, at the Plenary Session of the Peace Conference on February 14, 1919, when he asked for a more robust declaration in favor of the abolition of private manufacture.[9]

[7] Miller, *Covenant*, I, 172-173. Compare Merze Tate, *The United States and Armaments* (Cambridge, Mass., 1948), p. 67.

[8] In Wilson's second draft of the Covenant (first Paris draft), January 10, 1919. For text see Appendix C.

[9] Miller, *Covenant*, II, 575.

In his unofficial plan of December, General Smuts had come out against private manufacture and suggested nationalization of arms production and inspection by League officials. The British government, nevertheless, consistently opposed mention of the subject in their League drafts, while President Wilson stubbornly retained the proposal in all four of his drafts.

The effect of British opposition was evident in two drafts of the Covenant drawn up in Paris. On January 27, Miller of the American delegation and Lord Cecil of the British delegation jointly produced a draft of the disarmament article which conformed with Wilson's second Paris draft in all respects except that it omitted the reference to private manufacturing.[10] During the next few days, Sir Cecil Hurst, legal adviser to the Foreign Office, scrutinized the Cecil-Miller draft, and his changes were accepted by Miller. While Wilson did not like this draft very much, he modified his own draft on February 2 in accordance with it, yet again retained his clause on private manufacturing which the Hurst-Miller draft had also omitted.[11]

The League of Nations Commission, which was appointed on January 25 to draw up the Covenant, did not discuss Article VIII until the Fourth Meeting on February 6.[12] Although the Hurst-Miller draft was used as the basis of discussion, President Wilson at this meeting succeeded in inserting a paragraph on private manufacture into Article VIII:

The High Contracting Parties further agree that munitions and implements of war should not be manufactured by private enterprise, and direct the Executive Council to advise how this practice can be dispensed with.[13]

[10] Miller, *Covenant*, II, 131–141. For text, see Appendix C.

[11] Text of Hurst-Miller draft in Miller, *Covenant*, II, 142–144, and of Wilson's draft of February 2 in *ibid*, II, 145–154.

[12] The members of the League Commission included: President Wilson, Colonel House (U.S.); Lord Robert Cecil, General Smuts (Great Britain); Mr. Bourgeois, Mr. Larnaude (France); Mr. Orlando, Mr. Scialoja (Italy); Mr. Reis (Portugal); Baron Makino, Viscount Chinda (Japan); Mr. Pessoa (Brazil); Mr. Wellington Koo (China); Mr. Vesnitch (Serbia). Miller, *Covenant*, II, 229–230.

[13] Miller, *Covenant*, I, 172.

On this date, according to Miller, Cecil appeared ready to yield to Wilson and to include a strongly worded clause on private manufacture.[14] On the next day, however, the Naval Section at Paris presented to Cecil a memorandum which strongly opposed inclusion of this proposal and indeed urged that the whole question of arms limitation be reviewed independently of the Covenant of the League.[15] This was the same memorandum which had been prepared in the Admiralty in December. In spite of Admiralty opposition, Cecil agreed to retain the clause concerning private arms manufacture in Article VIII, although its wording was modified during the revision of the Covenant text by the Drafting Committee on February 12: instead of agreeing to the abolition of private manufacture, the High Contracting Parties were to agree that:

... the manufacture by private enterprise of munitions and implements of war lends itself to grave objections and direct the Executive Council to advise how the evil effects attendant upon such manufacture can be prevented.[16]

The Admiralty memorandum had also pointed out the difficulties of smaller nations which were not self-sufficient in munitions production.[17] In the Drafting Committee an amendment to this effect was added to Article VIII by the Portuguese delegation:

... due regard being paid in such recommendations to the necessities of those countries which are not able to manufacture for themselves the munitions necessary for their safety.[18]

With a few minor changes in wording, this was Paragraph 5 of Article VIII as it finally stood. Although a compromise, it did in part satisfy Wilson's insistence on the importance of private armaments production and its relation to disarmament.

The French attitude toward limitation of armaments under the League emerged clearly in three proposals made by Léon Bourgeois in the League Commission. The French considered general limitation desirable only insofar as it contributed to future French security.

[14] Miller says that Cecil handed Wilson a draft of this clause which Wilson then read. Miller, *Covenant*, I, 172.
[15] Miller, *Covenant*, I, 286–289.
[16] Miller, *Covenant*, II, 310.
[17] Miller, *Covenant*, I, 288.
[18] Miller, *Covenant*, I, 221.

The main purpose of disarmament in their opinion was the prevention of military aggression, in particular, German aggression.

Only one of these French proposals was accepted in principle by the British and American delegations. This was the suggestion by Bourgeois at the Eighth Meeting of the League Commission that not only the relative power of a state should be considered in limiting its armaments, but also the risks to which a state is exposed by its geographic position. Cecil reworded this French amendment and referred it to the Drafting Committee where it was accepted.[19]

The fate of the other two proposals was very different. While there was general support of the use of diplomatic, legal, and economic sanctions to enforce the League's decisions, the French suggestion of military sanctions—an International Force at the disposal of the League—met stiff opposition from the United States and Britain. This proposal first appeared in the draft of the Covenant adopted by the French Ministerial Commission for the League of Nations, presented by Bourgeois at the First Meeting of the Commission.[20] As the Hurst–Miller draft rather than the French or Wilsonian drafts was used in the Commission, the French were obliged to propose the "International Force" as an amendment to Article VIII in order to secure its consideration. This was done by Bourgeois at the Eighth Meeting on February 11. The idea of an international force in any form was never acceptable either to the British or to Wilson. Bourgeois nevertheless argued for the amendment and for the French conception of the League: "a force so superior to that of all nations or to that of all alliances that no nation or combination of nations can challenge or resist it."[21] Wilson answered that every possible provision should be made for the national security of League members, but an international force under international control was contrary to the United States Constitution.[22] Cecil added that the British people "would have many objections to accepting a control which insisted on a certain number of British soldiers being maintained under arms."[23] In order to

[19] Miller, *Covenant*, II, 292, 296.
[20] Miller, *Covenant*, II, 241–243.
[21] Miller, *Covenant*, II, 291–292.
[22] Miller, *Covenant*, I, 209–210.
[23] Miller, *Covenant*, II, 291–292.

conciliate the French, he suggested that a less strict arrangement might be adopted which would permit the preparation of agreements for an international force whenever the need for it should be felt. He proposed as an amendment:

A Permanent Commission shall be established to advise the League of Nations on naval and military matters.[24]

Both the Bourgeois and Cecil proposals were submitted to the Drafting Committee which drew up the February 14 draft of the Covenant. Bourgeois's amendment was again found unacceptable, but Cecil's suggestion was adopted as Article IX of the Covenant where it remained essentially intact in the final draft.[25]

In spite of the fact that the Cecil amendment was obviously as far as the British and American delegations would go toward meeting the French point of view, Bourgeois persisted in reintroducing the idea of an international force in subsequent meetings, although he later modified the proposal by suggesting the establishment of a body which amounted to an international General Staff. Such a body would prepare a military and naval program by which in urgent cases the obligations of the Covenant could be enforced.[26] This proposal was as unacceptable to the British and American representatives as the first. The Commission held to Cecil's Article IX, and French persistence in championing the international force idea, in all its disguises, went unrewarded.

Another French proposal met much the same fate, and again it reflected France's concern with security and her conception of a League whose authority should transcend the authority of the member states. In none of the drafts or discussions of Article VIII had

[24] Miller, *Covenant*, II, 296.

[25] Article IX was later modified in the 10th Meeting: the Permanent Commission's powers were broadened to include advising the League on the execution of Article VIII. On March 28, this was extended to cover the execution of Article I as well.

[26] Miller, *Covenant*, I, 253, 260. Bourgeois introduced this proposal successively in the Plenary Session of the Peace Conference on February 14; at the 12th Meeting of the League Commission, March 24; at the 13th Meeting of the League Commission, March 26; and finally at the Plenary Session of the Conference on April 28.

the principle of publicity of national armaments been questioned. A reference to publicity had been included in the earliest American drafts and had survived both the Cecil–Miller and Hurst–Miller drafts, where the private manufacture proposal had fallen. Indeed the Admiralty memorandum to Cecil gave "the fullest acceptance" to the proposal of full and frank publicity.[27] The French, moreover, had every reason to support the idea, which, if faithfully executed, would add immeasurably to their security.

The problem arose, then, not over the principle of publicity itself, but rather over the means of its execution. At the Tenth Meeting of the Commission, Bourgeois proposed a commission of verification or inspection under the League for the purpose of obtaining the necessary data on the scope of military and naval armaments and capacities for munitions production. He argued that exchange of information on armaments depended on the good faith of nations, and although at the present time this mutual trust could not be doubted, there would come a time when other (enemy) nations would enter the League. Bourgeois contended that the necessary safeguards should now be made lest the good faith of nations should later be taken advantage of. The proposal was rejected by the League Commission, but Cecil, again by way of compromise, suggested the insertion of a few words in Article IX, enlarging the powers of the Permanent Commission: "to advise the League on the execution of Article VIII."[28] Although this concession to the French point of view was adopted, Bourgeois continued to propose his commission of verification in subsequent meetings of the League Commission and at the Plenary Session of the Peace Conference on April 28.[29] He argued that the important thing was that the principle of verification be accepted, but against his successive appeals the opposition remained firm. Wilson told him that in view of the principles upon which the League was established, such a commission would seriously offend the susceptibilities of sovereign states. Eleutherios Venizelos of Greece moreover pointed out that such an amendment

[27] Miller, *Covenant*, I, 287.   [28] Miller, *Covenant*, II, 317–319.
[29] Proposed at the 11th Meeting, March 22; at the 13th Meeting, March 26; see Miller, *Covenant*, II, 343, 706f; I, 350–351.

might compromise the fate of the League in many countries and especially in the United States.[30] The French proposal, like the proposal for an international force, found no support.

There was one further issue upon which the Anglo-American and French delegations differed: the question of compulsory military service. Neither Wilson's nor House's original drafts of the Covenant had mentioned conscription, and it was not until Smuts's plan of December that its abolition was suggested. As we have seen, the idea impressed Wilson greatly, and he incorporated it in his January 20 draft. The proposal again appeared in the Cecil–Miller draft a week later, but, due to Italian objections, Wilson and Cecil agreed that Wilson's wording must be modified.[31] Accordingly, the Hurst–Miller draft suggested an inquiry "into the feasibility of abolishing compulsory military service," instead of a direct statement on its abolition.

The proposal was, however, destined to meet more opposition and finally defeat at the Fourth Meeting of the League Commission. Bourgeois objected to any allusion to a possible abolition of conscription, arguing that compulsory military service seemed to France to be a fundamental issue of democracy and a corollary of universal suffrage,[32] words echoed later in the Supreme Council by Marshal Foch on the question of the status of the postwar German army. Vittorio Orlando of Italy voiced his opposition, and the reference to conscription was dropped from Article VIII.

The drafting of Article VIII in the League Commission therefore revealed the principal American, British, and French attitudes toward disarmament, but, despite compromises or conflicting views on the points we have mentioned, Article VIII emerged as an affirmation of the principle of general arms limitation as one of the aims of the League of Nations. In its final form, the Article read:

[30] Miller, *Covenant*, II, 343, 72.
[31] Miller, *Covenant*, I, 65, 67. Orlando, in a conference with Wilson, argued that the abolition of conscription would hurt the smaller powers who could not afford to pay a voluntary army enough to keep it well filled.
[32] Miller, *Covenant*, II, 264.

(1) The Members of the League recognize that the maintenance of peace requires the reduction of national armaments to the lowest point consistent with national safety, and the enforcement by common action of international obligations.

(2) The Council, taking account of the geographical situation and circumstances of each State, shall formulate plans for such reduction for the consideration and action of the several Governments.

(3) Such plans should be subject to reconsideration and revision at least every ten years.

(4) After these plans shall have been adopted by the several Governments, the limits of armaments therein fixed shall not be exceeded without the concurrence of the Council.

(5) The Members of the League agree that the manufacture by private enterprise of munitions and implements of war is open to grave objections. The Council shall advise how the evil effects attendant upon such manufacture can be prevented, due regard being had to the necessities of those Members of the League which are not able to manufacture the munitions and implements of war necessary for their safety.

(6) The Members of the League undertake to interchange full and frank information as to the scale of their armaments, their military, naval and air programmes and the condition of such of their industries as are adaptable to warlike purposes.

Pressure on Lloyd George

During the final and most critical period of the Conference, from the time of Wilson's return in mid-March until the presentation of the Treaty to the Germans on May 7, there were signs in the British press and in Parliament of a growing uneasiness concerning the proceedings in Paris. The public was becoming impatient. In the four months since the conclusion of the Armistice little seemed to have been accomplished beyond an early draft of the Covenant and an outline of the military terms. The more difficult problems—territorial, economic, and financial—were yet to be faced by the Peace Conference, and after all the Premiers had returned to Paris, there seemed to be no excuse for the apparent delays. Certain sections of the press had charged that the problems encountered in drafting the League Covenant were holding up progress.[33] Although this was denied by President Wilson, the public was not enlightened as to the true causes of the delays. Indeed, a curtain of secrecy seemed to surround the proceedings of the Conference. The press received day-to-day "doles" from the officials of the Conference, but these progress reports contained insufficient information to satisfy the thirst for news. The press and Parliament complained of the violation of Wilsonian "open diplomacy," [34] and there were inevitable leaks of information upon which the press built distorted reports of the proceedings.[35] Furthermore, suspicions were aroused about the content of these secret negotiations. William Adamson, the Labour leader in the House of Commons, spoke for much of the country when he said that he had misgivings as to whether the proper steps were being taken in Paris to safeguard the interests of the country.[36] The public sensed that the apparent delays and the policy of silence during this period were due to serious dissension among the Allied delegations, which was in fact the case. The newly established Council of Four had nearly disintegrated in the face of such problems as the Saar, the Polish frontiers, and Italy's demands for Fiume.

The British Conservative press, particularly the *Morning Post* and the Northcliffe-controlled *Daily Mail* and *The Times*, ever critical of Lloyd George's attempts at moderation, seized this new opportunity to launch an attack upon the Prime Minister. If this campaign was partly justified by the extraordinary secrecy which surrounded the Conference, Lloyd George did little to calm his critics. Against the advice of his British colleagues, he refused to give out more information on the difficulties that were being faced.[37] The press cam-

[33] See the *London Globe*, March 20, 1919, quoted in Baker, *Woodrow Wilson and World Settlement*, II, 32. See also *The Times*, March 18, 1919, p. 11.

[34] *H.C. Debates*, 5th series, CXIV, col. 3003. April 16, 1919; *The Times*, April 16, 1919, p. 13.

[35] See *Lord Riddell's Intimate Diary of the Peace Conference and After, 1918-1923* (New York, 1934), pp. 39-40, 86.

[36] *H.C. Debates*, 5th series, CXIV, col. 2956. April 16, 1919.

[37] *Riddell's Diary*, pp. 39-40.

paign then followed the old lines: demanding a hard peace; clamoring for Allied demobilization; condemning Bolshevism; and crying for total indemnities. It was the policy of *The Times* during this period to publish extracts from the most extreme German conservative newspapers which illustrated the Hun's lack of humility, his arrogance, and his general opposition to Allied plans and an imposed peace.[38] The Northcliffe press, according to one observer, "surrendered themselves gleefully" to the propagandists of the French Ministry of War.[39] *The Times* quoted a French article which deplored the inclination in present British policy to return to the prewar attitude of "satisfying German ambitions by feeding them."[40] Leading articles sought to steer Lloyd George away from moderation in drawing up the peace terms:

> Attempts to soften these conditions with a view to mitigate German hatred and German hostility would be childish... Tenderness towards her, or at least compromise with her desires, would be construed by her as mere cowardice and folly.[41]

The *Daily Mail* commented:

> It is not our business to ask what Germany will think of the terms. Our duty is to dictate such terms as shall give a material guarantee for security, and let the Hun think what he likes about them.[42]

In a neat little box on the front page, the *Daily Mail* printed for several weeks the epigraph, "The Junkers will cheat you yet."[43] *The Times* charged Lloyd George with engaging in Germanophile and pro-Bolshevik activities,[44] an attack which enraged the Prime Minister, who remarked privately that he considered bringing an action for libel against Northcliffe.[45]

In the first week of April the pressure on Lloyd George, both in the press and in Parliament, centered around the issue of reparations. The press reported widespread suspicion that Britain would

---

[38] See *The Times*, April 15, 1919, p. 11.
[39] Harold Nicolson, *Peacemaking, 1919* (London, 1939), p. 62.
[40] *The Times*, April 5, 1919, p. 13. [41] *The Times*, April 21, 1919, p. 11.
[42] Nicolson, *Peacemaking*, p. 62. [43] Nicolson, *Peacemaking*, p. 62.
[44] *The Times*, April 5, 1919, p. 13. [45] *Riddell's Diary*, p. 46

not get her "full measure."[46] In Parliament a majority of the Conservative members signed the famous Lowther telegram, which was sent to Lloyd George in Paris and demanded that he keep his reparations pledges to the country. *The Times* had more subtle methods. Printing excerpts from five statements by Lloyd George on reparations, a leading article on the same page hoped that the Prime Minister had not aroused in the public mind expectations which he could not fulfill.[47]

Public unrest and suspicion had reached a high pitch by the time Lloyd George returned to England and spoke to Parliament on April 16. The speech was a masterpiece, for, although he avoided concrete statements upon the real issues of the peace, the Prime Minister succeeded in pacifying his Parliament and winning back its support. He spent much time on the problem of Russia, and he defended the delays of the Conference and the lack of publicity. He reaffirmed the fact that the Conference was proceeding on the basis of the Fourteen Points, but told little of the actual negotiations. He did, however, declare that, "one of the most beneficent results of peace ... will be that the great continental menace of armaments will be swept away," and that German forces would be reduced to a mere police force.[48] Then, he cleverly shifted attention away from the Peace Conference by an extremely dexterous and biting attack upon Lord Northcliffe and his press. Bonar Law commented later that the speech was open to serious Parliamentary criticism, had there been anyone to criticize, but the fact was that nine-tenths of the House of Commons hated Northcliffe and were glad to see Lloyd George go after him.[49]

It was clear after the Prime Minister's speech that no official reports would be given on the peace terms by any of the Allied governments until the day they were presented to the Germans. Meanwhile, the press continued its pressure on the British delegation

[46] Compare *The Times*, April 12, 1919, p. 15.
[47] *The Times*, April 11, 1919, p. 13.
[48] *H.C. Debates*, 5th series, CXIV, cols. 2954–2955. April 16, 1919.
[49] *Riddell's Diary*, pp. 66–67.

for a "stern" peace, and the House of Commons lapsed into comparative silence.

There had been little interest or debate in the press or Parliament on the disarmament question during this period. The assumption was that German disarmament would follow the lines indicated by the predictions of the military terms in the press in March. These predictions turned out later to have been fairly accurate.[50] It was also assumed that German disarmament was a necessary prerequisite to general disarmament, and general disarmament would be a matter for the League of Nations. However, no one was very concerned with the actual details of general disarmament, with the exception of certain Labour and Socialist groups who had long advocated disarmament as a part of their war aims programs. In early April, a Committee of the Bern Labour and Socialist Conference, including Ramsay MacDonald, met with Lord Robert Cecil in Paris. They suggested several amendments to the Covenant, including continuous international inspection of armaments.[51] Two days later, in a speech before a special conference of the Trade Union Congress and the Labour Party, J. H. Thomas advocated "national disarmament and no conscription" and condemned private armaments manufacturers as "a danger to the world."[52] And, on April 29, the International Socialist Conference, meeting at Amsterdam, talked of the necessity of total disarmament on land and sea and of the abolition of conscription.[53]

A few days later, the Treaty was presented to the Germans, and an official summary of the terms was given to the press. Comment on the Treaty was loud and varied in British circles, but after the beginning of May it was only possible for Conservative opinion to stage a holding action. The time for stiffening the terms by pressure upon the British delegation had passed. Now, instead of defending Lloyd George against the attacks of the Conservatives, the Liberal and Labour groups began an attempt to influence the peace by

[50] See *The Times*, March 20, 1919, p. 11.
[51] *The Times*, April 2, 1919, p. 14.
[52] *The Times*, April 4, 1919, p. 14.   [53] *The Times*, April 30, 1919, p. 10.

crying moderation while the German counterproposals were being considered.

The German Counterproposals

The Germans, before the 1918 Armistice, had been concerned about the interpretation of Wilson's Fourth Point. Prince Max, in a Reichstag speech on October 3, had pointed out that disarmament in order to be effective should be general and not one-sided. During the winter, while the Allies were meeting in Paris, the German government was studying the problems of peace which they expected to discuss with the Allied governments before a final treaty was concluded. The technical problems were examined by a group of experts under Count von Bernstorff, called the "Paxkonferenz," while a second body charged with preparations for the coming negotiations was a committee appointed in the Constituent National Assembly on April 14, 1919. This "Committee for Peace Negotiations" served as the intermediary between the National Assembly, the Cabinet, and the various parties. Its chairman was Konstantin Fehrenbach, the president of the National Assembly and leader of the Centrist Party.[54]

At the first session of the committee on April 15, Ambassador Edgar Haniel von Haimhausen from the Foreign Office spoke on the preparations for the peace and the probable conditions to be expected. About disarmament, he said that first the Allies were agreed on the complete disarmament of Germany, but apparently had not yet decided whether compulsory military service should be abolished. He predicted complete demilitarization of the left bank of the Rhine and possibly also that of a zone fifty miles east of the Rhine. He also expected that Germany would be permitted a small navy only, with the destruction of the fortifications of Heligoland and the Kiel Canal. Further, he was sure that Germany would be forbidden to have a military air force.[55] While his predictions were in line with the actual provisions which Germany was forced to accept, the final Allied conditions were, in fact, more severe.

[54] Luckau, *German Delegation*, p. 6.
[55] Luckau, *German Delegation*, pp. 182–184.

General Disarmament and the Peace Treaty

The actual instructions to the German delegates on the subject of disarmament were somewhat more optimistic than was warranted by von Haimhausen's predictions. First of all, these stipulated that a one-sided obligation upon Germany to disarm must be rejected:

Germany is prepared, however, in line with the Wilson program, to give guarantees for the future that these armaments will be reduced to the minimum required for security, provided that other countries, especially former opponents and neighboring states, are willing to give equal guarantees.[56]

With this as a basis, certain specific concessions were to be allowed: first, "extensive disarmament on land with a reciprocal and simultaneous abolition of compulsory military service"; second, "the razing of fortifications on the left bank of the Rhine may be conceded, but not the withdrawal of all troops. Readiness to evacuate the left bank of the Rhine only if France and Belgium establish a corresponding demilitarized zone." The instructions on these points had no chance of success. The third point, that a demand for destruction of German railroads on account of their strategic importance must be refused, was never asked of the Germans. In the instructions there also appeared a curious suggestion for "the creation of an international marine police, in which all seafaring nations shall have a proportional part; this is to be accompanied by an international prohibition of armed ships at sea except for the said marine police."[57] Beyond this there was a general declaration for freedom of the seas. This suggestion for an international marine police does not appear elsewhere, but is prophetic of similar proposals for an international air force which later became widespread.

The German delegation, led by Count Brockdorff-Rantzau, received the final text of the Treaty from the Allies at a formal meeting on May 7 at Versailles. On hearing the first report of the Treaty after it had been translated, the delegation was unanimous in declaring that unless it could be fundamentally revised, the Treaty could not be accepted. Their reaction to the document as a whole was well

---

[56] Luckau, *German Delegation*, p. 207.
[57] Luckau, *German Delegation*, p. 207.

expressed by Dr. Hans Simons, a member of the delegation, and later foreign minister:

> The treaty which our enemies have laid before us is, in so far as the French dictated it, a monument of pathological fear and pathological hatred; and in so far as the Anglo-Saxons dictated it, it is the work of a capitalistic policy of the cleverest and most brutal kind. Its shamelessness does not lie in treading down a brave opponent, but in the fact that from beginning to end all these humiliating conditions are made to look like a just punishment, while in truth there is in them neither shame, nor any respect for the conception of justice.[58]

A note was sent to the President of the Peace Conference two days later, protesting the fact that the basis of peace mutually agreed upon had been abandoned and stating that the Treaty included demands which were intolerable to any nation. Clemenceau replied that he could not admit discussion of the Allied right to establish the fundamental conditions of the peace. The Allies would consider only "suggestions of a practical kind." [59] Thereafter, the German delegation sought to break down the Allies with a barrage of notes, attacking numerous sections of the Treaty. When the period of examination ran out on May 22, the Allies granted a seven-day extension. The final, comprehensive German note on the counterproposals was presented to the Allies on May 28.

As far as the military clauses of the Treaty were concerned, the German counterproposals were mainly occupied with asking for concessions in return for their agreement to disarm first. It is significant that the question of disarmament—Part V of the Treaty—was considered under the heading of proposals on the League of Nations. The German government stated that they were prepared to agree to the fundamental ideas for the regulation of army, naval, and air forces, as proposed in Part V, on the expectation that Germany might enter the League with equal privileges immediately upon the conclusion of the peace. Further, they would agree to the abolition of compulsory military service on the condition that, "this measure be the beginning of a general reduction of armaments by

[58] Quoted in Luckau, *German Delegation*, p. 71.
[59] Luckau, *German Delegation*, pp. 225, 234.

all nations," and that within two years after the conclusion of peace the other states, under Article VIII, were to reduce their armaments and to abolish compulsory service. Under these conditions, the German government agreed to reduce their army to 100,000, dismantle their fortresses in the west, and establish a neutral zone. As for the naval terms, Germany was prepared to surrender not only the surface warships demanded, but also all ships of the line under the condition of a financial regulation.[60]

Concerning this promise of disarmament, however, the Germans contended that an extension of the period of execution allowed in Part V was essential. According to the terms submitted to Germany on May 7, all the disarmament provisions were to be carried out within two months of the coming into force of the Treaty. The Germans pointed out that this was technically impossible to fulfill. Therefore, changes in the clauses relating to this period of transition were asked for. The German government further proposed oral negotiations on these details.[61]

The reply of the Allies to the German counterproposals was submitted on June 16. The section on the military clauses began with a paragraph which explained the Allied position with regard to German disarmament and which may be considered as a gloss on the preamble to Part V of the Treaty. The statement reads as follows:

The Allied and Associated Powers wish to make it clear that their requirements in regard to German armaments were not made solely with the object of rendering it impossible for Germany to resume her policy of military aggression. They are also the first steps towards the general reduction and limitation of armaments which they seek to bring about as one of the most fruitful preventives of war, and which it will be one of the first duties of the League of Nations to promote.[62]

If the preamble is considered in the light of these assertions, it is not surprising that in future years many people contended that the preamble constituted an obligation on the part of the Allies to disarm.

[60] Luckau, *German Delegation*, p. 322.
[61] Luckau, *German Delegation*, p. 323.
[62] Luckau, *German Delegation*, p. 436.

While no concessions of permanent duration were made, in the military clauses the Allies did agree to modify the stipulations in regard to the period during which disarmament should be carried out. They recognized the contention of the Germans that the requirement of complete disarmament within two months was, in fact, technically impossible. They therefore submitted to the Germans the following modification which was to appear in the final treaty:

(a) Germany will be allowed to reduce her army more gradually than at present stipulated, i.e., to a maximum of 200,000 men within three months; at the end of that three months, and every subsequent three months, a conference of military experts of the Allied and Associated Powers shall fix the strength of the German army for the coming three months, the object being to reduce the German army to the 100,000 men stipulated in the treaty as soon as possible, and in any case by the expiration of the Law of the Reichswehr, i.e., by the 31st of March, 1920.[63]

The Allied reply refused Germany's request for immediate admission to the League and pointed out the provisions in the Covenant which determined admission of states not members of the League. When the German government had given clear proofs of its stability as well as of its intention to observe international obligations, particularly the Treaty, she would be admitted. Provided these conditions were fulfilled, the Allied governments saw no reason why the Germans should not enter the League "in the early future."[64]

As for Germany's demands for general reduction of armaments, the Allies would accept no modifications of Article VIII. They repeated their intention of opening negotiations immediately toward a scheme of general limitation and again emphasized that the success of German disarmament would greatly facilitate the accomplishment of this scheme.

Lloyd George, in a book on the Treaty, later commented, however, that there was much to be said for the German plea of disarmament:

The Allies could not in fairness impose permanent disarmament on

[63] Luckau, *German Delegation*, p. 437.
[64] Luckau, *German Delegation*, pp. 423-424.

Germany whilst all her neighbours across the frontiers glistened with weapons which on the slightest dispute could be turned on a defenceless Germany.[65]

The Allied pledge of general arms reduction, both in the Covenant and in the preamble, therefore, became the means by which the disarmament section of the Treaty could be justified. The accomplishment of this pledge would have removed part of the stigma which the Treaty later acquired.

The German delegation, on the receipt of this Allied reply which covered many other questions as well, recommended refusal of the Treaty to their government. Brockdorff-Rantzau resigned as Foreign Secretary. A Cabinet crisis followed; and the Scheidemann government was replaced by a government formed by Otto Bauer. On June 22, the German representatives at Versailles were instructed to send a note to the Allies saying that Germany was prepared to yield before the threat of force, but would not answer for the consequences of certain Allied demands, particularly the cutting off of the districts in the east. Nor would Germany recognize her sole responsibility for the war, and she asked that the Treaty be submitted for revision to the League Council, in which Germany should have a part, in two years.[66] The Allied reply was a sharp refusal: the time for discussion had passed, and the German government had less than twenty-four hours to declare whether they would sign and accept the Treaty as a whole.

On June 23, two hours before Foch's armies were to begin their advance on Germany, news reached the Allied leaders of Germany's acceptance. The Treaty was signed five days later at Versailles.

The Treaty and its Critics

The final Treaty did not differ greatly in content from the terms which were summarized and published on May 8. Even at this date, however, the main outlines of the settlement were already known to the public, particularly the terms relating to disarmament. The

[65] Lloyd George, *Truth about the Peace Treaties*, I, 687-688.
[66] Luckau, *German Delegation*, pp. 479-481.

military, naval, and air terms had been predicted in the press in March, shortly after the final debate on the Foch report, and the Covenant in its final form became public after its presentation at the Plenary Session of the Conference on April 28.[67] Thus, by the beginning of May, the lines of opinion in Great Britain on the Treaty in general, and on these sections in particular, had begun to take shape. After May 8, numerous articles appeared in newspapers and periodicals defending or condemning the terms, and a few significant comments were made by members of Parliament.

On the whole, the military, naval, and air clauses were received with general approbation in the press and in Parliament. *The Times* thought them well-designed and carefully thought out for obtaining the main objects pursued and not "a whit more stringent than the safety of Europe and the world requires."[68] If the Treaty was to be strong and durable, *The Times* considered the disarmament of Germany as the first guarantee of peace, with the provisions of the Covenant and the proposed assistance pact to France as further guarantees.[69] The Fabian *New Statesman*, far more critical of the Treaty as a whole, was in agreement with *The Times* on the sections concerning the disarmament of Germany and the League, which were "so important and so valuable as to outweigh [the] far greater mistakes." The indispensable preliminary to the disarmament of Europe—the disarmament of Germany—has been carried out."[70] The Conservative *Spectator* believed that the military and naval terms would mean the "end of militarism," the first goal on the road to "an Elysium of Peace."[71]

A full-scale debate in Parliament was postponed until after the Prime Minister's return from Paris and, in fact, did not take place until almost one month after the Treaty was signed. Nevertheless, the Parliamentary Correspondent of *The Times* reported several interviews with members of Parliament in which both Coalition and

[67] See the leading article in *The Times*, April, 29, 1919, p. 18.
[68] *The Times*, May 7, 1919, p. 13.   [69] *The Times*, May 10, 1919, p. 13.
[70] "The Peace," *New Statesman*, XIII, no. 318, 132–133 (May 10, 1919).
[71] "The Peace Terms," *The Spectator*, CXXII, no. 4741, 584 (May 10, 1919).

General Disarmament and the Peace Treaty 153

Opposition members declared themselves satisfied with the military, naval, and air clauses.[72]

As has already been suggested, however, the announcement of the terms on May 8 marked a shift in the forces defending and attacking Lloyd George and the Treaty as a whole. Moreover, there was a corresponding change in the country where the voices of moderation began to be heard above the clamor for a hard peace. Both these tendencies were symbolized by the victory of a Liberal, Commander Kenworthy, in an April by-election over a distinguished Conservative opponent, Lord Eustace Percy. If Kenworthy's election signified a resurgence of moderation in public opinion, his presence in Parliament had an even more remarkable effect. The non-Coalition Liberals, who had defended Lloyd George against the Conservatives during the drafting of the peace terms, now moved in to attack. Led by Commander Kenworthy and Colonel Wedgwood, they declared that the militarists in Paris had turned the peace into a "just and durable war."[73] It is significant that Kenworthy was the one Englishman who voted against the Treaty in the final debate on July 21.[74]

In the country, the passions of the election of 1918 had given way with the necessity for making further concessions to the Germans sign; and second, if they were forced to sign, would the peace thus established be a lasting peace? Both questions indicated that there was developing in England a certain uneasiness concerning the final form of the Treaty and that a revision of the harsher terms might, at some point, be necessary. In Paris, these considerations were affecting the attitude of the British delegation. Smuts was obsessed with the necessity for making further concessions to the Germans on the basis of the counterproposals; G. M. Barnes, the Labour representative, believed in conciliation; and even Lloyd George, himself, suddenly fearful that Germany would not sign, urged

[72] *The Times*, May 9, 1919, p. 13.
[73] H.C. Debates, 5th series, CXVI, col. 2474. June 6, 1919.
[74] H.C. Debates, 5th series, CXVIII, cols. 1113–1116. July 21, 1919. The other five M.P.s who opposed the bill were Irish. Compare McCallum, *Public Opinion and the Last Peace*, pp. 51–52.

concessions.[75] Reports in early June that the British delegation was weakening in the face of German demands caused alarm in many British circles. *The Times* expressed astonishment at these rumors and declared that "nothing could be more disgraceful to a British statesman than such weakening."[76] Conservatives and Coalition Liberals in Parliament asked assurance from the government that the rumors were false.[77] The fears of the British delegation were nevertheless short-lived; by June 13 Lloyd George had returned to the other extreme and was advocating military and economic coercion if the German government would not accept the terms.

The second consideration—whether the Treaty would lay the framework for a lasting peace—became a more important topic of debate. The question at issue had been concisely summed up by Lloyd George in an unpublished memorandum on the Treaty in March 1919:

You may strip Germany of her colonies, reduce her armaments to a mere police force and her navy to that of a fifth-rate power; all the same in the end if she feels that she has been unjustly treated in the Peace of 1919, she will find means of exacting retribution from her conquerors.[78]

The gravity of this question was complicated by another consideration, the implications of which were soon realized by the British people. If the peace were to be "imposed," as it undoubtedly would be, the Allies had taken upon themselves the full responsibility for the justice of its terms and their success.

Although the probable effect of the Treaty on the future peace of Europe was vigorously debated in Great Britain, particularly in Labour circles, this issue was not the primary focus of attention for certain groups where the attitudes of the Khaki Election had not

[75] *Riddell's Diary*, p. 86; compare Baker, *Woodrow Wilson and World Settlement*, II, 517–518.

[76] *The Times*, June 6, 1919, p. 13.

[77] H.C. Debates, 5th series, CXVI, col. 2202. June 5, 1919.

[78] Lloyd George's memorandum of March 25, 1919, which was not made public until 1922. See Parliamentary Papers, Command Paper 1614, 1922. The text of the memorandum is in Baker, *Woodrow Wilson and World Settlement*, III, 449–458.

died. These groups, predominantly Conservative in political affiliation, debated the "justice" of the Treaty on other grounds: the manner in which the peace terms dealt with the nation which, in their view, not only was responsible for the war's outbreak, but which had been soundly defeated by Allied armies and should accept the consequences of that defeat. On this basis, in press and Parliament, these men rose to defend the form and terms of the Treaty against its critics. *The Spectator* remarked that "the Peace is a good Peace; it is what it ought to be—a dictated peace." [79] In the House of Lords, the justice of an imposed peace was explained by Lord Curzon:

> The Peace Conference at Paris assumed the attributes and the functions of an international tribunal. It really represented... the collective moral judgment of mankind. It attempted for the first time to treat Germany as we treat an ordinary guilty individual in every-day life. Germany therefore could not be let off merely because she had laid down her arms.[80]

In the House of Commons, the Conservative views were most clearly represented by Colonel Claude Lowther, Brigadier General Page-Croft, and Horatio Bottomley, whose statements during May and June brought to light another facet of Conservative opinion: concern over the amount of reparations to be paid by Germany.[81] If, as was assumed, the Peace Conference had played the role of an international tribunal, it logically followed that reparations should be the punishment borne by the guilty party.

One cannot say that Parliament contributed greatly to the debate on the Treaty or to the formation of public opinion on the justice of the peace. Lord Riddell, after a visit to England in May, remarked to Lloyd George that the British public was losing faith in Parliamentary institutions. "Parliament does not seem to be interested in itself,

---

[79] "The Peace Terms," *The Spectator*, 584 (May 10, 1919).

[80] *H.L. Debates*, 5th series, XXXV, col. 167, July 3, 1919. Compare "Peace without Honour," *New Statesman*, XIII, no. 319, 156–157 (May 17, 1919), for a discussion of "criminal justice" in the Treaty.

[81] See the questions by Bottomley and Lowther, *H.C. Debates*, 5th series, CXV, cols. 1110–1111 (May 8, 1919); col. 1334 (May 12, 1919); and CXVI, cols. 1819–1820 (June 3, 1919).

and the public certainly are not interested in it."[82] This was partly due to the fact that the House of Commons was unable to debate the Treaty until Lloyd George returned and until they received the text of the terms. Nevertheless, when the moment finally arrived, the debate lasted only one day, a fact which Commander Kenworthy deplored.[83] Furthermore, the composition of Parliament contributed to its lack of influence. As Bonar Law put it: "The House of Commons is an amorphous body with no nerves or joints and no real parties, with the exception of the Labour Party, and no objective."[84]

The Labour Party was indeed the exception, although little credit is due those members of the party who sat in the House of Commons. With the more dynamic leaders—Henderson and MacDonald—defeated in the Khaki Election, the initiative in formulating Labour's views now came more from the outside groups: the Independent Labour Party, the Union of Democratic Control, and the National Executive of the Labour Party. These groups, rather than the Parliamentary Labour Party, led the attack on the terms of peace. Together with the Fabian *New Statesman* and the courageous Liberals, Wedgwood and Kenworthy, they were among the first to say that:

...the Treaty...only partially expresses the spirit of the Fourteen Points; and in many of its sections is the result not of the application of any political theory, but of a mere process of more or less crude bargaining.[85]

Moreover, it was in Labour circles that the most serious consideration was given to the terms of the Treaty relating to disarmament and to the problems involved in their implementation.

It has been suggested that, if the real leaders of the Labour Party had not been exposed to electoral defeat with all its bitterness, they might not have become the martyrs who denounced the Treaty with

---

[82] *Riddell's Diary*, p. 80.
[83] *H. C. Debates*, 5th series, CXVIII, col. 1028. July 21, 1919.
[84] *Riddell's Diary*, p. 67.
[85] "The Peace," *New Statesman*, XIII, no. 318, 132 (May 10, 1919).

such fury.[86] The fact was that these attacks had a profound effect on British public opinion as a whole and made many enemies of the peace in an extraordinarily short time.

The Labour Party's attack began on the day the peace terms were announced in May, in a vigorous manifesto issued by the National Executive. In this document, the Labour Party Executive objected to certain features of the Treaty which did not conform to the Wilsonian declarations, particularly the Saar settlement, the applications of the principle of self-determination, and the disposal of the colonies. The manifesto further regretted that "the Treaty, which imposes a drastic measure of disarmament upon Germany, does not include provision for progressive limitation of the armaments of the other signatories of the Treaty."[87] *The Times* commented that this manifesto was not representative of the opinions of the Labour Party in Parliament,[88] which may well be true. However, it might be further suggested that the Parliamentary Party was no longer representative of Labour opinion in the country.[89] The moderation of the Parliamentary Party in criticizing the terms was not echoed by other groups who exercised more influence in the formation of Labour opinion. In May, the I.L.P. issued a resolution against the Treaty phrased in far stronger terms than the National Executive manifesto. The resolution declared that the provisions of the peace:

... expose the real aims of the Allies and the reason for the prolongation of the war as being the complete smashing of Germany, both politically and economically ... They do not bring an end to militarism, but fasten the system more firmly on the people of the Allied countries ... [The Treaty] aggravates every evil which existed before 1914.[90]

Moreover, the Executive Committee of the U.D.C. denounced the

---

[86] McCallum, *Public Opinion and the Last Peace*, p. 42.

[87] *Report of the Nineteenth Annual Conference of the Labour Party, Southport, 1919* (London, 1919), p. 216.

[88] *The Times*, May 10, 1919, p. 14.

[89] Compare W. M. Jordan, *Great Britain, France, and the German Problem* (London, 1943), p. 40.

[90] Quoted in William P. Maddox, *Foreign Relations in British Labour Politics* (Cambridge, Mass., 1934), p. 89.

Treaty as an "indefensible breach of... international morality"; and the *Labour Leader* and the *Herald* joined in the chorus of disapproval.

In the House of Commons, the volume and intensity of comment by the Labour members under the leadership of Adamson was very different. Although Adamson himself displayed caution in giving the terms of the Treaty his full support, his colleagues, Clynes and Stephen Walsh, sounded less like Labour members than Conservatives. Walsh is reported to have said in May: "None can maintain that the terms imposed by the victors upon the vanquished are too severe. If anything, they err on the side of clemency." [91]

In early June, an effort was made in Labour circles to clarify Labour's rather confused stand on the Treaty. When the National Executive and the Parliamentary Party got together on a joint declaration of policy, the strength of the Executive's views became apparent. There were few words in this declaration resembling the earlier statements of the members of Parliament. It gave little support to the Treaty which "accepts and indeed is based upon the very political principles which were the ultimate cause of the war." As far as disarmament was concerned, the declaration was not optimistic on the chances of its accomplishment:

> The Treaty... is likely to impose fresh burdens of [armaments] upon the peoples as a consequence of the military occupation of the west bank of the Rhine for a period of 15 years and possibly longer. In such circumstances it will be impossible to take full advantage of the enforced disarmament of Germany in order to secure general disarmament and demilitarization.[92]

The declaration further called for the prohibition of private manufacture of armaments and compulsory military service.

A few days before the signing of the Peace Treaty, the Annual Labour Party Conference was held at Southport. The Treaty was discussed and the terms relating to disarmament particularly noted.

In the debate in the House of Commons after the presentation of

[91] *The Times*, May 9, 1919, p. 13.
[92] *Report of the Nineteenth Annual Conference of the Labour Party, 1919*, p. 217.

the terms of peace to Parliament on July 3, Adamson reported on the features with which Labour did not agree. Besides certain territorial adjustments and the exclusion of Germany from the League, Adamson mentioned the omission of provisions for the abolition of conscription in the Allied countries, as well as in Germany. He further regretted that the question of disarmament had not been dealt with in the machinery of the terms of peace "in the way certain other matters had been dealt with." When the Prime Minister pointed out that it was in the League of Nations, Adamson replied: "But not exactly in the way Labour would like."[93]

In the full-scale debate on the Treaty on July 21, Clynes summed up the Labour view on disarmament. The terms of peace had killed conscription in Germany; he hoped that the Prime Minister could reassure the working class in Great Britain that it could also be abolished here. Moreover, it was essential that the government should assume full responsibility, control, and ownership of the manufacture of armaments. He pointed to an Allied statement to Germany in June in which reduction of armaments was preached as an economy measure as well as a prerequisite of peace, and he stated that the same argument could be applied to disarmament in Great Britain.[94]

In the final vote on the Treaty, only one Labour member opposed it. The reason for Labour's support of the Treaty can perhaps be found in the resolution adopted by the Party Conference in June and quoted by Clynes in his speech: that the Conference was in favor of "the immediate revision by the League of Nations of the harsh provisions of the Treaty."[95] In signing the Treaty in June, General Smuts had given his assent for much the same reason: that although he opposed many of the terms, the Treaty established a League of Nations through which the injustices might be redressed.[96]

[93] *H.C. Debates,* 5th series, CXVII, cols. 1232–1233. July 3, 1919.
[94] *H.C. Debates,* 5th series, CXVIII, cols. 958–964. July 21, 1919.
[95] *H.C. Debates,* 5th series, CXVIII, col. 959.
[96] See Smuts's letter to Wilson on May 30, criticizing the Treaty and asserting that it "is against the letter and spirit of your points." Baker, *Woodrow Wilson and World Settlement,* III, 466–468. Compare Seymour, *House Papers,* IV, 466–467.

The same conviction, together with the idea that this peace was better than no peace, was no doubt in the minds of many other members of the Allied delegations and of Parliament who found much in the final terms to criticize.

The final terms of the Treaty were, in fact, at variance with that which the delegations in Paris had anticipated or wished. Despite the prominent part taken by the military men in drawing up Section V of the Treaty, none of the military leaders appeared satisfied with it. Sir Henry Wilson thought the terms too harsh. The restrictions on the German Army were based on a completely different principle from that desired by Marshal Foch; in fact, it is doubtful whether he favored any long-term measures of disarmament forced on Germany, if such German disarmament would necessarily entail eventual French disarmament as well. The admirals expected the clauses they drew up to be of temporary duration only, rather than a permanent limitation on the German Navy.

Nor were the political leaders better satisfied. President Wilson had characterized the framework of the military terms which first appeared in the Loucheur report as a "panic program"; and, according to General Sir Henry Wilson, the President all but refused to accept them at the last moment.[97] Lloyd George, as is indicated in the memorandum addressed to Clemenceau in the crucial days of the Conference, foresaw many of the later difficulties which would result from imposing a treaty that the defeated nation felt to be unjust.[98] Clemenceau, due to objections quite different from the other statesmen, accepted the Treaty terms only because he expected the Treaty of Guarantee with the United States and England to come into force with it: a treaty which never lived, but was stillborn. When the final military terms had actually been submitted to the Germans, President Wilson and others still expected that the Inter-Allied Military Control Commission, which would enforce them, would function for perhaps six months. It was, however, not withdrawn from Germany until January 1929.

Nor were these universal dissatisfactions and misunderstandings

[97] Callwell, *Sir Henry Wilson*, p. 174.
[98] See above, p. 154.

with the final Treaty due solely to irreconcilable differences between the delegations of the three great powers who really determined the results. Two other factors which have already been mentioned contributed to the already difficult reconciliation of conflicting views. The first of these was the lack of a well worked out agenda and plans of procedure on the basis of which the Conference might work. The second was the difficulties produced by the press and public opinion on the negotiations of the Conference.

Postwar Europe and Disarmament

The "War to End War" was concluded, it has been said, by the "Peace to End Peace." As a durable formula for maintaining the peace of Europe, the Treaty of Versailles was not a success. The causes of the failure of the disarmament movement, as well as the roots of many other problems and disappointments of the next twenty years, may be traced in part to certain provisions of the Treaty and to the immoderate climate of opinion in which it was conceived. Because the Treaty was largely a product of compromise, no one of the countries affected by it, victors or vanquished, found it wholly satisfactory in its final form. Moreover, in deciding that Germany should be excluded from the Conference and that the terms should be imposed rather than negotiated, the Allies had taken upon themselves full responsibility for the justice of the settlement and for its success. To a large extent the durability of the settlement depended on laying down moderate terms about which Germany should have no cause to complain, if the peace were to be imposed. Or, alternatively, given a set of harsh terms, the tranquility of Europe could be maintained only if those terms enjoyed the wholehearted support of Allied public opinion, so that a breach of the Treaty by Germany would instantly be met by the united action of Great Britain, France, and the United States. The final terms were, however, a compromise between these alternatives, because neither alternative in its pure form could satisfy the different forces of Allied opinion. While a peace sufficiently moderate by German standards would be largely unacceptable in most Allied circles, there was enough Allied sentiment against an extremely harsh peace to make impossible the continued and effective enforcement of its terms. The final Treaty, as a compromise, thus lacked the support of vanquished and victors alike and was a failure in securing peace for Europe.

If the Treaty was unsuccessful in establishing a tranquil Europe and if successful limitation of armaments depends greatly upon a reduction in tension among major powers, the Treaty also contributed to the eventual failure of the disarmament movement. Nevertheless, the terms of the Treaty relating to disarmament were important milestones in the history of the movement. By the preamble to the military clauses, by Article VIII of the Covenant, and by the Allied statements in reply to the counterproposals, the intention of general reduction of armaments became part of the public law of Europe. The disarmament of Germany, a prerequisite of the peace and of general disarmament, was soon to be carried out. The machinery for the accomplishment of general reduction, the League of Nations, had been established and enjoyed the full support of European public opinion. And people seriously desired to see the burden of arms lifted from their shoulders. If there was any time in this century when there existed an opportunity, however slight, to realize the ideal of disarmament, it was in the dozen years after the Treaty of Versailles.

But the vicious circle could not be broken: disarmament seemed impossible while the possibility of a resurgent Germany remained, and, conversely, the failure of the Allies to fulfill their pledge of general arms reduction greatly intensified the German feeling of insecurity, encirclement, and resentment. In a country as much subjected to foreign control as Germany in the twenties, the course of domestic politics was determined to an abnormal extent by what was happening in international politics. Thus the inability of Allied statesmen during these years to unite in facing and finding solutions for the problems of the peace, especially the problem of arms reduction, had a profound effect upon German internal politics, contributing to the downfall of the forces of reason and playing directly into the hands of the extremist parties.

Equally, though indirectly, damaging to the future of disarmament was the lack of enthusiasm with which the Treaty was received in the Allied countries, particularly in Great Britain. The attack by certain liberals upon the Treaty, immediately following the Peace Conference, created a body of opinion hostile to the settlement as a whole. However just this attack may have been, it was unfortunate that the settlement fell into general disfavor, for those sections of the Treaty which merited approval were also adversely affected.

The unwillingness of Great Britain, as well as of other nations, to attack directly the problem of arms reduction was partly due to diverse pressures at home, both within the major political parties and from the press, and also due to Britain's traditional policy of reluctance in entering upon long-term international commitments, a reluctance strengthened by the mixed feelings with which British public opinion viewed the entire settlement.

The issue of disarmament in this period was intimately connected with many of the other problems of the peace—financial, political, and psychological. Had the movement for disarmament been successful, as it nearly was, it would have been an important force in the stabilization of the international community. As mounting arms expenditure prior to 1914 increased international tensions and, as Viscount Grey has contended, made World War I inevitable, so disarmament in the postwar period would have immeasurably improved the conditions of international politics, to an extent where reason instead of force might have become the basis of diplomacy. Aside from its relation to international stability, disarmament offered a tremendous aid, if not in fact a solution, to the most critical problem which domestic statesmanship faced in all countries: economic disorganization. Reduction of military expenditure would have gone far to alleviate conditions in this sphere, as well as to enable the national treasuries to meet the mounting pressure for increased expenditure on the social services.

All of these factors tended to make limitation of armaments an issue of practical politics, and, while the technical barriers to drawing up an acceptable agreement were great, they were not insurmountable. The study of the problem by military men at the

Peace Conference in drawing up the disarmament clauses for Germany had pointed the way. The obstacles to a solution were political and psychological, and in spite of temporary successes for naval limitation, a series of delays and unwise diplomatic moves brought failure to the general disarmament conference of 1932, at a time when reduction was both possible and vitally important for the future of Europe.

Appendix A

The Liberal and Labour Members of Parliament Who Voted in Opposition to the Government from May 1917 to February 1918

LIBERALS

Arnold, Sydney
Baker, J. A.
Barlow, Sir John E., Bt.
Beale, Sir William P., Bt.
Birrell, Rt. Hon. Augustine
Bliss, Joseph
Bryce, J. A.
Burns, Rt. Hon. John
Buxton, Noel E.
Chancellor, Henry G.
Collins, Maj. Godfrey P.
Denman, Hon. R. D.
Harvey, T. E.
Hogge, James Myles
Holt, R. D.
King, Joseph
Lamb, Sir Ernest H.
Lees-Smith, H. B.
Lough, Rt. Hon. Thomas
McMicking, Maj. Gilbert
Mallalieu, Frederick William
Martin, Joseph
Mason, David Marshall
Morrell, Philip E.
Nuttal, Harry
Outhwaite, Robert Leonard
Ponsonby, Arthur A. W. H.
Price, Charles Edward
Pringle, W. M. R.
Roch, Walter F.
Rowntree, Arnold S.
Runciman, Sir Walter, Bt.
Shortt, Edward
Trevelyan, Charles P.
Watt, Henry A.
Whitehouse, John Howard
Wilson, Rt. Hon. J. W.

LABOUR

Anderson, W. C.
Bowerman, Rt. Hon. C. W.
Jowett, Frederick W.
MacDonald, J. Ramsay
Richardson, Thomas
Snowden, Philip
Thomas, Rt. Hon. James H.
Thorne, William J.
Wilson, William Tyson

Appendix B

Liberal Members of Parliament, Interested in a Moderate Peace, Who Were Industrialists, Merchants, or Bankers, 1917 to 1918

Arnold, Sydney
Baker, J. A.
Barlow, Sir John E., Bt.
Bliss, Joseph
Bryce, J. A.
Chancellor, Henry G.
Collins, Maj. Godfrey P.
Holt, R. D.
Lamb, Sir Ernest H.

Lough, Rt. Hon. Thomas
Mallalieu, Frederick W.
Mason, David Marshall
Nuttal, Harry
Price, Charles Edward
Rowntree, Arnold S.
Runciman, Sir Walter, Bt.
Wilson, Rt. Hon. J. W.

Appendix C

Colonel House's Draft, July 16, 1918 (Article 21).

The Contracting Powers recognize the principle that permanent peace will require that national armaments shall be reduced to the lowest point consistent with safety, and the Delegates are directed to formulate at once a plan by which such a reduction may be brought about. The plan so formulated shall not be binding until or unless unanimously approved by the Governments signatory to this Covenant.

The Contracting Powers agree that munitions and implements of war shall not be manufactured by private enterprise and that publicity as to all national armaments and programmes is essential.

President Wilson's Second Draft (First Paris Draft), January 10, 1919 (Article IV).

The Contracting Powers recognize the principle that the establishment and maintenance of peace will require the reduction of national armaments to the lowest point consistent with domestic safety and the enforcement by common action of international obligations; and the Delegates are directed to formulate at once plans by which such a reduction may be brought about. The plan so formulated shall be binding when, and only when, unanimously approved by the Governments signatory to this Covenant.

As the basis for such a reduction of armaments, all the Powers subscribing to the Treaty of Peace of which this Covenant constitutes a part hereby agree to abolish conscription and all other forms of compulsory military service, and also agree that their future forces of defense and of international action shall consist of militia or volunteers, whose numbers and methods of training shall be fixed, after expert inquiry, by the agreements with regard to the reduction of armaments referred to in the last preceding paragraph.

The Body of Delegates shall also determine for the consideration and action of the several Governments what direct military equipment and armament is fair and reasonable in proportion to the scale of forces laid down in the programme of disarmament; and these limits, when adopted, shall not be exceeded without the permission of the Body of Delegates.

The Contracting Powers further agree that munitions and implements of war shall not be manufactured by private enterprise or for private profit, and that there shall be full and frank publicity as to all national armaments and military or naval programmes.

The Cecil–Miller Draft, January 27, 1919 (Article IV).

The Contracting Powers recognize the principle that the establishment and maintenance of peace will require the reduction of national armaments to the lowest point consistent with domestic safety and the enforcement by common action of international obligations; and the Executive Council is directed to formulate at once after expert inquiry plans by which such a reduction may be brought about. The plan so formulated shall be binding when, and only when, unanimously approved by the Governments signatory to this Covenant, but when so approved, it shall not be departed from by any signatory without the consent of all.

As the basis for such a reduction of armaments, all the High Contracting Powers hereby agree to abolish conscription and all other forms of compulsory military service, and also agree that their future forces of defense and of international action shall consist of militia or volunteers, whose numbers and methods of training shall be fixed, after expert inquiry, by the agreements with regard to the reduction of armaments referred to in the last preceding paragraph.

The Executive Council shall also determine for the consideration and action of the several Governments what direct military equipment and armament is fair and reasonable in proportion to the scale of forces laid down in the programme of disarmament; and these limits, when adopted, shall not be exceeded without the permission of the Body of Delegates.

The Contracting Powers further agree that there shall be full and frank publicity as to all national armaments and military or naval programmes.

Bibliography

DOCUMENTS

Official German Documents Relating to the World War (New York, 1923).
Papers Relating to the Foreign Relations of the United States, 1916–1919 (Washington, 1922–1947).
The Annual Register, 1916 (London, 1917).
The Parliamentary Debates, 5th series:
    House of Commons, 1914–1919.
    House of Lords, 1915–1919.

REPORTS

Report of the Annual Conference of the Independent Labour Party (London, 1915).
Report of the Fifteenth Annual Conference of the Labour Party (London, 1916).
Report of the Sixteenth Annual Conference of the Labour Party (London, 1917).
Report of the Nineteenth Annual Conference of the Labour Party (London, 1919).
General Staff, War Office, *Daily Review of the Foreign Press* (London, 1917).
Second Section, U.S. General Staff, G.H.Q.A.E.F., *(Confidential) Press Review* (1917).

NEWSPAPERS

Manchester Guardian   *The Times* (London)

PERIODICALS

The Economist   *English Review*
The Edinburgh Review   *The Nation* (London)
International Conciliation   *National Review*

The New Europe
New Statesman
Nineteenth Century

The Round Table
The Spectator
The Statist

PAMPHLETS

Maurice, Maj.-Gen. Sir Frederick, *Intrigues of War* (London, 1922).
Morel, E. D., *Truth and the War* (National Labour Press, Ltd., 1916).
Pollard, A. F., *The League of Nations: A Historical Argument* (London, 1918).
Ponsonby, Arthur, *Parliament and Foreign Policy* (U.D.C. Publication No. 5, 1914).
Union of Democratic Control, *The Morrow of War* (U.D.C. Publication No. 1, 1914).

BOOKS

Baker, Ray Stannard, *Woodrow Wilson: Life and Letters* (New York, 1939). A biography in eight volumes, written from Wilson's private papers and from documents, letters, diaries, and other material supplied by Wilson's associates and friends. The last two volumes, covering the war years and the Armistice, are arranged in chronological order.

——— *Woodrow Wilson and World Settlement* (New York, 1923). An account of the Peace Conference, of American policies, and of Wilson's attempts to apply them. Written by Wilson's later biographer from the collection of papers and documents which the President brought back from Paris, including the minutes of the Council of Four.

Berlau, A. J., *The German Social Democratic Party, 1914-1921* (New York, 1949). A solid and very detailed treatment of the ideas, policies, and attitudes of the Social Democrats up to the signing of the Versailles Treaty. A short chapter covers the new party programme of 1921.

Bernstorff, Count, *My Three Years in America* (New York, 1920). A narrative of the author's work as German Ambassador in Washington during the first years of the war, objectively written.

The Diary of Lord Bertie of Thame, 1914-1918 (New York, 1924). Lord Bertie's diary as British Ambassador in Paris during the war: a day-by-day record of his personal comments upon his experiences, upon people and events.

Brand, Carl F., *British Labour's Rise to Power* (Stanford, Calif., 1941). Eight studies summarizing basic developments in the Labour Party's history. The chapters on Labour's war aims, peace programs, and reactions to President Wilson are particularly relevant.

Brockway, A. Fenner, *Inside the Left* (London, 1942). Reminiscences of thirty years of Labour and Fabian activity.

Callwell, C. E., ed., *Field Marshal Sir Henry Wilson* (London, 1927). A biography, including parts of Wilson's diaries, of the British military representative on the Supreme War Council and chief of the General Staff. The diary excerpts, obviously not written with an eye to publication, contain frank comments upon people and events.

Cecil, Lord Robert, *A Great Experiment* (London, 1941). Although autobiographical in form, Cecil is relating the story of the League of Nations, its "making," "early years," and "downhill."

Churchill, Winston S., *The World Crisis; 1916–1918* (London, 1927). The third volume of Churchill's history of the war, covering the period when he was Minister of Munitions.

Clausewitz, The Living Thoughts of, (Philadelphia, 1942). Materials from the writings of the great German strategist.

Cockayne, George Edward, ed., *Complete Peerage of England, Scotland, Ireland, Great Britain and the United Kingdom* (London, 1893).

Cocks, F. Seymour, *The Secret Treaties and Understandings* (London, 1918). One of the very few commentaries on or publications of the secret treaties made between the European Allies.

Cole, G. D. H., *A History of the Labour Party since 1914* (London, 1948). A detailed account of the political events in the history of the Labour Party, up to the General Election of 1945.

Conwell-Evans, Thomas P., *Foreign Policy from a Back Bench* (London, 1932). A study based on the papers of Lord Noel Buxton, revealing parliamentary viewpoints on British diplomacy from 1904 to 1918.

Cripps, Charles Alfred (Lord Parmoor), *A Retrospect* (London, 1936). The memoirs of Lord Parmoor through the 1931 crisis, valuable as illustrating the attitude of a supporter of a moderate peace and of the League idea.

Dahlin, Ebba, *French and German Public Opinion on Declared War Aims* (Stanford, Calif., 1933). An interesting and valuable study of French and German reactions to and influences upon their governments' policies with regard to war aims.

Dickinson, Goldsworthy Lowes, *Documents and Statements Relating to Peace Proposals and War Aims* (London, 1919).

Fay, Sidney B., *The Origins of the World War* (New York, 1928). The outstanding work upon a controversial subject: a detailed and impartial study of the war's origins which exploded the myth of Germany's sole responsibility.

Forster, Kent, *Failures of Peace* (Philadelphia, 1941). A survey of the attempts to bring about a negotiated peace, discussed chronologically and by countries. Indispensable as a reference manual on this subject.

Gatzke, Hans W. *Germany's Drive to the West* (Baltimore, 1950). A systematic survey of German war aims during the course of the war, showing the political conditions and expansionist aims of certain parties and groups. The discussion of the failures of the successive peace feelers is especially valuable.

Gooch, G. P., *History of Modern Europe, 1878–1919* (New York, 1923). A useful survey of the relations of the great powers from the Triple Alliance to the Versailles Treaty.

Grey, Sir Edward (Lord Grey of Fallodon), *Twenty-Five Years, 1892–1916* (London, 1925). The memoirs of the diplomat and foreign secretary. The second volume includes the first two years of the war, with much to say of British–American relations, negotiations with Colonel House, and Wilson's mediation policy.

Hankey, Rt. Hon. Lord, *Diplomacy by Conference* (London, 1946). A volume of essays based on the author's experiences in and around Whitehall, including an essay on disarmament.

Lord Hardinge of Penshurst, *Old Diplomacy* (London, 1947). The autobiography of the Under Secretary at the Foreign Office, including an interesting chapter on the Peace Conference.

Hart, B. H. Liddell, *The Real War, 1914–1918* (Boston, 1930). Probably the best short history of the war, covering its tactical and strategic aspects in detail.

House, Edward M., and Charles Seymour, eds., *What Really Happened at Paris* (New York, 1921). A series of lectures, by American delegates to Paris, upon the most important subjects covered at the Peace Conference, including an essay by General Tasker H. Bliss on disarmament.

Hutchison Keith, *The Decline and Fall of British Capitalism* (New York, 1950). A liberal, but scholarly interpretation of British politics since the latter years of the nineteenth century, studying the history of the rise of Socialism.

Jordan, W. M., *Great Britain, France, and the German Problem, 1918–1939* (London, 1943). A study of Anglo-French relations in the making and maintenance of the Versailles Treaty.

Keynes, J. M., *Economic Consequences of the Peace* (London, 1919). The severe condemnation of the Peace Treaty, which pointed out the injustice and impracticality of the terms of the Treaty and predicted economic ruin in those countries which executed the terms. A book which did much to turn liberal opinion against the Treaty, especially in Great Britain.

Lansing, Robert, *The Peace Negotiations: A Personal Narrative* (Boston, 1921). A record of the relations and disagreements between Wilson and the Secretary of State during and after the Peace Conference.

Lippmann, Walter, *Public Opinion* (New York, 1922). An investigation of the forces which enter into the formation of public opinion and of the hindrances which operate to prevent a sound interpretation of the facts, by a member of The Inquiry.

Lloyd George, David, *The Truth about the Peace Treaties* (London, 1938). A defense of the Prime Minister's own work during the Paris Peace Conference, and valuable to the historian for the reason that it is a personal narrative and interpretation of the Conference.

——— *War Memoirs of David Lloyd George* (Boston, 1933), vols. I and II, 1914–1915 and 1915–1916. The first two volumes of his memoirs, carrying the story up to his premiership in 1916, with valuable contributions to the history of the period, although with a tendency toward self-vindication and self-glorification.

Luckau, Alma, *The German Delegation at the Peace Conference* (New York, 1941). A comprehensive collection of published and unpublished documents concerned with the German preparations for and activities at the Peace Conference, together with a long introduction narrating the story of the German delegation.

Lutz, R. H., ed., *Fall of the German Empire* (Stanford, Calif., 1932). A careful and comprehensive collection of German documents, from the outbreak of the war to the collapse of the Empire, including Reichstag debates and periodical and newspaper extracts.

Maddox, William P., *Foreign Relations in British Labour Politics* (Cambridge, Mass., 1934). A useful study of political ideology and of the forces motivating Labour foreign policy.

Marston, F. S., *The Peace Conference of 1919* (London, 1944). A monograph dealing with the organization and procedure of the Peace Conference, rather than with the content of the negotiations for the Treaty: an extremely valuable account of the organizational confusion and lack of preparation.

Maurice, Major General Sir Frederick, *The Armistices of 1918* (London, 1943). A concise factual narrative of the steps by which the armistices were negotiated in 1918 with the Central Powers, exploding the German "stab-in-the-back" explanation of defeat in the field.

McCallum, R. B., *Public Opinion and the Last Peace* (London, 1944). A careful study of the merits of the Versailles Treaty and of the attitudes of various elements of British public opinion toward the settlement, 1919-1936.

McCurdy, Charles A., *A Clean Peace: The War Aims of British Labour* (New York, 1918). The complete text of the official war aims memorandum of the Inter-Allied Labour and Socialist Conference, held in London, February 23, 1918.

Miller, David Hunter, *The Drafting of the Covenant* (New York, 1928). The detailed account of the origins and drafting of the Covenant of the League of Nations during the meetings of the League Commission at the Paris Peace Conference, by a member of the American staff who was present at the meetings of the League Commission. Numerous documents relating to the origins and formation of the Covenant are included, as well as minutes of the meetings of the League Commission. Invaluable as a reference work.

——— *My Diary at the Conference of Paris* (New York, 1924). The diary of a prominent member of the American Commission in Paris, covering the period of the Conference and many phases of the negotiations. Also invaluable as a reference work on the Paris Peace Conference.

Nicolson, Harold, *Peacemaking, 1919* (London, 1939). Impressions of the Peace Conference, including excerpts from the author's diary of 1919. A delightful portrayal of the general atmosphere of the Conference, and an indictment of vague diplomacy and of diplomacy by conference.

Noble, George Bernard, *Policies and Opinions at Paris, 1919* (New York, 1935). Probably the definitive work upon the influences of the opinion of the French press upon the negotiations of the Peace

Conference. The author was attached to the American Peace Commission.

Noel-Baker, Philip, *The Private Manufacture of Armaments* (New York, 1937). Basing his thesis on carefully assembled facts and documents, the author argues that private arms manufacture was a principal factor in the creation of the huge armaments which, he says, necessarily lead to war.

Notter, Harley, *The Origins of the Foreign Policy of Woodrow Wilson* (Baltimore, 1937). Written from President Wilson's private papers, this is an extremely detailed analysis of Wilson's foreign policy: neutrality, plans for world peace, and the decision to enter the war.

Oxford and Asquith, The Earl of, *Memories and Reflections, 1852–1927* (Boston, 1928). The second volume of Asquith's reminiscences includes a review of the conduct of the war during his premiership and contains much valuable material.

Pease, Edward R., *The History of the Fabian Society* (New York, 1916). An authoritative history of the Fabian Society by its secretary for 25 years, revised by Sidney Webb and G. B. Shaw.

Lord Riddell's Intimate Diary of the Peace Conference and After, 1918–1923 (New York, 1934). The diary of the official representative of the British press at the Peace Conference, an intimate associate of Lloyd George. It contains a number of entertaining and informative observations upon statesmen, politicians, and other notables at the Conference.

Robertson, Sir William, *Soldiers and Statesmen, 1914–1918* (London, 1926). A straightforward account of British strategy during the war and of the relations and difficulties between the Cabinet and General Staff.

Selections from the Correspondence of Theodore Roosevelt and Henry Cabot Lodge, 1884–1918 (Boston, 1925). A valuable source book for the historian. The letters deal largely with public affairs.

Rudin, Harry R., *Armistice, 1918* (New Haven, Conn., 1944). A detailed and sound study of the discussions of and negotiations for the armistice, from the summer of 1918 through November 11, with special emphasis upon the political struggles in Germany.

Scott, James Brown, ed., *Official Statements of War Aims and Peace Proposals* (Washington, 1921).

Seeckt, General Hans von, *Thoughts of a Soldier* (London, 1930). Reminiscences of the German general.

Seymour, Charles, ed., *The Intimate Papers of Colonel House* (Boston, 1926-1928). Selected papers from the House collection at Yale, arranged and interpreted by the later president of Yale. Invaluable as source material for the war years.

Sitwell, Osbert, *Those Were the Days* (London, 1938). Essays and impressions.

Snowden, Philip Viscount, *An Autobiography* (London, 1934). The autobiography of the Labour Party leader. The first volume goes through the Peace Treaties.

Somervell, D. C., *British Politics since 1900* (New York, 1950). A lively but sometimes too cursory survey of British party politics.

Swanwick, H. M., *Builders of Peace* (London, 1924). An account of the growth, vicissitudes, and achievements of the Union of Democratic Control from its birth in 1914, written by an active woman member.

Tate, Merze, *The Disarmament Illusion* (New York, 1942). The definitive study of the disarmament movement up to 1907, part of which is republished in her subsequent *United States and Armaments*.

—— *The United States and Armaments* (Cambridge, Mass., 1948). A monograph summarizing American participation in disarmament conferences and plans since the nineteenth century: one of the few historical works on disarmament.

Walters, F. P., *A History of the League of Nations* (London, 1952). The definitive history of the accomplishments and failures of the League, by a former assistant to Lord Robert Cecil, later with the League Secretariat.

Webb, Beatrice, *Our Partnership* (London, 1948). The Fabians and British politics.

—— *Beatrice Webb's Diaries, 1912-1924* (New York, 1952). Mrs. Webb's journals covering the period of World War I, the decline of the Liberal Party and the rise of the Labour Party.

Webster, C. K., *The League of Nations in Theory and Practice* (Boston, 1933). A historical and descriptive survey of the development, organization, and activities of the League by a prominent English authority.

Wester Wemyss, Lady, *The Life and Letters of Lord Wester Wemyss* (London, 1935). The biography of the First Sea Lord and original architect of the naval terms of the Versailles Treaty, including much valuable material previously unpublished.

Willis, Irene Cooper, *England's Holy War* (New York, 1928). An analysis of the course of liberal idealism before, during, and after the war, particularly as it found expression in the *Daily News*.

Winkler, Henry R., *The League of Nations Movement in Great Britain, 1914-1919* (New Brunswick, N.J., 1952). A valuable survey of the efforts of English journalists and public officers which contributed to the realization of the League. Particularly valuable to a student of British press opinion.

Woolf, Leonard S., ed., *The Framework of a Lasting Peace* (London, 1917). A collection of the different League plans or proposals available in 1917.

Zimmern, Sir Alfred, *The League of Nations and the Rule of Law* (London, 1936). An examination, from the political point of view, of the methods of international cooperation, the role of the League in these processes, and the case for the League, ably presented by a well-known political scientist, Foreign Office and League official.

Index

Adamson, Rt. Hon. William, 142, 158–159
Admiralty memorandum on munitions industry, 97, 132, 136, 139
Air terms of Versailles Treaty, 76, 120, 123n, 124–125, 128–130, 152; German predictions of, 146; German views on, 148; period of their execution, 149–150. *See also* Aviation
Alexander I, Czar of Russia, 2
Alsace-Lorraine, 19, 45–46, 49, 56, 63, 83, 85
Amiens, battle of, 76
Amsterdam, Netherlands: International Socialist Conference at, 145
Anderson, W. C., 165
Andrássy, Count Julius, 24
Angell, Norman, 29, 72
Arbitration Alliance of Great Britain, 8
Arbitration of disputes, 48, 52, 73
Armaments, private manufacture of: effects on government policy, 5–7; opposed by Labour Party, 6, 56, 134, 145, 158, 159; opposed by Socialists, 10, 95, 145; opposed by U.D.C., 17; opposed by Wilson and House, 42, 70, 71, 94, 101, 135; opposed by Smuts, 100, 135; favored by British Admiralty, 97, 132, 136; in Article VIII, 101, 103, 131, 134–136. *See also* Disarmament
Armaments, publicity of national: favored, 71, 100–101; in Article VIII, 103, 131–132, 138–140; and international inspection, 138–140, 145

Armaments expenditure, high costs of, 95, 119, 159, 163
Armistice, 1918: negotiations for, 76–83; terms of, 83–86; renewal of, 107, 108, 109, 111, 114–115, 118–119
Armistices, history of, 84
Arnold, Sydney, 165, 166
Asquith, Rt. Hon. Herbert H., 4–5, 29, 52, 61, 62, 68, 91; his government, 5, 7, 13; on conscription, 24; on a negotiated peace, 27, 31–32, 62–66 *passim*; his Cabinet replaced, 33–34; his section of the Liberal Party, 61–66 *passim*, 88, 90n, 91, 153; on a League, 40–41, 52, 66; on the Maurice motion, 62, 65; on the Lansdowne letter, 65
Austro-Hungarian Empire, 24, 37, 38, 48, 54, 61
Aviation, commercial, 96, 129

Baker, J. A., 165, 166
Baker, Newton D., 70–71
Baker, Ray Stannard, 117
Baldwin, Stanley, 92
Balfour, Rt. Hon. Arthur James, 85, 115–116; memorandum to Cabinet (1917), 45; and Lansdowne letter, 53; and terms of German disarmament, 107, 113, 115, 122, 124–126; and general disarmament in Covenant, 106, 107, 122
Ballin, Albert, 26
Baltic Sea, fortifications on, 113
Barlow, Sir John E., 165, 166
Barnes, Rt. Hon. George N.: in Coalition Cabinet, 56; on the Kaiser, 88; on private arms manu-

179

Index

facture, 134; at Peace Conference, 153
Bauer, Otto, 151
Beale, Sir William P., 165
Beaverbrook, 1st Baron, 20, 33
Belgium, 12, 19, 35, 63, 81, 83
Benedict XV, Pope, 24, 47–52 *passim*
Benson, Admiral William S., 113, 115n, 128
Berliner Tageblatt, 49
Bern, Switzerland: Labour and Socialist Conference at, 145
Bernstorff, Count J. H. von, 28, 31, 34–37, 146
Bertie of Thame, 1st Viscount, 20, 31, 32, 45–46, 69
Bethmann-Hollweg, Chancellor Theobald von, 4n, 22, 33, 46, 48, 52; on peace negotiations, 24, 27, 28, 34, 35; on a League, 35; on German war aims, 35; opposes unrestricted submarine warfare, 42; resignation, 47
Birrell, Rt. Hon. Augustine, 165
Bliss, Joseph, 165, 166
Bliss, General Tasker H.: and disarmament, 71, 94–96; and Armistice negotiations, 77–78; and terms of German disarmament, 109, 111, 114n, 115n, 122, 123, 124
Blockade of Germany, 84, 115, 127
Board of Trade (British), 25
Bolshevism, 143, 144
Bonar Law, Rt. Hon. Andrew. *See* Law, Rt. Hon. Andrew Bonar
Bottomley, Horatio W., 155
Bourgeois, Léon, 135n, 136–140
Bowerman, Rt. Hon. C. W., 165
Bowman, Professor Isaiah, 70n
Briand, Aristide, 54
Bright, John, 3
Bristol, England: Lloyd George's speech at, 88–89
British Empire, 61, 100
Brockdorff-Rantzau, Count Ulrich von, 147, 151
Bryan, William Jennings, 70

Bryce, 1st Viscount, 19, 44, 66
Bryce, J. A., 165, 166
Bryce Group. *See* League of Nations Society
Bryce Plan, 44, 66. *See also* League of Nations Society
Buckmaster of Cheddington, 1st Baron, 44
Burn, Colonel Charles R., 92n
Burnham, 2nd Baron (of the *Daily Telegraph*), 54
Burns, Rt. Hon. John, 13, 165
Buxton, Noel: on a moderate peace, 43–44, 64; associated with Foreign Affairs group, 64; joins Labour Party, 65n

Campbell-Bannerman, Rt. Hon. Sir Henry, 18, 65
Caporetto, battle of, 54
Castlereagh, Lord, 2
Catholic Center Party (German), 27, 46–47, 146
Causes of World War I. *See* World War, origins of the
Cavallero, General Ugo, 114n, 115n
Cecil, Rt. Hon. Lord Robert, 60, 114n, 145; memorandum on the war (1916), 32, 33; correspondence with House, 72, 96, 97; on disarmament, 88; his League plans, 98–99, 100, 101, 106–107, 132, 135, 139, 140; on League Commission, 135–140 *passim*
Cecil-Miller draft of Covenant, 106–107, 135, 139, 140
Chancellor, Henry G., 165, 166
Chinda, Viscount Sutemi, 135n
Churchill, Rt. Hon. Winston S., 21, 33, 51, 52, 87–88, 109n; as First Lord of Admiralty, 5; on League of Nations, 87–88; his "Mansion House" speech, 119n
Civil Servants, 69, 74, 96–97, 98
Clausewitz, General Carl von, 50
Clemenceau, Georges, 115, 116, 117, 160; and Armistice negotiations, 77–81 *passim*, 84, 85; and terms of

German disarmament, 108, 114, 115, 122, 124, 125, 126; opposed to negotiation with Germany, 112, 114, 148
Clementel, Etienne, 114n
Clynes, Rt. Hon. John Robert, 158, 159
Coalition Cabinet: formed, 33-34; its war and peace aims, 38-39, 45, 52, 53-54, 59, 60-61, 93; on a League, 41, 68-69
Coalition, Lloyd George's, 87-92, 154
Cobb, Frank, 81-82
Cobb-Lippmann memorandum, 81-82, 133
Cobden, Richard, 3
Coblenz, Germany, 83, 84
Collins, Colonel Godfrey P., 59-60, 165, 166
Cologne, Germany, 83, 84
Colonies (German): in Allied war aims, 21, 39; in drafts of naval terms, 113, 127; in Treaty, 157
Committee for Peace Negotiations (German), 146
Common Sense, 43
Compulsory military service: in Great Britain, 24, 119, 121; abolition favored by Czernin, 50; by Smuts, 51, 100; by Labour Party, 56, 145, 158, 159; by Wilson, 101; by Socialists, 145; Lloyd George on, 58, 87, 121; for postwar German army, 120-123, 146; French views on, 121, 140; debated in League Commission, 140; German views on, 147, 148-149. *See also* Disarmament
Concert of Europe, 2
Conferences, Allied official: Economic conference at Paris (1916), 25-26; Inter-Allied conference at Paris (1917), 58; at Versailles (1918), 59. *See also* Peace Conference
Congress of Vienna, 2
Conscription. *See* Compulsory military service

Conservative Party (British), 6, 33; and war aims, 13-14, 16, 60; in Khaki election, 88, 91; on Treaty terms, 154, 155
Control Commission, Inter-Allied, 109, 120, 124-126, 160
Corbett, Sir Julian S., 68n
Council of Four, 126-127, 142
Council of Ten, 104, 106-116, 120-130. *See also* Supreme War Council
Counterproposals to Versailles Treaty (German), 127, 145-146, 146-151; content of, 148-149; Allied reply to, 149-150, 162
Covenant of League of Nations, 116, 123, 141-142, 152; procedure in drafting, 106, 107; Article I of, 138n; Article VIII of, 11, 103, 138n, 150, 151, 162; drafting of Article VIII, 71, 72-73, 100, 101, 131-141; text of Article VIII, 141; German views on Article VIII, 148-149; Article IX of, 137-138, 139; drafts of, 66, 97 (League of Nations Society); 66, 97 (League to Enforce Peace); 68-69 (Phillimore Plan); 96-98 (Zimmern memorandum); 98-99 (Cecil's plan); 71, 72-73 (House draft); 101 (Wilson's draft); 99-101 (Smuts's proposal); 106-107, 135 (Cecil-Miller draft); 135 (Hurst-Miller draft); 101-102 (French and Italian drafts). *See also* Disarmament; League, concept of a; League of Nations; League of Nations Commission
Coupon election. *See* Khaki election
Courtney of Penwith, 1st Baron, 23-24
Crespi, Silvio, 114n
Croft, Brigadier-General Henry Page, 88n, 92n, 155
Crowe, Sir Eyre, 68n
Curtis, Lionel, 21, 61
Curzon of Kedleston, 1st Earl, 69, 97-98, 155

Customs union, proposed for Balkans, 56
Czernin, Count Ottokar von, 48, 50, 51

Daily Express, 20, 53
Daily Mail: jingo views of, 20, 21; in Khaki election campaign, 88, 89–90; during Peace Conference, 142–143
Daily News (Chicago), 28
Daily News (London), 12
Daily Telegraph, 52–54, 89–90
Davis, Norman, 114n
de Bon, Vice-Admiral Ferdinand Jean Jacques, 113, 115n, 128n
Degoutte, General J. M. J., 114n, 115n
Delbrück, Hans, 22
Delcassé, Théophile, 20
Demobilization, Allied, 106, 114, 115, 117–118, 127, 143
Democracy: war for, 21–22, 28, 43, 46; in Germany, 46, 61, 80
Denman, Hon. R. D., 165
Diaz, General Armando, 109n
Dickinson, Goldsworthy Lowes, 19, 44
Dickinson, Rt. Hon. Sir Willoughby Hyett, 60, 67. *See also* League of Nations Society
"Diplomacy by conference," 98, 100
Disarmament Conference of 1932, 105, 164
Disarmament, general: definition of, 1–2; prewar proposals regarding, 1–4, 95; Labour Party on, 6, 44, 56, 59, 132, 134, 145, 156–159; and British liberalism, 8–9, 95, 132; in League Covenant, 11, 71, 72–73, 100, 101, 103, 131–141, 150, 151, 162; British groups favoring, 17, 42, 67, 132 (U.D.C.); 18 (I.L.P.); 22, 42 (Fabian Society); 60, 67, 132 (League of Nations Society); British opinion on, 22, 26, 41, 42, 69, 74, 87, 88, 94, 106, 132, 152, 163; German opinion on, 26, 49, 57, 146–149 *passim*; Wilson's views on, 29, 39–42, 59, 69, 71, 82–83, 94, 101, 126, 132; Grey on, 41, 58, 132, 163; American opinion on, 42, 70, 71, 72–73, 82, 93–96, 101, 132; Smuts on, 44–45, 51–52, 100–101, 132; in Pope's proposals, 48–50; Lloyd George on, 58, 87, 94, 150–151; Foreign Office views on, 68, 69, 94, 96–97, 99, 132; and "total war," 75; Cobb-Lippmann memorandum on, 82; its effect on peace settlement, 83, 162, 163; technical problems of, 96, 100, 104–105, 129, 146, 163–164; British Admiralty opposed to, 97, 132, 136; French views on, 101–102, 121, 140; Allied obligations toward, 103, 126–127, 131, 149–150, 151, 162; as a condition of German disarmament, 122, 126–127, 145, 146, 149–152 *passim*; League's responsibility for, 133, 145, 149, 162. *See also* Armaments, private manufacture of; Armaments, publicity of national; Air terms; Covenant; Fourth Point; Military terms; Naval terms; "National Safety," Part V; Peace proposals
Disarmament, terms of German. *See* Air terms, Military terms, Naval terms, Part V
"Domestic safety." *See* "National safety"
Drafting Committee of the Peace Conference, 136, 138
Dreadnought, 5
Dundee, Scotland: Churchill's speech at, 88
Duval, General, 115n, 128

Ebert, President Friedrich, 57, 114, 118
Economic war aims (British), 14, 25–26, 53, 60
Economist, The: Hirst as editor of, 19, 43; reports discussion of peace, 24; protests economic warfare, 25; on disarmament, 42

Edinburgh Review, 26
Empire, British. *See* British Empire
Erzberger, Matthias, 6n, 46-47
Essen, Germany, 110
Etonians, Old, 53

Fabian Society, 7; and war aims, 14-16, 21-22, 61; plans for a League, 19-20, 41, 56, 61-62, 97, 98; on disarmament, 42
Fay, Sidney B., 74n
Federalism: advocated by *Round Table* group, 61, 74
Fehrenbach, Konstantin, 146
"Fight to the finish," 14, 20-22
Fiume, Italy, 142
Foch, Marshal Ferdinand, 151; and the Armistice, 76-79, 83-86 *passim*; and terms of German disarmament, 106, 108, 109, 111, 120-126 *passim*, 140, 160
Foch Joint Committee on German disarmament, 115, 119-124, 127-128, 152
Foreign Office (British): 1916 memorandum on peace aims, 68; November 1918 memorandum on a League, 96-97, 132
Foreign policy: democratic control of, 17, 43, 64, 73, 74
Fourteen Points: set forth by Wilson, 58-60, 66; in Armistice negotiations, 76, 77, 80, 81-83, 92-93; Cobb-Lippmann memorandum on, 81-82, 133; Allied reservations to, 81-82; question of Treaty's conformity with, 144, 147, 156, 157, 159
Fourth Point of Wilson's Fourteen Points: text of, 59; British reaction to, 59-60; accepted by belligerents as basis of peace, 82; divergence of views on, 93-97, 146; incorporated into Covenant, 131-141. *See also* Disarmament; Covenant
France: prewar arms firms in, 5-7; and outbreak of the war, 10, 12; war aims in, 20, 23, 31, 45-46, 85, 93, 109, 110, 116, 136-137; secret treaty concluded by, 26; war weariness in, 36, 45; views on a League, 74, 101-102, 136-140; and Armistice negotiations, 77-86 *passim*; fears German resurgence, 117; views on general disarmament, 101-102, 136-140; views on German disarmament, 106-116 *passim*, 120-130 *passim*, 160. *See also* Alsace-Lorraine, Clemenceau
Freedom of the seas, 40, 53, 81
French Revolution, 1, 2
Fry, Rt. Hon. Sir Edward, 95

General Staff, Allied. *See* High Command, Allied
General Staff, German. *See* High Command, German
Geographical position: relation to risks of disarmament, 137
German delegation to Peace Conference: instructions to, 147; at Paris, 146-151; reaction to the Treaty, 147-149, 151
Germany: prewar naval expenditures in, 4-5; at Hague Conference of 1907, 4n; private arms firms in, 5-7; and war's outbreak, 10, 12, 30, 73-74; war aims in, 22-23, 49; opinion on a moderate peace in, 24, 27-28, 31, 34-37, 46-47, 48, 50; opinion on disarmament in, 26, 49, 57; and unrestricted submarine warfare, 30-31, 42, 46, 78; U.S. diplomatic relations with, 30-31, 42-43; reaction to Allied war aims, 39; democracy in, 46, 61, 80; armistice with Russia, 54; and Armistice negotiations, 76-86 *passim*; blockaded, 84, 115, 127; feared in post-Armistice period, 116-119 *passim*, 143; opinion on peace terms in, 143, 146-151; its admission to the League, 148, 150, 159; in the 1920's, 162. *See also* Counterproposals; Colonies; Bethmann-Hollweg; Max of Baden, German

delegation; High Command, Part V

Gladstone, William E., 13, 33-34, 65

Gontard, Paul von, 6n

Goschen, Rt. Hon. Sir W. E., 4n

Grassi, Admiral, 115n

Great Britain: liberalism in, 2-3, 7-9, 13, 23-24, 25-26, 34; at Hague Conferences, 3-4; prewar naval expenditures in, 4-5; private arms firms in, 5-7; and war's outbreak, 10, 12-16, 73-74; development of war aims in, 16-22, 25-27, 36-39, 45-46, 56-58, 60-65, 77; opinion on a League in, 17, 19-20, 41, 44-45, 52, 56, 58, 60-62, 66-69, 72-74, 87-88, 96-101, 106-107, 135; opinion on general disarmament in, 17, 18, 22, 26, 41-42, 44-45, 51-52, 56, 58-60, 62, 67-69, 74, 87, 88, 92, 94, 96-97, 99, 100-101, 106, 132-140 *passim*, 136, 150-151, 152, 163; secret treaties concluded by, 20, 26; discussion of a moderate peace in, 27, 28, 30, 32-33, 35-37, 43-45, 47, 51-54, 55; "knock-out" policy of, 31-34 *passim*, 50-51, 59; opinion on Fourteen Points in, 59-60, 81-83, 92-94; and Armistice negotiations, 77-86 *passim*; Khaki election campaign in, 86-92; views on German disarmament in, 106-116 *passim*, 120-130 *passim*, 150-151; fears of German resurgence in, 117-118, 119; opinion on Peace Conference and Treaty in, 141-146, 150-160, 163; fails to implement postwar general disarmament, 163. *See also* Admiralty; Asquith; Cecil; Foreign Office; Grey; Lloyd George; Parliament

Greek delegation at Peace Conference, 139-140

Gretton, Colonel John, 92n

Grew, Joseph C., 35

Grey, Sir Edward (1st Viscount Grey of Fallodon): 1916 press interview, 28; correspondence with House, 29, 71, 132; on a negotiated peace, 32; retires from Cabinet, 33; on concept of a League, 41, 66, 73; on disarmament, 41, 58, 132, 163

Grieg, Colonel James William, 92n

Guarantee, proposed treaty of, between France, Great Britain, and U.S., 152, 160

Guinness, Colonel Walter Edward (Lord Moyne), 92n

Hague Conferences of 1899 and 1907, 3-4, 95, 104

Haig, Field-Marshal Sir Douglas, 83

Haimhausen, Edgar Haniel von, 146, 147

Haldane of Cloan, 1st Viscount, 4n, 5

Hankey, Sir Maurice, 69, 74

Hardinge, Sir Charles (1st Baron Hardinge of Penshurst), 4n, 53-54

Harvey, T. E., 165

Haskins, Professor Charles H., 70n

Heligoland, fortification of, 113, 146

Henderson, Rt. Hon. Arthur, 156; leads Parliamentary Labour Party, 16; resigns from Cabinet, 56; and 1917 Labour Party memorandum, 56; on a League, 74

Hensley Rider to U.S. Appropriation Bill of 1915, 95

Hewart, Rt. Hon. Sir Gordon, 39

Herald (Labour), 158

High Command, Allied, on Armistice terms, 76, 79, 80, 83, 84

High Command, German, 34, 37, 77, 79, 80

Hindenburg, General Paul von, 34, 77, 80

Hirst, Francis W., 19, 43, 64

Hogge, James Myles, 165

Holt, Richard Durning, 64n, 165, 166

House, Colonel Edward M., 28, 35, 41, 44, 46, 49, 58, 64, 66, 69, 70, 96, 97, 135n; his correspondence with Grey, 29, 71, 132; on disarmament, 42, 70, 94; his Covenant draft, 71-73, 97, 132, 133, 140;

secures Allied acceptance of Fourteen Points, 80-83, 85-86, 92; and terms of German disarmament, 115, 122, 123n
House of Commons. *See* Parliament
Howard, Roy, interviews Lloyd George, 31
Hughes, Rt. Hon. William M., 25, 26
Hurst, Cecil J. B., 68n, 135, 137, 139, 140
Hurst-Miller draft of League Covenant, 135, 137, 139, 140
Hyndman, H. M., 62

Indemnities. *See* Reparations
Independent Labour Party, 6, 14-18 *passim*, 27, 47, 55, 64, 156; 1915 resolution on war aims, 18, 56, 62; resolution attacking Treaty, 157
Industrial Revolution, 1, 2, 8
Inquiry, The, 70, 72, 81, 94
Inspection of national armaments, international, 138-140, 145
Inter-Allied Military Control Commission. *See* Control Commission
International General Staff advocated by French, 74, 101-102, 138
International law, 42, 71, 72
International Marine Police, 147
International Military Force advocated by French, 137-138
International organization. *See* League, concept of a; League of Nations
International Socialist Conference (Amsterdam, 1919), 145
International trade, 14, 25, 74
Irish Nationalists, 63n, 90n, 153n
Italy, 54; London Treaty with, 20, 26; her war aims, 81, 142; favors compulsory military service, 140

Japan: war with Russia, 4; at Peace Conference, 134
Jaurès, Jean Léon, 6n
John, E. T., 65
Jowett, Frederick W., 165
Jutland, battle of, 30

Kaiser. *See* Wilhelm II
Karl of Austria, Emperor, 48
Kennedy, A. R., 68n
Kenworthy, Commander J. M. (1st Baron Strabolgi), 153, 156
Kerr, Philip Henry, 21
Khaki election (1918), 65, 86-92, 154, 156, 157
Kiel Canal, 113, 127, 146
King, Joseph, 165
Kitchener of Khartoum, 1st Earl, 24
"Knockout blow" statement by Lloyd George, 31-34 *passim*, 52, 59
Koo, Wellington, 135n
Krupp industries, 110
Kühlmann, Baron Richard von, 54

Labour Leader, 15, 158
Labour and the New Social Order, 56
Labour Party, 7, 18, 56, 57, 65-66, 142; war aims of, 14-16, 55-57, 61, 63-66 *passim*; 1917 memorandum on war aims, 56, 57, 58-59, 134; conferences of, 41, 55, 56, 57, 145, 158, 159; on a League and disarmament, 41, 56, 62, 132, 134, 145, 156-159; on Fourteen Points, 58-59, 94; in Khaki election campaign, 88, 90n, 91; its views on the Treaty, 154, 156-159. *See also* Fabian Society; Independent Labour Party; Parliamentary Labour Party
Labour and Socialist Conference (Bern, 1919), 145
Lamb, Sir Ernest H., 165, 166
Lancken, O. von der, 54
Lansdowne, 5th Marquess of, 47; memorandum to Cabinet, 32-33; retires from Cabinet, 33-34; letter to *Daily Telegraph*, 52-54, 58, 65

Index

Lansing, Robert, 72; reply to Pope's proposal, 49-50; and terms of German disarmament, 112, 115, 122, 123n, 130

Larnaude, Ferdinand, 135n

Latin America, 94

Law, Rt. Hon. Andrew Bonar, 32, 41, 66, 144, 156

League, concept of a, 19, 59, 72; U.D.C. on, 17; Fabian Society on, 19-20, 56, 61-62, 97; Wilson on, 29, 36, 39-42, 59, 71-73, 101; Bethmann-Hollweg on, 35; Asquith on, 40-41, 62; Bonar Law on, 41, 66; Smuts on, 44-45, 99-101; favored by Labour Party, 41, 56, 62; Lloyd George on, 58, 66, 87; growing acceptance of, 66-75, 97-102; League to Enforce Peace on, 66, 97; Bryce group on, 66, 97; Phillimore Committee on, 68-69, 72, 96, 97; House on, 71-73, 97, 101, 132; Churchill on, 87-88; Zimmern memorandum on, 96-97, 98-99, 100; and disarmament, 106; Cecil on, 98-99, 100, 106-107, 135; Miller on, 106-107, 135; French government on, 74, 101-102, 136-140. *See also* Covenant; Disarmament; League of Nations; League of Nations Commission; Peace proposals

League to Enforce Peace, 41, 49; Wilson's speech to, 28-30, 71; its plan for a League, 66, 97

League of Nations, 114, 117n, 122, 124, 125, 128; responsibility for general disarmament, 133, 145, 149, 162; Germany's admission to, 148, 150, 159; revision of Versailles Treaty by, 159. *See also* Covenant; Disarmament; League, concept of a

League of Nations Commission, 105, 107, 131-141. *See also* Covenant

League of Nations Society, 19, 41, 44-45, 60, 67, 132; its plan for a League, 44, 66, 97

League of Nations Union, 68, 132

Lees-Smith, H. B., 63, 65n, 165

Levée en masse: advocated by Ludendorff, 79

Liberal Imperialists, 7, 10, 15, 16, 21, 60

Liberal Party (British), 2-3, 7, 8, 10, 12, 17-18, 23-24, 29, 33-34, 64-66; in Coalition Cabinet, 33-34; Lloyd George faction of, 60-61; Asquith faction of, 61-66 *passim*, 88, 90n, 91, 153; Foreign Affairs group of, 64; and Khaki election campaign, 87-91; on the Treaty, 152-154, 156-157. *See also* Liberal Imperialists; Lloyd George; Asquith, Nonconformism

Liebknecht, Karl, 6n

Limitation of armaments. *See* Disarmament

Lippmann, Walter, 70, 81-82, 93

Lloyd George, Rt. Hon. David, 29, 41, 45-46, 50, 52, 54, 55, 60-65 *passim*, 115, 116, 119, 131, 155, 156, 159; his 1909 budget, 7; his "knockout blow" statement, 31-34 *passim*, 52; on Lansdowne, 32-33; becomes Prime Minister, 33-34, 89; his 1918 speech to T.U.C., 57-58, 66, 94; on general disarmament, 58, 87, 94, 150-151; on a League, 58, 66, 87; and Armistice negotiations, 77-81 *passim*, 85, 86; during Khaki election campaign, 86-92 *passim*; on compulsory military service, 58, 87, 108, 121; and terms of German disarmament, 107-108, 111, 112, 123, 125, 126, 160; his relations with press and Parliament during Peace Conference, 118, 142-145; his views on Treaty's justice and durability, 150-151, 153-154, 160. *See also* Coalition Cabinet; Coalition, Lloyd George's; Liberal Party.

Lodge, Senator Henry Cabot, 78

London Chronicle, 89-90

London Treaty with Italy, 20

Long, Rt. Hon. Walter Hume, 39

Index

Loucheur, Louis, 108–111, 115, 118, 160
Lough, Rt. Hon. Thomas, 165, 166
Lowther, Colonel Claude, 92n, 144, 155
Ludendorff, General Erich F. W., 77, 79, 80
Luxembourg, 83

Macaulay, Thomas Babington, 17
MacDonald, J. Ramsay, 156, 165; and Parliamentary Labour Party, 16; in U.D.C., 18; on Reichstag resolution, 47; and 1917 Labour Party memorandum, 56; favors a moderate peace, 64; on disarmament, 145
McKenna, Rt. Hon. Reginald, 5, 6
McMaster, Donald, 92n
McMicking, Major Gilbert, 165
McNeill, Ronald (Lord Cushendun), 92n
Mainz, Germany, 83, 84
Makino, Baron, on League Commission, 135n
Mallalieu, Frederick William, 165, 166
Manchester Guardian, 12, 44, 53
Manchester school, 3
"Mansion House" speech by Churchill, 119n
Manufacture of armaments, private. *See* Armaments, private manufacture of
Martin, Joseph, 165
Mason, David Marshall, 165, 166
Massingham, H. W., 26
Maurice, General Sir Frederick B., 65
"Maurice motion," 62, 65, 91
Max of Baden, Prince, 77–80, 146
Mexico, 42
Mezes, President Sidney E., 70n, 93
Michaelis, Chancellor Georg, 47, 50
Military terms of the Versailles Treaty, 76, 103, 105, 106, 128, 145, 152; drafting of, 104, 107–116, 120–127, 130; Allied views on, 160; German views on, 146, 148–149; period of their execution, 149–150. *See also* Part V; Preliminary Peace Treaty; Peace Conference
Miller, David Hunter, 70n, 72, 93, 99, 129n, 130n, 134, 136; his memorandum to Bliss on disarmament, 94–95; his Covenant draft with Cecil, 106–107, 135, 139, 140; his Covenant draft with Hurst, 135, 137, 139, 140
Milner, 1st Viscount, 21, 61, 112, 116, 125
Moderate peace. *See* Negotiated peace
Moderate peace settlement: pressure against, 116–119, 141–145, 161
Morel, E. D., 30
Morley of Blackburn, 1st Viscount, 13
Morning Post, 117, 142
Morrell, Philip E., 53, 64, 165
Mulliner, H. H., 6
Munitions manufacture, postwar German, 109, 110–111, 115, 120, 129. *See also* Armaments, private manufacture of
Murray, Gilbert, 73

Nation, The, 25–26, 30, 53, 95
"Nation in arms," 2
National Review, 21, 60, 112
"National safety," disarmament consistent with, 82, 131, 133–134
National Socialist Party (British), 62
Naval Committee on Treaty terms, 113–114, 119, 120, 127
Naval Council, Allied, 80, 83
"Naval holiday" proposals, 5, 95
Naval terms of the Versailles Treaty, 76, 120, 123n, 125, 130, 152; drafting of, 113–114, 127–128; report of Naval Committee on, 113–114, 119, 127; German views on, 146, 148–149; period of their execution, 149–150; Allied views on, 160. *See also* Part V
Navies, 4–5, 88, 128n. *See also* Naval terms

Negotiated peace: Parliamentary discussion of, 23-24, 27, 44, 47, 53, 63-65; German government on, 24, 27-28, 31, 34-35, 36-37, 47, 48, 50; Asquith government on, 31-33; Lloyd George government on, 33, 36-37, 38-39, 52; Wilson on, 28-30, 34-37, 39-42, 44, 49-50; Lloyd George's views on, 31, 32-33; unofficial British groups on, 43-44, 62-65, 79; Reichstag Resolution for, 46-47; Pope Benedict's proposal of, 47-51 *passim*; Austrian government favors, 48, 50-51; Smuts favors, 51-52; Lansdowne letter on, 52-54; secret moves toward, 54-55; Labour Party's efforts on, 55, 63, 64, 65; relation to disarmament, 75. *See also* Armistice; Versailles Treaty; Peace proposals

Netherlands, 83, 145

New Europe, The, 61

New Statesman, 15-16, 22, 30; and League plans, 19-20, 56, 61-62; on the Fourteen Points, 58-59; on the Treaty terms, 152, 156. *See also* Fabian Society

Nicholas II, Czar of Russia, 3-4

"No Annexations, No Indemnities," 44, 58

Nonconformism (British), 3, 10

Northcliffe, 1st Viscount, 14, 20-21, 33, 60, 142-145; and Asquith's resignation, 89; and the Khaki election campaign, 88-90

Northcliffe press: war aims of, 14, 20-21, 33, 60; in the Khaki election campaign, 88-90; on German aggressiveness, 117, 119; pressures on Lloyd George during Peace Conference, 142-145

Nuttal, Henry, 165, 166

Open diplomacy, 58-59, 73, 81, 142. *See also* Diplomacy by conference

Orlando, Vittorio E., 135n, 140

Ottoman Empire: in Allied war aims, 26, 37, 38

Outhwaite, Robert Leonard, 165

Page, Walter Hines, 29

Parliament: debates on war policies and peace aims, 23-24, 25, 27, 41, 43, 44, 62, 63-66 *passim*; debate on Reichstag Resolution, 47; debate on Fourteen Points, 59; debate on Maurice motion, 62n, 65; character of House of Commons, 64, 90n, 91-92, 155-156; debates on Peace Conference and Treaty, 142, 144-145, 152-156, 158-159.

Parliamentary Labour Party, 14, 16, 142, 157-158

Parmoor, 1st Baron, 43, 44

Part V of the Versailles Treaty, 76, 103-105, 152, 162; preamble to, 103, 126-127, 131, 149, 151; German views on, 148-149; period of its execution, 149-150; Allied opinion on, 160. *See also* Air terms; Military terms; Naval terms

Patrick, General Mason M., 115n

Paxkonferenz: studies problems of peace, 146

Peace Conference, Paris, 1919, 100, 119; effect of Khaki election on, 86-87, 91, 92, 102; procedure at, 104-110 *passim*, 113-116, 118-119, 129-130, 161; secrecy of its proceedings, 142, 144; as an international tribunal, 155. *See also* Versailles Treaty

Peace Negotiations Committee of Labour Party, 55

Peace proposals: U.D.C. manifesto, 17; I.L.P. resolution, 18, 56; Fabian Society proposals, 19-20, 56, 61-62, 98; Bryce League plan, 44, 66; 1917 Labour Party memorandum, 56; Wilson's Fourteen Points, 58-60; League to Enforce Peace plan, 66; 1916 Foreign Office memorandum, 68; Philli-

Index

more League plan, 68–69; House's Covenant draft, 71, 72–73; Zimmern memorandum on League and disarmament, 96–98; Cecil's League plan, 98–99; Wilson's Covenant draft, 101; Smuts's League plan, 99–101; Cecil-Miller draft, 106–107, 135; Hurst-Miller draft, 135; French draft, 101–102, 136–140. *See also* Covenant; League, concept of a

"Peace without victory," 39–42, 49, 72

Penn, William, 1
Percy, Lord Eustace, 153
Pershing, General John J., 83, 124
Pessôa, Epitacio, 135n
Pétain, General Henri Philippe, 45, 83
Phillimore, Sir Walter G. F. (1st Baron Phillimore), 68–69
Phillimore Plan for a League, 68–69, 72, 96, 97, 98, 99, 132
Phillimore Committee, 41n, 68–69
Poland, 38, 115, 142
Pollard, Albert Frederick, 68n, 74
Ponsonby, Arthur A. W. H., 18, 23, 53, 64, 65n, 165
Portuguese delegation at Peace Conference, 136
Poutiloff Affair, 6n
Preliminary Peace Treaty: Armistice as a, 84; military terms as a, 107, 108, 113–116, 119, 129–130
Press, British: on war's outbreak, 12, 15–16; favors a fight to the finish, 14, 20–22, 26, 32, 47, 50–51, 60; on a moderate peace, 24, 25–26, 30, 43, 48, 64; on a League, 42, 61; on the Lansdowne letter, 53; on the Fourteen Points, 58–59, 92–93; during the Khaki election, 88–90; on disarmament, 94, 152; campaigns against moderation at Conference, 105, 116–119, 142–145, 161
Press, French, 23, 117, 143
Press, German, 22–23, 49, 118, 143

Preussische Jahrbücher, 22
Price, Charles Edward, 165, 166
Pringle, W. M. R., 165
Private manufacture of armaments. *See* Armaments, private manufacture of
Procedure in drafting Treaty terms. *See* Peace Conference
Progressive Party (German), 46
Psychological warfare, 73–74
Publicity of national armaments. *See* Armaments, publicity of national

Reconstruction, British domestic, 88
Reichstag Resolution of July 1917, 46–47, 48
Reis, Batalha, 135n
Reparations, 105, 106, 116, 119n; British opinion on, 37, 60, 88–90, 91, 92, 118, 143–144, 155; Allied reservations to Fourteen Points on, 81; in Armistice terms, 84; in Treaty drafts, 113
Responsibility for World War I. *See* World War, origins of the; War criminals
Rhineland: in Armistice terms, 83, 84, 85; in terms of German disarmament, 110, 146; German views on, 147
Ribot, Alexander F., 54
Richardson, Thomas, 165
Riddell, Sir George, 155–156
Robertson, General Sir William: 1916 memorandum on the war, 32
Roch, Walter F., 165
Rose, J. Holland, 68n
Roumania, 34, 38
Round Table, The, 21, 61, 74, 96
Rowntree, Arnold S., 165, 166
Ruhr: in French policies, 109, 111
Runciman, Rt. Hon. Walter, 25, 165, 166
Rush-Bagot agreement (1817), 95
Russia, 26, 43, 44, 45, 54, 58, 60, 85; at Hague Conferences, 3–4; civil war in, 117, 144
Russo-Japanese war, 3–4

Saar, 85, 142, 157
Sanctions: economic, 73; military, 73, 137–138
Scheidemann, Philipp, 24, 151
Scialoja, Vittorio, 135n
Secret treaties, Allied, 20, 26
Seeckt, General Hans von, 1
Self-defense, national. *See* "National safety"
Self-determination, principle of national, 17, 19, 52, 56, 58, 68, 157; advocated by Wilson, 29, 40, 59
Senlis, France, 83
Shaw of Dunfermline, Baron, 19, 68
Shelburne, 2nd Earl of, 34
Shortt, Edward, 165
Shotwell, James T., 70n
Simon, Rt. Hon. Sir John, 24
Simonds, Frank, 118
Simons, Dr. Hans, 147–148
Smuts, General Jan Christian: on disarmament, 44–45, 51–52, 100–101, 132; on a League, 45; on a negotiated peace, 51–52; his League plan, 99–101, 132, 140; and drafting the Treaty, 135n, 153–154, 159
Snowden, Philip: and prewar private arms manufacture, 6, 44; in debates on peace terms, 27, 44, 64, 165; regarding disarmament, 44, 59
Social Democratic Party (German), 22–23, 27, 46, 57
Socialist Party (British), 55, 62
Socialists: on private arms manufacture, 5–7, 10, 95, 145; and war's outbreak, 7, 10; relation to the Labour Party, 7, 14–15; on war aims, 10, 23, 57; conferences of, 14–15 (Stuttgart); 19, 62–63 (London, 1915); 56 (Stockholm); 57 (London, 1918); 145 (Bern); 145 (Amsterdam). *See also* Socialist Party; National Socialist Party; Labour Party; Social Democratic Party
Somme, battle of the, 30
Sonnino, Baron Sidney, 54
Southport, England: Nineteenth Annual Labour Party Conference at, 158
Spectator, The, 27, 30, 152, 155
Statist, The, 30
Steed, H. Wickham, 26, 90
Stockholm Conference of Socialist parties, 56
Stuttgart Conference of the Second International, 14–15
Submarine warfare, 30–31, 34–35, 42, 78, 79
Suffrage in Khaki election, 91
Sully, Duc de, 1
Supreme War Council: draws up Armistice terms, 83, 85–86; wartime co-operation in, 98; draws up terms of German disarmament, 104, 106–116, 120–130. *See also* Council of Ten
Switzerland, 28, 77, 145
Sykes, Major-General Frederick Hugh, 115n

Talleyrand-Périgord, Charles Maurice de, 34
Tardieu, André P. G. A., 112, 122n
Temps, Le, 23
Territorial integrity, principle of, 29, 42, 72, 73
Thomas, Albert, 6n
Thomas, Rt. Hon. James Henry, 145, 165
Thorne, William J., 165
Thwaites, Major-General William, 114n
Times, The (London), 14, 21, 29, 32, 47, 48, 50–51, 53, 157; on Fourteen Points, 59, 60, 92–93; in Khaki election campaign, 89, 90; on German post-Armistice threat, 117–119, 143; on Peace Conference proceedings, 142–144, 154; approves terms of German disarmament, 152
Tirpitz, Admiral von, 5
"Total war": definition of, 7n–8n; developments toward, 22, 23–27 *passim*, 38–39, 86, 100; and "total solutions," 52, 75

Trade, Board of. *See* Board of Trade
Trade, international. *See* International trade
Trade Union Congress: early views on the war, 16; Lloyd George's speech to (1918), 57–58; special conference with Labour Party (1919), 145
Trevelyan, Charles P.: as a U.D.C. leader, 17–18; on a negotiated peace, 35, 64, 165; joins postwar Labour Party, 65n; his correspondence with House and Wilson, 35, 72
Trevelyan, Rt. Hon. Sir George Otto, 17
Turkey. *See* Ottoman Empire
Tyrrell, Sir William G., 68n

Union of Democratic Control, 29, 30, 35, 41, 42, 72, 74, 94, 132, 156; formation of, 17–18; its 1914 manifesto, 17, 62; on a negotiated peace, 23, 44, 64; attacks the Treaty, 157–158
United States: on a negotiated peace, 28–30, 34–37, 39–42, 49–50; views on a League, 29, 36, 39–42, 59, 66–67, 71–73, 74, 97, 101, 117, 132–140 *passim*; views on general disarmament, 29, 39–40, 42, 59, 69–72, 82–83, 92, 93–96, 101, 126, 132–140 *passim*; diplomatic relations with Germany, 30–31, 42–43; development of war aims in, 45, 49–50, 58; and Armistice negotiations, 77–86 *passim*; views on German disarmament, 106–116 *passim*, 120–130 *passim*, 160. *See also* Bliss, Tasker; Wilson, Woodrow; House; League to Enforce Peace

Venizelos, Eleutherios, 139–140
Verdun, battle of, 30
Versailles, Treaty of, 11, 76, 83, 103, 116; its imposition on or negotiation with Germany, 112, 114, 118, 125, 143, 148, 154–155, 160, 161; its reception in Allied countries, 145–146, 152–160, 163; German reaction to, 147–149, 151; justice of, 148, 154–155, 156–160, 161–162; durability of, 153–154, 161–162; future League revision of, 159. *See also* Air terms; Covenant; Disarmament; League of Nations; Military terms; Part V; Reparations; Peace Conference
Vesnitch, Milenko, 135n
Victoria, Queen, 8
Vorwärts, 22–23
Vossische Zeitung, 49

Walsh, Stephen, 158
War, 1914–1918. *See* World War
War Cabinet. *See* Coalition Cabinet; Lloyd George
War criminals, 23, 88–90, 118
"War to end war," 11, 13
Watt, Henry A., 165
Webb, Beatrice, 15
Webb, Sidney: and Fabian Society, 15; and 1917 Labour Party memorandum, 56
Wedgwood, Colonel Josiah C., 153, 156
Wemyss, Vice-Admiral Sir Rosslyn (Lord Wester Wemyss), 77, 83, 113–114, 115n, 127
Whitehouse, John Howard, 35, 72, 165
Wilhelm II, Kaiser, 4n, 22–23, 34, 39; demands for removal of, 78; his punishment advocated, 88, 89, 90, 92
Wilson, Lieutenant-General Sir Henry H., 109n, 115n, 122–123, 160
Wilson, Rt. Hon. J. W., 165, 166
Wilson, William Tyson, 165
Wilson, President Woodrow, 17, 18, 38, 44, 46, 52, 90, 115, 116, 135n, 142; on terms of a negotiated peace, 28–29, 34–37, 45; his speech

to League to Enforce Peace, 28–30, 36, 71; exchange of notes on terms of peace, 34–37, 38, 49–50, 52, 93; "peace without victory" speech, 39–42, 72; on disarmament, 39–42, 69–71, 93–94, 126; "Fourteen Points" speech, 58–60, 66; views on a League, 66, 71–73, 74, 97, 99, 101; in Armistice negotiations, 77–83 *passim*; drafting Article VIII, 101, 133–140 *passim*; drafting terms of German disarmament, 109–113 *passim*, 122–126 *passim*, 130, 160. *See also* Fourteen Points

Women's Labour League, 55

Woolf, Leonard, 19

World War, origins of the: Allied views on, 11–12, 16, 29–30, 36, 37, 42–43, 73–74; relation of armaments to, 95–96; German responsibility for, 151, 155

Zimmermann note, 42

Zimmern, Sir Alfred E., memorandum, 96–97, 98–99, 100, 132

Harvard Historical Monographs

* Out of print

1. Athenian Tribal Cycles in the Hellenistic Age. By W. S. Ferguson. 1932.
2. The Private Record of an Indian Governor-Generalship. The Correspondence of Sir John Shore, Governor, with Henry Dundas, President of the Board of Control, 1793–1798. Edited by Holden Furber. 1933.
3. The Federal Railway Land Subsidy Policy of Canada. By J. B. Hedges. 1934.
4. Russian Diplomacy and the Opening of the Eastern Question in 1838 and 1839. By P. E. Mosely. 1934.
5. The First Social Experiments in America. A Study in the Development of Spanish Indian Policy in the Sixteenth Century. By Lewis Hanke. 1935.*
6. British Propaganda at Home and in the United States from 1914 to 1917. By J. D. Squires. 1935.*
7. Bernadotte and the Fall of Napoleon. By F. D. Scott. 1935.
8. The Incidence of the Terror During the French Revolution. By Donald Greer. 1935.
9. French Revolutionary Legislation on Illegitimacy, 1789–1804. By Crane Brinton. 1936.*
10. An Ecclesiastical Barony of the Middle Ages. The Bishopric of Bayeux, 1066–1204. By S. E. Gleason. 1936.
11. Chinese Traditional Historiography. By C. S. Gardner. 1938.*
12. Studies in Early French Taxation. By J. R. Strayer and C. H. Taylor. 1939.
13. Muster and Review. A Problem of English Military Administration, 1420–1440. By R. A. Newhall. 1940.
14. Portuguese Voyages to America in the Fifteenth Century. By S. E. Morison. 1940.*
15. Argument from Roman Law in Political Thought, 1200–1600. By M. P. Gilmore. 1941.*
16. The Huancavelica Mercury Mine. A Contribution to the History of the Bourbon Renaissance in the Spanish Empire. By A. P. Whitaker. 1941.
17. The Palace School of Muhammad the Conqueror. By Barnette Miller. 1941.

Harvard Historical Monographs

18. A Cistercian Nunnery in Mediaeval Italy: The Story of Rifreddo in Saluzzo, 1220–1300. By Catherine E. Boyd. 1943.
19. Vassi and Fideles in the Carolingian Empire. By C. E. Odegaard, 1945.
20. Judgment by Peers. By Barnaby C. Keeney. 1949.
21. The Election to the Russian Constituent Assembly of 1917. By Oliver H. Radkey. 1950.
22. Conversion and the Poll Tax in Early Islam. By Daniel C. Dennett, Jr. 1950.*
23. Albert Gallatin and the Oregon Problem. By Frederick Merk. 1950.
24. The Incidence of the Emigration During the French Revolution. By Donald M. Greer. 19551.*
25. Alterations of the Words of Jesus as Quoted in the Literature of the Second Century. By L. E. Wright. 1952.*
26. Liang Ch'i-Ch'ao and the Mind of Modern China. By J. R. Levenson. 1953.*
27. The Japanese and Sun Yat-sen. By Marius B. Jansen. 1954.
28. English Politics in the Early Eighteenth Century. By Robert Walcott, Jr. 1956.*
29. The Founding of the French Socialist Party (1893–1905). By Aaron Noland. 1956.
30. British Labour and the Russian Revolution: 1917–1924. By Stephen R. Graubard. 1956.
31. RKFDV: German Resettlement and Population Policy. By Robert L. Koehl. 1957.
32. Disarmament and Peace in British Politics, 1914–1919. By Gerda Richards Crosby. 1957.